DISCOVERING
DANIEL

AMIR TSARFATI

WITH DR. RICK YOHN

HARVEST PROPHECY
An Imprint of Harvest House Publishers

Cover design by Faceout Studio, Molly von Borstel
Interior design by KUHN Design Group

For bulk, special sales, or ministry purchases, please call 1-800-547-8979.
Email: CustomerService@hhpbooks.com

This logo is a federally registered trademark of the Hawkins Children's LLC. Harvest House Publishers, Inc., is the exclusive licensee of this trademark.

Discovering Daniel
Copyright © 2024 by Amir Tsarfati
Published by Harvest House Publishers
Eugene, Oregon 97408
www.harvesthousepublishers.com

ISBN 978-0-7369-8838-4 (pbk)
ISBN 978-0-7369-8839-1 (eBook)

Library of Congress Control Number: 2023947084

Printed in the United States of America

24 25 26 27 28 29 30 31 32 / BP / 10 9 8 7 6 5 4 3 2 1

I dedicate this book…

to God, whose presence is the only source of perfect peace during the darkest of times.

to my family, friends, and ministry partners. It is your love, prayers, and support that give me the strength and resources to carry out that to which God has called me.

to the innocent civilians who were killed and those who were taken hostage by the terrorist group Hamas on October 7, 2023. I also acknowledge the sorrow and pain of my nation as we seek to heal from this twenty-first century holocaust. We will fight, we will heal, and, with the help of the one true God, we will emerge stronger than ever before. Hamas believed it could win this fight, but, as we can clearly see in the book of Daniel, God has a different plan.

ACKNOWLEDGMENTS

What a blessing it is to be given the opportunity to study and teach the Holy Scriptures. Thank You, Lord, for Your precious truth as written in Your perfect, powerful Word.

I want to thank Dr. Rick Yohn for his partnership in coming alongside me for this book. I also want to express my sorrow for the loss of Linda, your beloved wife of 63 years. She was a joy to know and a great teacher in her own right. She will be missed. Finally, thank you to Steve Yohn for your assistance in the writing of this book.

My love and appreciation go out to my wife, Miriam, my four children, and my daughter-in-law for your love and encouragement through the long workdays and the extended absences.

Thank you, Behold Israel team, for your love, support, and dedication—Mike, H.T. and Tara, Gale and Florene, Donalee, Joanne, Nick and Tina, Jason, Abigail, Kayo, and Steve. Also, thanks to all your spouses and children, who often sacrifice their family time with you to further the spreading of God's Word.

Thank you to Bob Hawkins, Steve Miller, and the wonderful team at Harvest House for all your hard work in making this book happen.

Finally, thank you so much to the hundreds of thousands of followers, prayer partners, and ministry supporters of Behold Israel. This ministry would not exist without you.

CONTENTS

HOME IN A
FOREIGN LAND

H ope.
 Such a beautiful word filled with excitement and anticipation. Hope feels like spring, like something new and better is on the
horizon. Hope says that no matter how life looks now, you just need
to be patient. You just need to endure. Soon enough, the situation
will change, the tide will turn. Righteousness will prevail. The pain
will disappear. Justice and peace will take the upper hand and all will
once again be right for you and for everyone around you.

There was a time not long ago that hope was brimming all over
our world. The Berlin Wall had fallen. Communism had collapsed.
The Cold War was extinguished. Optimism was in the air. Old enemies started to become friends, then partners. Political disagreement
existed but was carried out with an air of civility.

But that is not what we find now. Today, we are living in a world
of hatred, disagreement, warfare.

Contrary to many times in our history, most modern wars are not
fought on the battlefield. The conflicts do not involve bullets or mis-
siles. Instead, the armies are unleashed in the entertainment industry, in the classroom, and on social media. The lines of division are

drawn up on many fronts. Subjectivity is pitted against truth. Relativism stands against absolutism. Aberration fights tradition, and individual expression wars against morality.

Because the fight is in the realm of ideas and standards, allegiances can be easily blurred. Those in the church often find themselves on both sides of the front, aiming their weapons at one another. Life used to be so much easier when we had an enemy that we could easily define. In those days, when we saw the enemy faltering, our hope quotient went up. When the enemy gained a victory, hope waned.

Today, in our world where the enemy is powerful but often clandestine, discouragement about the future comes much easier. We feel the adversary's forces all around us, and we can't help but see defeat after defeat at the ballot box, on the movie screen, in the television news, and on the streets of our cities. The enemy's victories are even reaching into the church as one denomination after another kowtows to public mores in the name of relevance and evangelism.

Daniel lived in a time when the enemy was much more tangible. They were easily recognized as the burly men with the swords who were bursting into your house, killing your father, kidnapping your sister, and absconding with all your possessions. Yet we find in the book of Daniel hope during the darkest of times. And even though Daniel's enemy was flesh and blood, Daniel's attitude and actions set a precedent for how we can deal with our foes despite them being cultural and spiritual.

What does it look like to live in a way that will bring you hope in this decaying society of moral relativism, subjective truth, and a total disregard for God's Word? And how can you get through to those on the other side when the animosity is so great? This is a question that believers must answer. The darkness of sin is a global phenomenon. The devil is at work in every corner of the world. But it is because of this darkness that hope shines so brightly.

Ramat Gan, near Tel Aviv, is the hub of Israel's lucrative diamond industry. Beautiful stones from all over the world pass through the Diamond Exchange District on their way to jewelry stores. From there, they will eventually hang around the necks, clasp to the wrists, or encircle the fingers of men and women from all backgrounds and nationalities and ethnicities. When the purveyors of these gems want to show off their luster, they will often place a piece of black velvet on a table. Then, taking a pair of tweezers, they will carefully lift a stone and place it on the cloth. The stark contrast between the stone and the black background will cause the diamond to shine and sparkle, clearly showing its brilliance and beauty.

That is the hope and mission of the believer in this dark culture. When you find someone who truly has the light of Christ in them, the brilliance of their spiritual optimism draws people in. Why? Because others want it too. In this book, we will look at how we can live a life of hope in this confused world. And we will also see how we can shine that glory of Christ in us in such a way that we can lead family, friends, neighbors, coworkers, all those we love to find that same peace, joy, and satisfaction.

Is it possible to find hope for today in words that a prophet wrote 2,500 years ago? Absolutely, because the two key elements of this book are as relevant today as they were back then. In fact, today they are even more relatable. First, Daniel set an example through his life of standing strong for God when you are living surrounded by the enemy. Second, Daniel's prophecies of the end times only gain in significance as we rapidly near their fulfillment.

But before we can dig too deeply into the life and teachings of this great prophet, we need some background. In one of my previous books, I said that it was important for me to tell you where I sit before I tell you where I stand. In other words, learning a little about me will help you as you process what I am teaching. The same is true for Daniel. To truly understand what he wrote, we need to learn more about him and the times in which he was living.

The Thousand-Foot View

Daniel is different than most prophetic books of the Bible. Typically, what you'll find are men chosen by God to speak words of truth and warning to the kings of Israel and Judah. They were the "turn or burn" preachers of their day, passing on God's words to the Jews, saying, "Hey, you remember that covenant we made long ago when I said that if you obey Me I'll give you blessings, but if you don't then it'll be curses? Well, since you ditched obedience a long time back, here come the punishments."

Daniel's charge from God was different. Jeremiah and Ezekiel were already doing a bang-up job telling God's chosen people how they had failed and warning them that the hammer was about to come down. No need to add another voice to their ranks. Instead, God moved this young prophet into a unique position in which he had access to the most powerful king in the world at that time—King Nebuchadnezzar of Babylon. The first eight chapters of Daniel's book are filled with words of warning to this great king, along with a couple other monarchs thrown in for good measure. His job was to remind them that there is a God in heaven who is truly in charge. Sure, these kings were pretty special, but there is One who is much, much greater than they.

Then, in chapters 9–12, Daniel left the present time completely. His focus shifted forward generations and then two-and-a-half millennia as he received directly from God His divine plan for the nation of Israel. But on his way to our era, Daniel made a pit stop during which he predicted with absolute precision the day that the Messiah would enter Jerusalem riding on the back of a donkey. It's truly mind-blowing.

Throughout the book we are reminded that our God is sovereign. He rules over the affairs of mankind. He will set one ruler in place as He puts down another. As supreme over creation, He also has a purpose and a plan for nations and for individuals, and He carries them out in His time and in His way. He is a faithful God who can and will fulfill all that He has promised.

But God is not just the Big Picture God. He also cares about each individual, particularly when those people are following Him. We see this in His loving care for Daniel and his companions. Daniel was a man who stood above his peers. He never compromised his convictions and never wavered in his faith. Because of his fidelity to the Lord, God gave him the amazing ability to understand and interpret dreams. Then the Lord miraculously placed this young man in the remarkable situation of using this gift to impact the Babylonian king.

The format and layout of Daniel is unique within the Bible—half historical narrative and half prophetic utterance. In this book, I will walk you through Daniel's writings chapter by chapter, just as I did in my previous book *Revealing Revelation*. As we go through, we'll come across some passages that are difficult to interpret. If there is any place where, even after careful study, the meaning remains ambiguous, I'll let you know that. I will not speculate without telling you that I'm doing so, and I will never be dogmatic about something that isn't clearly spelled out in Scripture. Ultimately, my prayer is that by the time you finish this book, the hope that you will find in this kidnapped exilic Jew will grant you peace and stoke your anticipation for the plans that God has for you and for all His people.

Invasion

Imagine a young teenager huddling with his family in the palace. The small closet is dark and cold. The only sounds are the whimpers of his younger sister, the soft prayers of his mother, and the screams of the people out in the street.

When newly crowned King Nebuchadnezzar of Babylon came marching to Jerusalem, Daniel and his friends had crowded along the top of the city walls to see this great fighting force and its mighty king. It had only been a short time since word had reached the royal courts of Judah that Nebuchadnezzar, crown prince at the time, had secured a resounding victory against the Egyptians and the few remaining Assyrians in a battle at Carchemish in Syria. Babylon's King Nabopolassar, Nebuchadnezzar's father, had died soon after, and the most powerful crown in the world had passed to the man who was now approaching Jerusalem's gates.

Those with more common sense than a group of teenage boys had found them up on the walls and hurried them away from their exposed location to a place of safety. Daniel was of royal blood, so his place of safety was the palace. The growing screams from outside the luxurious dwelling were the first indication that Nebuchadnezzar had not come on a social call. Soon, young Daniel could hear a skirmish—metal on metal, metal on wood. Then the crash of doors being kicked in echoed through the palace, the sound bouncing from one marble wall to another. He began shaking, pressing tightly up against the side of his mother.

Door after door was slammed open. Still, Daniel jumped and cried out when theirs was flung wide. A soldier, his uniform splattered with blood, stepped in, and Daniel's mother began to plead for her children. Ignoring her, the soldier scanned their faces, finally locking eyes with Daniel. Stepping forward, he grabbed the boy by his wrist and yanked him to his feet. Daniel's sister screamed. Before he had time to turn and say goodbye, he was pulled out the door and dragged across the palace floors. That was the last time he ever saw his mother.

Daniel soon found himself on the city streets. The scene was awful. The bodies of men, soldiers, and civilians were strewn everywhere. Some had their wives and children weeping over them, others were alone, draped over a stall or splayed across stone steps. The path Daniel and his captor were taking retraced his earlier steps back toward the gates of the city.

As they neared their destination, Daniel spotted a group of young men—all in their teens like he was. Each of them had some sort of connection to the crown, be it direct or indirect. They had all been lined up facing toward the gate. The soldier who was holding Daniel's arm roughly pulled him to the end of the line and indicated that he should stand there. Soon, several others were deposited next to him, extending the row even further.

Daniel sweated as he stood, partly due to the sun and partly due to fear. To his right stood his cousin, Azariah.

"Do you know what's going on here?" he asked.

Azariah shook his head, then he motioned with his chin and said, "No, but look over there."

On a raised platform beyond a phalanx of guards, a man in his mid-twenties sat on a travel throne. One after another, men approached him, dropped to their knees, said a few words, then were dismissed with a short comment or a simple wave. Having been raised around the royal family, Daniel had seen kings in the past. But none had the presence, the stateliness, the sheer power of the young man he saw on that throne.

Soon, several Babylonian men approached the line of Judean youths. They were not dressed as soldiers. Instead, they looked more like men of the court—soft and clean-shaven. One by one, they examined the teens. They had each pull at their hair and show their teeth. There were a few they had remove their tunics so that they could examine their physiques more closely. At the end of each examination, one of the men either pointed toward the gate or toward the city. Immediately, a soldier stepped forward, took hold of the young men, and removed them in the direction indicated.

The men came to Azariah. After a thorough examination, he was pointed toward the gate. Daniel saw terror in his cousin's eyes as he looked back before passing outside the walls. Then it was Daniel's turn. Behind him was the palace and his mom. But for some reason, he had an unshakable feeling that his place was through the gate.

Maybe it was because Azariah went that way, maybe it was because the soldiers who were taking teens back into the city seemed to be much rougher with them. Or maybe it was something bigger.

Ultimately, he didn't have time to analyze his feelings. The Babylonian pointed toward the gate, and Daniel was led through. As he passed the throne where Nebuchadnezzar sat, he turned toward him. For a moment, his eyes locked with those of the king, who just happened to be looking his way. A flood of emotion flowed through Daniel unlike anything he had experienced before. Something deep inside this teenage boy told him that this would not be the last time that he would stare into the eyes of this king.

God had given Daniel a mission: to be a light to the Gentiles. Chances are the teen who was deported from his comfortable life in Jerusalem to a court in a foreign land was completely unaware of this plan for his life. But what we do see with Daniel and his friends was that despite not understanding God's plan, they still trusted that He had one. So when God shifted their location and living circumstances because He needed them elsewhere, they didn't kick or scream. They accepted their new normal, remained true to God, and waited for opportunities to be used by Him.

Throughout Scripture, we see God using difficult times to accomplish His will. We never would have heard of Moses if God had not allowed the Egyptians to enslave Israel. Gideon would never have made the pages of the Bible if God didn't give the Midianites freedom to oppress His chosen people. And VeggieTales never would have made Jonah the lead asparagus in their first feature-length movie if the prophet hadn't spent three long, smelly days being digested by a fish.

God has given each of His followers a mission based on how He has created and gifted them. By mission, I'm talking about the reason that God placed each of us on this planet. You may have one great mission, or you may have numerous charges that change and evolve as you go through life. Either way, what is clear is that we are here for a reason. Paul emphasized that point when he wrote, "We are [God's] workmanship, created in Christ Jesus for good works, which God prepared beforehand that we should walk in them" (Ephesians 2:10).

Daniel and his friends couldn't accomplish their mission lounging in the comfort of the Jerusalem palace. In the same way, there are times when God needs to move us around or shake us up a bit to ensure we are perfectly staged to accomplish His will. Often, we don't understand what God is doing or why. Usually it is only when we look back, in hindsight, that we can make sense of the difficult times.

Because of the struggles within my parents' marriage, my brother and I were first sent to relatives, then into the foster care system. It was not an easy life. I was provided for and I had a roof over my head, but there was no love for me within my foster family. When I was a teen, this aloneness led me to despair, and I prepared to take my own life. But God stayed my hand, and it was at my lowest point that I was introduced to the true Messiah through the *Jesus* movie. If I had been reared in a happy, traditional home, I don't know that I would have ever come to the point that I was ready to accept something as radical to a Jewish boy as faith in the Messiah. So while I do not relish those difficult days, I am so thankful for them because they brought me to the point of my salvation.

That's why it is so important, particularly in the bad times, to be looking for God. Always He is there to walk us through the difficulty as a loving Father would. But we also need to keep our eyes and ears tuned in because He may be opening doors that will allow us to make a difference in the lives of those around us.

God moved Daniel, and He did so for a reason. But what was it that led to King Nebuchadnezzar marching on Jerusalem and stealing away the best and the brightest of the city's youth?

A Promised Punishment

Israel had become a great nation under the leadership of King David and his son, Solomon. But the greatness was short-lived. For all the wisdom Solomon had been given by God, there was still one area in which he was a complete idiot—women.

> King Solomon loved many foreign women, as well as the daughter of Pharaoh: women of the Moabites, Ammonites, Edomites, Sidonians, and Hittites—from the nations of whom the Lord had said to the children of Israel, "You shall not intermarry with them, nor they with you. Surely they will turn away your hearts after their gods." Solomon clung to these in love. And he had seven hundred wives, princesses, and three hundred concubines; and his wives turned away his heart. For it was so, when Solomon was old, that his wives turned his heart after other gods; and his heart was not loyal to the Lord his God, as was the heart of his father David (1 Kings 11:1-4).

Solomon knew the rule. He knew the reason for the rule. He knew the potential consequences for breaking the rule. Yet he said to himself, "It'll be different for me." How many people over the millennia have approached sin with that same arrogance? Just one drink, just one kiss, just one look at that website. Solomon thought he could handle the temptations. Turns out he couldn't, and he brought the nation down with him.

When Solomon died, he turned over his spiritually struggling nation to his spiritually bankrupt son, Rehoboam. The wisdom of Solomon was legendary, the wisdom of Rehoboam—not so much. It wasn't long before the kingdom was split in two. Ten tribes rebelled against Jerusalem to form the northern kingdom of Israel. Two remained with the house of David to form Judah. The northern kingdom was quick to reject the God of Abraham, Isaac, and Jacob, creating two golden calf gods and setting one each at the top and bottom of the nation for easy idol-worshipping access.

Despite their rebellion, though, God still loved the people of the north. He sent Elijah, Elisha, Amos, Hosea, and other prophets to tell His people to come back to Him. But Israel was having none of it. The Lord finally had enough, and, in 722 BC, He brought the Assyrians down on the kingdom. The result was utter devastation, and most of the Jews were removed from the land. In their place, Assyria's King Shalmaneser filled the population vacuum with Gentiles from other conquered lands. Soon, the region came to be known as "Galilee of the Gentiles" (Isaiah 9:1).

From their homes to the south, the people of Judah watched the demise of their sister, Israel. But rather than heed the warning and straighten up their ways, their attitude was, "Wow! Stinks to be them. Probably ought to go sacrifice a child to Molech in the Valley of Hinnom, just to stay safe." Once again, God sent prophets to turn them around. Isaiah, Micah, Jeremiah, Zephaniah, Habakkuk, and Joel all took their shots at bringing the nation to repentance. But the people didn't listen to them.

By this time in 605 BC, as mentioned above, the Assyrians were no more. In their place was the military juggernaut of Babylon. God tapped Nebuchadnezzar on the shoulder and pointed him toward Jerusalem. The king came, the city fell, and Daniel, along with many other Jews, was removed from the land and taken to Babylon in this first of three deportations spread over a period of two decades. It is during this event that the book of Daniel opens.

CHAPTER 1

SETTING THE STANDARD

Outside your window, the view is black as pitch. But what the night is lacking in light, it is more than making up for in sound. You can hear the rain pounding, followed by what feels like the clatter of a million BBs as hail pelts the roof. You huddle your family close together and try to calm your children by singing little refrains like, "We love the thunder 'cause the thunder brings rain." Every rural, small-town kid knows that rain is always a good thing.

Suddenly, a siren pierces through the din. Tornado! You and your wife each scoop up one of the little ones, while your oldest leaps to her feet. You scramble for the steps that lead to the basement. Just before you follow your wife down the stairs, you hear a growing rumble. It's close. Once underground, you hold each other tightly in a small, protected cement alcove as what sounds like a freight train approaches. Soon, the noise is deafening, and you hear glass smashing and wood snapping overhead. The floor above you gives way and crashes around your hideaway. Rainwater begins to cover the floor. Your children are crying, your wife is loudly telling them it will be okay, and you are praying with everything you have for the protection of your family.

Then it's passed. The blast of the tornado pulls away. The rumble of the thunder grows fainter. Soon, all you can hear is rain hitting the debris around you and the sound of dozens of car alarms. You tell your wife to wait with the children as you step out to explore. The view is devastating. You look up and see stars peeking through the clouds—stars where the ceiling of your basement should be. Your house is gone. Your possessions are gone. All that's left of your former life is huddled with their arms around one other in a corner of your basement. You pause for a moment and thank God for such a marvelous blessing.

I've never gone through a tornado. Dr. Rick Yohn, my writing collaborator on this book, has experienced several, and he has also seen firsthand the aftermath of some very devastating twisters. As he and his wife, Linda, drove through some recently hit areas and talked with survivors, many of whom had lost everything, they witnessed differing reactions. Some were in complete shock. Others expressed inconsolable sorrow. But there were many more who, despite their loss, were feeling incredible relief. "We may have lost everything," they would say, "but at least we have each other."

The Babylonians swept through Jerusalem like a tornado. Death, destruction, and loss trailed behind them. By the time Daniel and his friends began their long trek to the capital city, they had nothing left of their former lives. And when I say nothing, I don't just mean they lost their possessions and their comfortable royal lives. After a tornado hits, at least there is the hope that between insurance money and some help from the government, people can rebuild their homes and their businesses. Maybe life can one day get back to normal again.

But for Daniel's gang, normal was a state of being that no longer existed. They had been in the line of nobility to become somebody in the nation of Judah. They were being groomed for high positions, name recognition, and a life of power in their line of service. Those dreams were now shattered, and all that faced them was an uncertain future that might include slavery, servitude, or possibly a quick death.

One has to believe that the question of "Why?" crossed Daniel's mind. Why would God have allowed a heathen nation like Babylon to invade and enslave God's chosen people? But because of Daniel's upbringing, the answer to this seemingly huge conundrum was quite easy. Daniel was brought up with a knowledge of the Word of God. He would be familiar with the warnings of the prophets like Isaiah and Jeremiah. Being within the royal circle, he had seen how the kings since the days of Josiah had rebelled against the God of their fathers and were following pagan deities. What had been promised since the days of Moses was coming to pass. If the nation rebelled, God would bring punishment. And, as so often happens, the children were about to pay the price for the sins of their fathers.

Daniel and his friends could have been angry at God and bitter against the generations that came before them. That is how so many people react when they are innocent victims of other people's sins. And, for those who have been victimized, it is totally understandable that they may descend into long-lasting anger and depression. But what Daniel shows us is that there is a better path. There is a way that lifts one up, rather than letting past circumstances grind one into the ground. It is the way of hope, the way of faith, the way of God.

Death March to Babylon

We don't know what the journey was like for Daniel and his friends. Often, when prisoners were transported, they were stripped naked, chained together, and forced to walk the distance, likely barefooted. You may have heard the term *death march*, a forced march of prisoners of war during which those who cannot continue are killed or simply left along the roadside to die. One of the most famous of these in recent history was World War II's Bataan Death March. In April 1942, 66,000 Filipino and 10,000 American prisoners of war were forced to trek 66 miles through horrific conditions. Those who fell by the wayside were beaten, bayoneted, or shot. Only 54,000 of the original 76,000 made it all the way to the destination.

Think of how violent and cruel that forced journey was. Now, let's look at the Babylonian death march. Instead of 66 miles, the straight-line distance between Jerusalem and Babylon is more than 550 miles. But nobody traveled in a straight line between the two cities, because lying in the gap was the vast Arabian Desert. Those making the journey were forced to travel north, then arc over the desert in what was known as the Fertile Crescent. Only then could one make the descent southward to Babylon.

So how long of a journey did they make? Rather than look at distance, the best way to estimate the length of the trip is in time. Somewhat less than a century after Daniel and company travelled east to Babylon, Ezra the priest brought a contingent of exiles back west, going home to Jerusalem. We read of his journey, "On the first day of the first month he began his journey from Babylon, and on the first day of the fifth month he came to Jerusalem, according to the good hand of his God upon him" (Ezra 7:9). Feel free to check my math, but by my calculation, that was a four-month road trip. But Ezra and his cohorts were likely in much better shape than the prisoner-of-war crew that was being shuffled into exile. Daniel's trip probably took a little longer and cost many more lives. Were Daniel and his friends forced to walk the whole way, or were they carted in caged wagons because of their royal pedigree? That's a question we can't answer. What we do know is that it had to have been a world-shattering experience for these teens.

And the shake-ups didn't end when they arrived.

A Whole New World

Everything was different. Have you ever visited a foreign country on vacation, one with a different language, culture, and government structure? Very quickly, you realized that you had some challenges ahead of you. It's likely you had moments of stumbling through asking for directions or ordering meals. Your one consolation through the embarrassment was that you would soon be back in your own country, surrounded by people who thought like you and spoke your language.

Daniel and his friends didn't have that luxury of return. When they arrived in Babylon, they knew that this was where they would stay. They didn't even have the comfort of remaining with the rest of the Jewish exiles. Nebuchadnezzar had a plan for them, and holding on to their roots and their identities was not part of it.

> Then the king instructed Ashpenaz, the master of his eunuchs, to bring some of the children of Israel and some of the king's descendants and some of the nobles, young men in whom there was no blemish, but good-looking, gifted in all wisdom, possessing knowledge and quick to understand, who had ability to serve in the king's palace, and whom they might teach the language and literature of the Chaldeans (Daniel 1:3-4).

Young King Nebuchadnezzar had done some traveling during his military campaigns. Something he had learned as he moved from city to city and culture to culture was that there were some very smart, high-quality young men out in the world. Their only drawback was that they were not Babylonian—yet. His plan was to take their best and brightest and make them his best and brightest.

Who were these cream-of-the-crop candidates? We see from the above passage that they were young men. Old guys need not apply.

Second, they had noble blood flowing through their veins. Sorry peasants and all you riffraff, you're out. Third, they had to be good-looking and without a blemish. The king's court had its standards, after all. Finally, they had to be some smart cookies. Nebuchadnezzar wanted young men who not only had a strong grasp on their own culture's wisdom and knowledge, but who had the ability to quickly pick up the Chaldean language and literature.

One qualification that was not included was that they had to adhere to a common belief system. They were welcome to hold on to whatever gods they worshipped back in their home country. The only caveat was that their old ways could not interfere with Babylon's new ways. Go ahead and worship your gods, as long as you worship our gods first. For most polytheistic pagan cultures, this was no problem. For the Jews, it was *the* problem. Written long before in the number one slot on those stone tablets was the command, "You shall have no other gods before me" (Deuteronomy 5:7). There was no wiggle room allowed, even if it was at the demand of a king.

There was another major change facing Daniel and his friends. This one was life-altering and permanent. Several generations earlier, King Hezekiah became sick with a terminal illness. He cried out to God, and the Lord graciously extended his life. At that time, a fledgling kingdom sent envoys with some letters and a present to the king, congratulating him on his recovery. Hezekiah was feeling a little full of himself and decided he wanted to show off to these foreigners. So he gave them a tour of Jerusalem, including his gold and silver, his spices, and his armory. The kingdom these men came from was Babylon.

Soon after their departure, the prophet Isaiah paid Hezekiah a visit. He told the king that he had done a very foolish thing by letting his pride get the best of him and putting all his treasures on display. Then Isaiah prophesied to Hezekiah of a coming time:

> Hear the word of the LORD of hosts: "Behold, the days
> are coming when all that is in your house, and what your
> fathers have accumulated until this day, shall be carried to
> Babylon; nothing shall be left," says the LORD. "And they
> shall take away some of your sons who will descend from
> you, whom you will beget; and they shall be eunuchs in
> the palace of the king of Babylon" (Isaiah 39:5-7).

Daniel and his friends were the fulfillment of this prophecy. They were taken away to Babylon, where they would have been made eunuchs. As additional evidence of this fact, look back to Daniel 1:3. Who was it that was in charge of the young men at their departure? It was Ashpenaz, the master of King Nebuchadnezzar's eunuchs. Not only were these young men taken from their homes, transported to a faraway land, and placed in a culture that was the polar opposite of righteous and monotheistic, but they were also sexually mutilated so that they would never be able to have children. All their dreams about being a father, passing on the family name, bouncing a toddler on their knee, all gone with a cut. If Job's wife had been there, she would have concluded that they should just "Curse God and die!" (Job 2:9).

Yet still, we see Daniel and his friends holding on to their hope.

Acclimation and Assimilation

The king was now faced with a strategic decision. Here was a batch of freshly arrived Jerusalem eunuchs to join the ones he already had from Egypt and Assyria. If his plan were to work of using these young men as sources of wisdom and influence within his court, he had to make sure their loyalties lay with him. Assassination and intrigue were a constant within the halls of many palaces. If these guys were going to use their brains to plot and scheme, Nebuchadnezzar wanted to make sure they were plotting for him and not against him. He had to find a way to separate them from the loyalty they felt to the homes they left and direct it instead to the land in which they now lived.

There was one great advantage Nebuchadnezzar had with his future advisors. They were all young. Youthful minds are easier to reprogram. They are adaptable. It causes far less grief for a child or teen to acclimate to a new situation than it does an adult. Whereas a captured soldier may need to be compelled at the point of a sword to serve, a young person can be persuaded with a harsh word or, better yet, an incentive. Thus, what we find in Daniel 1 is a strategy of reprogram and reward.

The first part of the reprogramming was a rebranding. These young men were no longer Jews, they were Babylonians. Thus, they needed Babylonian names.

> Now from among those of the sons of Judah were Daniel, Hananiah, Mishael, and Azariah. To them the chief of the eunuchs gave names: he gave Daniel the name Belteshazzar; to Hananiah, Shadrach; to Mishael, Meshach; and to Azariah, Abed-Nego (Daniel 1:6-7).

Back in that time, names meant something. Today, few people understand the origin of their name or its meaning, beyond it maybe belonging to a family member, friend, or historical figure. In the time of Daniel, names were typically used to express character or, more frequently, to honor God. As part of the reprogramming process, Ashpenaz, chief of the eunuchs, instituted a significant change for these young Jews. Their names would still elicit praise, but to a different deity.

Marduk was the chief god of Babylon, the protector of the city. He was also known as Bel, which many might recognize from the Hebrew pronunciation of his name, Baal. His son, Nabu, was the god of wisdom and literature. Mount Nebo, Moses' vantage point of the Promised Land before his death, bears the name of this "announcer" god. A third god who was worshipped in Babylon was the moon god, Aku. It is these three gods who find their way into the appellations of our newly minted Babylonians.

Daniel's name means "God is my judge." In its place, he was given Belteshazzar, "Bel protect the prince." Imagine this young man, while striving to remain true to his Lord, being labeled with the name of Baal, the one false god who had likely been the greatest stumbling block for wayward Jews over the centuries. Hananiah, who at birth had been given the God-affirming name "Yahweh has acted graciously," was rechristened with one that celebrated creation rather than the Creator—Shadrach, the "command of Aku." Mishael's name became Meshach. "Who is like God?" became "Who is like Aku?" So similar, but so very different. Finally, there was Azariah, whose name celebrated the true God who lovingly comes alongside His people—"Yahweh has helped." His name became Abednego, or "Servant of Nabu."

Did this rebranding work to separate these young men from their past? That we are studying the book of Daniel instead of the book of Belteshazzar gives us a hint. With just a few exceptions, whenever Daniel mentioned his Babylonian name, he used some version of the formula "Daniel, whose name was Belteshazzar." The only times he didn't use that formula in his book was chapter 4, which is when King Nebuchadnezzar had taken the role of storyteller.

If Daniel insisted on using his own Jewish name in his book, why did he refer to his friends by their Babylonian names? First, we need to realize that there are only three contexts where Daniel talks about these three companions. One is when they are introduced, and we learn about their name conversions. The second is at the end of chapter 2, when the young prophet reveals to Nebuchadnezzar the meaning of his dream. At the end, we read:

> Daniel petitioned the king, and he set Shadrach, Meshach, and Abed-Nego over the affairs of the province of Babylon; but Daniel sat in the gate of the king (Daniel 2:49).

This refers to official court business, so it makes sense that Daniel would use the court names of his friends. The final usage is the entirety of chapter 3, in which we read the tale of the fiery furnace. His use of Shadrach, Meshach, and Abednego there is just good storytelling. From a writer's point of view, having to remind the reader who is who as Daniel switched from his narrative to Babylonian character's quotes would make the account unreadable. So, like the great author he is, the prophet streamlined his story by using his friends' Babylonian names, and let us all sit back to enjoy the action.

When deciding whether to fight against these new names, it seems like Daniel and friends decided to go with the flow. There's nothing in the Mosaic law that prohibited a certain kind of name. And, since they were likely brought up with a knowledge of Jewish history, they would know that having a foreign god in one's name wasn't unprecedented. The great hero judge Gideon, after he destroyed the altar of Baal, was given the name Jerubbaal, which means "contender with Baal" or "Baal judges." Certainly that was a different context, but ultimately, Belteshazzar and Jerubbaal shared the same false god in their names. So these young men took the "Call me anything you like, just don't call me late for dinner" approach. It turned out, though, that dinner was where the true test of their commitment to God would come.

A Change of Diet

Being raised among royalty had many privileges, one of which was good food. Daniel has been portrayed by some health-conscious folks as a committed vegetarian. I would call his vegetarianism more situational, because the chances that he stuck to the green stuff before he was hauled away to Babylon are very slim. In the palace at Jerusalem, food of all types was not a problem. King Solomon's spread was especially opulent:

> Now Solomon's provision for one day was thirty kors of fine flour, sixty kors of meal, ten fatted oxen, twenty oxen from the pastures, and one hundred sheep, besides deer, gazelles, roebucks, and fatted fowl (1 Kings 4:22-23).

Certainly the economic situation had changed since the Solomonic heyday, but I have no doubt that meat was still on the palace menu. Once he got to Babylon, Daniel became a vegetarian because he had to, not because he wanted to.

When Daniel arrived in Babylon, he wasn't thrown as a captive into a cell and fed bread and water. That would not work with Nebuchadnezzar's plan of having these young men "serve before the king" (Daniel 1:5). To get the best out of them, he needed them smart and healthy. So he ordered that these new court recruits be given "a daily provision of the king's delicacies and of the wine which he drank" (verse 5). For most of those who had been taken with Daniel, eating this royal food was wonderful. Mealtime would have included meats, fish, and vegetables cooked into amazing dishes using spices from all over the world. Babylon might have begun to feel more like a foreign study program at a royal university than forced captivity. Well, except for the whole eunuch thing. But imprisonment in a distant land certainly could have been a lot worse.

But while everybody else was celebrating the menu, Daniel was faced with a dilemma.

> Daniel purposed in his heart that he would not defile himself with the portion of the king's delicacies, nor with the wine which he drank; therefore he requested of the chief of the eunuchs that he might not defile himself (verse 8).

God was very specific in the Mosaic law about what animals could and couldn't be eaten. There would have been much from the king's table that didn't meet up with God's standards. Some might ask, "Why didn't Daniel just eat around the bad stuff? If they served him surf and turf, couldn't he just shove the lobster to the side and eat the steak?" That wouldn't have worked because the problem was more than just a kosher one. Most meat in those days was offered to the gods before it came to the plate. In Babylon, it seems this was also true of the wine because Daniel decided to reject it also.

Was eating this food really that big of a deal? Think about it: Daniel had been uprooted from his comfortable home. He had been forced on a four-month journey. Then when he arrived, he had been mutilated and told that he was to serve the one responsible for his mutilation. All in all, it had been a lousy period of his life. Could he really be blamed if he partook in some of the few pleasures still available to him? What if he still prayed, read the Scriptures, and tried to always do the right thing? Couldn't he compromise in this one little area? It's not like there were any rabbis around to condemn him. Besides, wasn't it God who had allowed this whole upheaval to happen?

This takes me back to the Garden of Eden and the satanic logic used to seduce Eve into compromise:

> [The serpent] said to the woman, "Has God indeed said, 'You shall not eat of every tree of the garden'?"

> And the woman said to the serpent, "We may eat the fruit of the trees of the garden; but of the fruit of the tree which *is* in the midst of the garden, God has said, 'You shall not eat it, nor shall you touch it, lest you die.'"

> Then the serpent said to the woman, "You will not surely die. For God knows that in the day you eat of it your eyes

will be opened, and you will be like God, knowing good
and evil" (Genesis 3:1-5).

First, the serpent challenged God's word—"Has God indeed
said…?" Then he challenged God's character—"You will not surely
die," implying that God had lied. The enemy likely used the same
tactic on Daniel. "Would compromising the dietary laws really be
that bad, given your situation?" And, "God is the one who got you
into this mess. See how He's repaid your righteousness?"

This same kind of spiritual seduction is rampant today, especially in
the church. "We're grown adults, and we've both been married before.
Is it really that big of a deal if we sleep together?" "God has let me get
into this financial mess. Surely, He can't expect me to tithe when I'm
already just getting by." There's a reason we are admonished to be wise as
a serpent (see Matthew 10:16). The devil is exceptional at using twisted
logic to make sin seem not only okay, but beneficial and our right.

But righteousness is not fluid. Morality is not situational. God
has called us to a standard, and when we flaunt that standard, it creates a barrier between ourselves and Him. Daniel was committed to
ensuring that his actions were never responsible for driving a wedge
between himself and God.

Though most of the captive Jews were unfaithful to God, those who
placed Him first in their lives did not go unnoticed by their Father in
heaven. After Daniel and his friends were confronted with the non-
kosher, idol-sacrificed diet, we see two very important words: "But
Daniel." That beautiful conjunction "but" is so often used in Scripture to contrast the unrighteous with the righteous, the bad news
with the good, destruction with hope.

Remember back in Genesis when God looked around the world
and saw how corrupt mankind had become? It grieved Him when
He compared the beauty of when it all started with the sinful ugli-
ness of what it had become.

So the LORD said, "I will destroy man whom I have created from the face of the earth, both man and beast, creeping thing and birds of the air, for I am sorry that I have made them." But Noah found grace in the eyes of the LORD (Genesis 6:7-8).

There was sin, sorrow, and impending destruction. Then came those future-altering words, "But Noah," and with them came hope and joy and an incredible glimpse into how holiness and love are perfectly balanced in the character of God.

Daniel would not give in like the others. He would not defile himself with the king's menu. He would stand for his beliefs. But he knew this was a risk. Standing against the orders of the king was a near foolproof method for getting yourself killed. So to pull this off, he and his buddies were going to have to be smart.

They formulated a plan.

But God was way ahead of them. Even before they had made their commitment, He was at work preparing their overseer to be open to their suggestion. "Now God had brought Daniel into the favor and goodwill of the chief of the eunuchs" (Daniel 1:9). This is why we never need to fear doing the right thing. Before we are even faced with a moral dilemma, God knows whether we will say yes to righteousness, and He has already begun working out the situation.

The Boys Make a Stand

Daniel and his boys determined to stand with God and not eat the food. They knew the potential consequences, but to them, faithfulness was more important than life. How did they approach it? Did they go on strike? Did they march around the dining hall with chants and signs? Absolutely not. Instead of using a negative approach to a negative situation, they turned it around to a positive.

> Daniel said to the steward whom the chief of the eunuchs
> had set over Daniel, Hananiah, Mishael, and Azariah,
> "Please test your servants for ten days, and let them give
> us vegetables to eat and water to drink. Then let our
> appearance be examined before you, and the appearance of
> the young men who eat the portion of the king's delicacies;
> and as you see fit, so deal with your servants." So he
> consented with them in this matter, and tested them ten
> days (Daniel 1:11-14).

The steward hesitated. He was afraid for his life. If anything went awry with his charges, it wouldn't just cause him a reprimand or even his job. A downturn in the health of Daniel, et al., said the man, "would endanger my head before the king" (verse 10). That's even worse than some of the punishments I and my fellow soldiers experienced in the Israeli Defense Forces, although only slightly. So Daniel made him a proposition he couldn't refuse: "Feed us vegetables and water for ten days, then see how we are." It was brilliant! No downside for the steward, only the potential of positive results. The man readily agreed.

Ten days passed, and it was time for the inspection. The steward looked the four young men over and saw that "their features appeared better and fatter in flesh than all the young men who ate the portion of the king's delicacies" (verse 15). So amazing were the results that the rest of the young men had their "delicacies" taken away and replaced with vegetables, instantaneously making Daniel, Shadrach, Meshach, and Abednego the most disliked members of the king's training program.

God's hand is so wonderfully evident in this account. A vegetarian diet can certainly bring noticeable changes in a person's health over time. But for there to be that significant a difference in only ten days shows that God was there quite literally tipping the scales in their favor. This takes us back to the point we discussed earlier. When we determine to do what is right, the Lord will be there with us 100 percent of the time. He won't just be watching us from a distance, rooting for us and hoping it all turns out okay. He will be intimately and intricately involved.

And the blessings for obedience are ongoing. God didn't just help out Daniel and his friends in this instance, then say, "See you around." As they kept their eyes on Him, He kept His eyes on them.

> As for these four young men, God gave them knowledge and skill in all literature and wisdom; and Daniel had understanding in all visions and dreams. Now at the end of the days, when the king had said that they should be brought in, the chief of the eunuchs brought them in before Nebuchadnezzar. Then the king interviewed them, and among them all none was found like Daniel, Hananiah, Mishael, and Azariah; therefore they served before the king. And in all matters of wisdom and understanding about which the king examined them, he found them ten times better than all the magicians and astrologers who were in all his realm (verses 17-20).

God caused them to excel through the program. Then, at graduation, they not only outshone the rest of their class, but these teens were far wiser than any of the seasoned wise men in the kingdom. Now, I'd like to attribute this to the fact that, like me, they were Jews of the tribe of Judah. However, quality of this type goes far beyond even that pedigree. These young men reaped what they had sown. They were faithful in their actions, and the Lord was faithful in His gifts and blessings.

It is unlikely that any of us will face a life-and-death decision over righteousness. But we do face situations every day when we have the choice to say yes to God or yes to ourselves. Some of these may be big decisions, but most will be small. In those lesser times, the enemy may whisper in our ear as he did to Eve, "It's really no big deal. Just this one time."

Every decision as to whether we sin or not is a big one, because every sin is big. Not only does it separate us from our closeness with God, but it has a cumulative effect. Jesus told His disciples, "He who is faithful in what is least is faithful also in much; and he who is unjust in what is least is unjust also in much" (Luke 16:10). I have seen far too many believers shipwreck their faith after giving in to little sinful compromises.

Peace comes from knowing you are right with God. Hope comes from holding on to the promises the Lord gives to us when we are right with Him. Daniel experienced a bounty of spiritual blessings because of his faithfulness. In the next chapter, we'll see that faithfulness take him into the throne room of the king.

CHAPTER 2

THE IMPOSSIBLE DREAM

It was the fall of 2015, and Behold Israel was in its second year. The ministry's board was meeting in Parker, Colorado, for the purpose of developing to a greater extent BI's vision. One of the members asked me a question: "Amir, when are you going to write a book so that more people can get your teaching?"

This wasn't the first time that I had heard the question. In fact, I had pondered the possibility many times before. Unfortunately, I knew the answer, which I then shared with the board. "I'm sorry, guys. What you're asking is impossible. You know that English is not my first language. I'm fine speaking it, but writing an entire book is a whole different thing. Besides, when am I supposed to find time to be an author? I'm constantly traveling. And the time that I'm in Israel, I'm leading tours or preparing messages. There's just no way."

No sooner had I finished my response than our finance director shouted out, "Steve Yohn!"

"What about him?" I knew Steve from a tour he had been on, but I knew his father, Rick, better.

"Steve wrote some books with Jason Elam, who used to be a kicker for the Denver Broncos. Maybe he can write the books with you."

It was an interesting idea. "Call pastor Rick, and see if he can get Steve down here for lunch."

Steve and I met. Then, for the next three days, we sat together in pastor Rick's basement and worked out the details for my first book, *The Last Hour*. Suddenly, the impossible was made possible, which shouldn't have been a surprise to me or anyone else. We serve a God who is in the business of making the impossible possible.

This is our theme as we step into Daniel 2. King Nebuchadnez-zar faced a problem, and he wanted to be sure that he was going to get the right solution. So he gave his advisors an impossible task—a task that, if they didn't accomplish it, would cost them their lives. Thankfully for them, there was someone in their midst who knew the One who dealt in the impossible.

It is in this chapter that we come to the first of the visions that we find in Daniel's book. This one and the two that follow come from Daniel the storyteller. When I say storyteller, I am not using it in the fictional sense. Daniel used real-life illustrations to communicate his points. When we get to the second half of the book, the style of writing shifts from storytelling to apocalyptic visions.

For some of you who prefer lecture to narrative, you may find yourself occasionally frustrated in the first half of Daniel. "Where's the meat, Amir? I feel like we're all application and no theology." Remember, in all that God does, there is order. In this book, we are going to follow the style and feel of the original author. There is a reason that the Holy Spirit guided Daniel to write this way. What I love about this book is that there is plenty throughout to keep both the right-brain people and the left-brain folk engaged and stimu-lated throughout.

The King Has a Dream

King Nebuchadnezzar tossed and turned in his bed. His eyeballs were dancing against the insides of his lids as his subconscious presented to him a vision that was awe-inspiring and terrifying. The tension built inside of him until suddenly he cried out, sitting up straight in his opulent bed chamber.

Looking around, he came to the realization that it had been a dream. But it had been no ordinary night journey. This one meant something. He was sure of it. Not caring about the hour—after all, he's the king—he called his servants and sent them out to rouse his wise men. He was about to present to them a challenge.

> Now in the second year of Nebuchadnezzar's reign, Nebuchadnezzar had dreams; and his spirit was *so* troubled that his sleep left him. Then the king gave the command to call the magicians, the astrologers, the sorcerers, and the Chaldeans to tell the king his dreams. So they came and stood before the king. And the king said to them, "I have had a dream, and my spirit is anxious to know the dream" (Daniel 2:1-3).

Before we get to the wise men's response, we've got a little housecleaning to do. Daniel tells us that this event took place in the king's second year. Remember, Daniel was taken right after Nebuchadnezzar became king, and was immediately put into a three-year training program. So how does that math work out with Daniel now being a full-fledged graduate of Babylon's Magi University?

Dr. John F. Walvoord, former president of Dallas Theological Seminary for more than three decades, gives us some insight:

> The Babylonian method of dating the reigns of kings was to use the ascension-year dating system that did not count

> Nebuchadnezzar's ascension year (September 7, 605 B.C.
> – April 1, 604 B.C.) as the first year of his reign. His "first
> year" would have been April 2, 604 B.C. to March 21,
> 603 B.C., and his "second year" would have been March
> 22, 603 B.C. to April 9, 602 B.C. The events of chapter
> 2 occurred at the end of the three-year course of the study
> mentioned in 1:5, shortly after Daniel entered the king's
> service. But it was officially the "second year of the reign
> of Nebuchadnezzar."[1]

So this would have been just after Daniel and his buddies had completed their training, which is likely why they were not included in the group of wise men that were gathered to the palace. Bleary-eyed and a little nervous at being pulled from their beds into the king's presence, the magi breathed a sigh of relief when they heard the request.

Nebuchadnezzar Demands the Impossible

Dreams. They'd done those before. They'd listen to the king tell his story. Then they'd give a little song, a little dance, a few random words of wisdom, and the king could go back to sleep with a cheery interpretation of his nightmare.

> The Chaldeans spoke to the king in Aramaic, "O king, live
> forever! Tell your servants the dream, and we will give the
> interpretation" (verse 4).

But the king broke the dream/interpretation protocol. He threw them a curveball, one with enough juice on it that it was impossible to hit.

> The king answered and said to the Chaldeans, "My decision
> is firm: if you do not make known the dream to me, and

its interpretation, you shall be cut in pieces, and your houses shall be made an ash heap. However, if you tell the dream and its interpretation, you shall receive from me gifts, rewards, and great honor. Therefore tell me the dream and its interpretation" (verses 5-6).

Nebuchadnezzar was a smart guy. He knew the wise men and their sketchy ways. It was time to put them to the test. "Maybe you guys didn't hear me right. I said I want you first to tell me my dream, then I'll listen to what it means. You do that, and you'll get rewarded beyond your wildest dreams. If you don't, then it's slice and dice time." It was a brilliant play. These men claimed they could do the impossible. They could look to the skies or into bowls filled with potions or at the bones of animals, and they could give the king insight into the future and the spirit world.

Nebuchadnezzar said, "Prove it."

They panicked.

> The Chaldeans answered the king, and said, "There is not a man on earth who can tell the king's matter; therefore no king, lord, or ruler has ever asked such things of any magician, astrologer, or Chaldean. It is a difficult thing that the king requests, and there is no other who can tell it to the king except the gods, whose dwelling is not with flesh" (verses 10-11).

And the truth came out. The claims of these magicians, astrologers, sorcerers, and Chaldeans, who were also soothsayers, to be able to see and understand the supernatural were all bogus. If these guys couldn't give the king what he asked for, then what good were they? He decided not to even wait for their inevitable failure. Furious, he "gave the command to destroy all the wise men of Babylon" (verse 12). The decree went out, and the wise men began to be put to death.

Daniel is such a brilliant storyteller. The reader is drawn in but can still manage an emotional distance. *Wow, kind of stinks to be Babylonian magi right about now*, they may think. And then a realization hits. "Wait, isn't Daniel one of the Babylonian magi?" And suddenly the reader has skin in the game. It's beautiful!

Word got to Daniel and his friends that a kill order had gone out and they were on the list. I love how they responded. Rather than panicking, the four friends talked it out. They "counseled" together. Once they agreed on a plan of action, Daniel stepped forward as the one to implement their strategy. The first step was to attempt to pause the killing.

> With counsel and wisdom Daniel answered Arioch, the captain of the king's guard, who had gone out to kill the wise men of Babylon; he answered and said to Arioch the king's captain, "Why is the decree from the king so urgent?" Then Arioch made the decision known to Daniel (verses 14-15).

Arioch was in charge of the slaughter, so Daniel went to him, which was a pretty bold move. He pled for his life and for those of his companions, telling the captain of the king's guard that he could stop the killing. He would tell Nebuchadnezzar the dream. Arioch pushed back. He had his orders, and only the king could tell him to pause. So, Daniel and Arioch likely went in to see the king together. Daniel promised Nebuchadnezzar a dream and an interpretation; he just needed a brief time-out. The monarch agreed, and Daniel rushed home to tell his friends.

Prayer Makes Possible the Impossible

The plan had worked perfectly. Now only one small step remained to save the wise men in Babylon. Daniel and his friends had to do the impossible. But remember, they served a God who dealt in the impossible, and that's who they turned to now.

> Daniel went to his house, and made the decision known to Hananiah, Mishael, and Azariah, his companions, that they might seek mercies from the God of heaven concerning this secret, so that Daniel and his companions might not perish with the rest of the wise men of Babylon. Then the secret was revealed to Daniel in a night vision. So Daniel blessed the God of heaven (verses 17-19).

These teenagers knew what most Christian adults forget. When you have a problem, the very first thing you do is get on your knees and pray. You don't work out the numbers. You don't Google opinions. You don't make a pros and cons list. Those options may all come into play later, but the number one action we must always take when faced with a difficulty of whatever magnitude is to immediately put it in the hands of the God who can do all things.

The companions prayed, and God answered. He revealed the dream to Daniel in a night vision. This is the first that we see of Daniel receiving a vision. When we get to the second half of this book, it will become evident that this is God's preferred methodology for communicating with this prophet.

Once they had their answer, they did the second thing that most Christian adults forget to do. They stopped and thanked God. Daniel prayed:

> Blessed be the name of God forever and ever,
> for wisdom and might are His...
> I thank You and praise You,
> O God of my fathers;
> You have given me wisdom and might,

and have now made known to me what we asked of You,
for You have made known to us the king's demand
(verses 20, 23).

The thanksgiving done, Daniel hustled to find Arioch. "Don't kill any more. I've got the interpretation," he told the captain. Arioch rushed Daniel back into the king's presence, where Nebuchadnezzar asked, "Are you able to make known to me the dream which I have seen, and its interpretation?" (Daniel 2:26). Daniel's answer tells us everything we need to know about the character of the young man.

Daniel answered in the presence of the king, and said,
"The secret which the king has demanded, the wise men,
the astrologers, the magicians, and the soothsayers
cannot declare to the king. But there is a God in heaven
who reveals secrets, and He has made known to King
Nebuchadnezzar what will be in the latter days" (verses
27-28).

Immediately, Daniel gave God credit. This is a pattern that we will see throughout his life. I wonder whether Daniel was thinking about the Hebrew hero, Joseph, as he stood before the king. Pharaoh had a frightening dream. Joseph was brought in. Pharaoh said to him, "I hear you can interpret dreams." Rather than taking any credit for himself, Joseph answered, "It is not in me; God will give Pharaoh an answer of peace" (Genesis 41:16). Despite all the books you might order from Amazon on the subject, accurate dream interpretation is the purview of God, not man. Nebuchadnezzar asked, "Are you the guy?" Daniel answered, "I'm not. But God is."

If you're a believer in the Lord Jesus Christ, Daniel's assertion above makes perfect sense. But in our secular society today, the idea that God reveals the future is a foreign notion. In fact, the very idea of miracles seems silly to the secular mind. John C. Lennox, professor of mathematics at the University of Oxford and a well-known Christian apologist, wrote:

> It goes without saying that Daniel's affirmative answer to that question constitutes a major challenge to contemporary secularism, in its atheistic insistence that the universe is a closed system of cause and effect.[2]

Lennox goes on to talk about evolutionary biologist Richard Dawkins, an outspoken member of the New Atheists, who wrote in his book *The God Delusion*:

> The nineteenth century is the last time when it was possible for an educated person to admit to believing in miracles like the virgin birth without embarrassment. When pressed, many educated Christians today are too loyal to deny the virgin birth and the resurrection. But it embarrasses them because their rational minds know that it is absurd, so they would much rather not be asked.[3]

Men like Dawkins mock believers who accept the supernatural. At the same time, they worship at the feet of rationalism, the god of the atheist. But we shouldn't expect anything different. An individual who does not possess the Holy Spirit cannot understand the supernatural. Dawkins lives in a closed system of the universe that believes if something cannot be proven scientifically, it cannot be trusted. Yet if you ask him to scientifically prove the origins of the universe or of life, he'll be forced to admit he can't.

Dawkins is convinced that he and those like him are intellectually far superior to those who believe a God exists who is able to perform miracles and make known future events. He and his fellow New

Atheists, who substitute ridicule and sarcasm for sound argument, remind me of the apostle Paul's words to the Corinthians:

> These things we also speak, not in words which man's wisdom teaches but which the Holy Spirit teaches, comparing spiritual things with spiritual. But the natural man does not receive the things of the Spirit of God, for they are foolishness to him; nor can he know them, because they are spiritually discerned. But he who is spiritual judges all things, yet he himself is rightly judged by no one. For "who has known the mind of the LORD that he may instruct Him?" But we have the mind of Christ (1 Corinthians 2:13-16).

Without the Holy Spirit, how can one be expected to understand spiritual things? Daniel was about to lift the veil between the natural and the supernatural, giving the king a glimpse of what the prophet was able to see with his spiritual eyes. Nebuchadnezzar was going to learn of "the times of the Gentiles."

The Times of the Gentiles

Before we move on, we need to understand what the times of the Gentiles is about because it is so significant to the understanding of this book. The Bible begins with Gentiles. Adam and Eve were Gentiles. Noah was a Gentile. Jews didn't come into being until Abraham. But also in those early chapters of Genesis, God began telling His story by looking at individuals and families. There were Adam and Eve and Cain and Abel. We read about Enoch, Methuselah, and, again, Noah. This microcosmic focus carries through the first 11 chapters of the Bible. Then comes Genesis 12, and the focus widens. The story becomes about the Jews and the nation of Israel, and this carries all the way through to the end of Malachi. It is true that other countries are mentioned. But they are discussed only in reference to their relationship with Israel.

That is why Daniel is unique. In a testament filled with Jewish focus, this book's tie-in with the times of the Gentiles unites it with the end times focus of Jesus on the Mount of Olives, of Paul in Romans 11, and of John in the book of Revelation. Daniel shows that God has a plan for those outside the nation of Israel, to use them as a means to draw His own people back to Himself.

God chose Israel to be a light to the nations. The Lord said to His people, "I will also give You as a light to the Gentiles, that You should be My salvation to the ends of the earth" (Isaiah 49:6). But God's chosen nation failed at its calling. Rather than standing out as a light, their desire was to be like all the other nations. Before opening the door to the Promised Land, God warned Israel that if they failed to follow Him, He would take this beautiful inheritance away from them. Still, they rebelled, and He acted. In 722 BC, the Assyrians removed the northern kingdom of Israel, and from 605 BC through 586 BC, He used the Babylonians to complete His process of evicting the southern kingdom of Judah. From that time forward, Gentiles have either dominated or had influence over the land of Israel. These are the times of the Gentiles.

The Dream Revealed

Back to our story. Daniel was standing in front of King Nebuchadnezzar. He had just made a bold statement by claiming that through the power of God he would not only interpret the king's dream, but he would accomplish the impossible feat of describing the nightmare first.

> You, O king, were watching; and behold, a great image!
> This great image, whose splendor was excellent, stood
> before you; and its form was awesome. This image's head

was of fine gold, its chest and arms of silver, its belly and thighs of bronze, its legs of iron, its feet partly of iron and partly of clay. You watched while a stone was cut out without hands, which struck the image on its feet of iron and clay, and broke them in pieces. Then the iron, the clay, the bronze, the silver, and the gold were crushed together, and became like chaff from the summer threshing floors; the wind carried them away so that no trace of them was found. And the stone that struck the image became a great mountain and filled the whole earth (Daniel 2:31-35).

Daniel had the king at "great image." The scary dream could have been about anything. He could have seen attacks by huge armies or had visions of ghosts and spirits or found himself making a speech in front of his city's great population in only his underwear. But as soon as Daniel talked about a statue, Nebuchadnezzar knew that he could trust everything else that came out of this young wise man's mouth.

Upon knowing the details of the dream, it is easy to understand why it was so troubling. The king knew that it had something to do with him, but he didn't know what. Was he the statue? Was he only a part of the statue? Maybe he was the rock, or more terrifyingly, maybe the rock was tumbling toward him. It makes sense why he wanted to be sure that he had the right interpretation, and why he was so frustrated when no one could meet his truthfulness challenge.

This idea of truth being so close yet so far away reminds me of Revelation and a different throne room. John the Revelator was standing before the court of the King of kings. A scroll was brought out with seven seals holding it closed. The anticipation of learning the wisdom that was contained therein filled the room. But then disaster struck:

> I saw a strong angel proclaiming with a loud voice, "Who is worthy to open the scroll and to loose its seals?" And no one in heaven or on the earth or under the earth was able to open the scroll, or to look at it (Revelation 5:2-3).

John couldn't believe his ears. *No one? We're in heaven in the very presence of God, and there is no one worthy to open the scroll?* He wept and wept, until one of the elders said to him, "Do not weep. Behold, the Lion of the tribe of Judah, the Root of David, has prevailed to open the scroll and to loose its seven seals" (verse 5). John looked, and there before him the great Lion stood in the form of a slaughtered lamb. This was the One that the Almighty had deemed worthy to reveal the truths written in the scroll.

Nebuchadnezzar was so close to learning the essential truth of his dream. Yet without someone worthy to unlock its wisdom, he was still impossibly far away. Imagine his excitement, his joy, when Daniel, one who was deemed worthy by God, stepped forward to reveal this all-important insight. After listening to the dream portion of this young man's message, Nebuchadnezzar readied himself for its interpretation.

The Dream's Interpretation—Five Kingdoms
Kingdom One—Babylon

Daniel began, "You, O king, are a king of kings. For the God of heaven has given you a kingdom, power, strength, and glory; and wherever the children of men dwell, or the beasts of the field and the birds of the heaven, He has given them into your hand, and has made you ruler over them all—you are this head of gold" (Daniel 2:37-38). The king's chest must have swelled when he heard those last words. Of course he's the head of gold. Who else would be? It certainly wasn't Pharaoh Necho II or whoever that schmo was who was leading the last of the Assyrian rabble at Carchemish. Nebuchadnezzar knew there was no one else who deserved to be that head of gold. It was good to hear that Daniel's God agreed with him.

The king's position at the top was the good news. The bad news was that it wouldn't last. Daniel continued, "But after you shall arise another kingdom inferior to yours" (verse 39). While many might focus on the flattering word "inferior, it's likely that Nebuchadnezzar's mind locked on to "after." When you're on top, it's hard to imagine a time when you will no longer be there. But it happens to everyone. You may have climbed to the top of the corporate ladder, but there is a limit to your time in charge. Eventually, you will walk out of your office for the last time, and the next day, someone else's family picture will be on the desk.

This is why Jesus, in the Sermon on the Mount, told His listeners to focus on what is most important in life. He said, "Do not lay up for yourselves treasures on earth, where moth and rust destroy and where thieves break in and steal; but lay up for yourselves treasures in heaven, where neither moth nor rust destroys and where thieves do not break in and steal" (Matthew 6:19-20). There is nothing wrong with excelling in business or in any other earthly endeavor. Just keep it in perspective. It is temporary, here one day and gone the next. Only what you do for the Lord is eternal.

For the king, there was a silver lining to the black cloud of "after." The temporal nature of the word implied that everything would remain dandy while he was king. He wouldn't have to deal with the eventual decline and fall of the Babylonian Empire. But once he was gone, his dreams of an ongoing dynasty would go with him. The fact that Nebuchadnezzar didn't immediately call for Daniel to be executed for this treasonous utterance shows the respect that the king had quickly developed for this young man. He recognized that his wise man was not speaking his own words, but those of the God he served. And since this was obviously the God who had given him his dream to begin with, it was best he hear Him out.

Kingdoms Two, Three, and Four—Medo-Persia, Greece, Rome

Having survived the bombshell of the temporal kingdom revelation, Daniel pressed on:

> After you shall arise another kingdom inferior to yours; then another, a third kingdom of bronze, which shall rule over all the earth. And the fourth kingdom shall be as strong as iron, since iron breaks in pieces and shatters everything; and like iron that crushes, that kingdom will break in pieces and crush all the others (verses 39-40).

The first kingdom and the last, which we'll hear about in a moment, are identified in the interpretation. These middle three are not. However, a look at history clearly shows us what empires God has connected to the torso and legs of the statue. Babylon would be superseded, but not in grandeur. The inferior kingdom of silver was the Medo-Persian Empire that conquered Babylon in 539 BC. Although lasting for two centuries, this second empire did not live up to the beauty and opulence of Nebuchadnezzar's kingdom. Between 334 and 330 BC, the Greek "kingdom of bronze," led by Alexander the Great, defeated the Medo-Persians, and Alexander extended his empire far to the east.

Although Alexander died young, his empire lasted another two-and-a-half centuries before the Romans took over in 63 BC. Why did Nebuchadnezzar's vision picture the mighty Roman Empire as iron mixed with clay? Because the history of Rome is one of division. There were times of unity, but so often one general was pitted against another, or the emperor was embattled against the senate. Eventually, this discord led to a splitting of Rome into an eastern and a western empire. Like iron, there was massive strength in the Roman Empire, but dissension, disunity, and eventually, distance corroded its power, leading to its collapse.

Kingdom Five—God's Kingdom

Now Daniel came to the most intriguing of the kingdoms—one unlike any of the previous. Like a bowling ball hurled toward a porcelain pin, this stone kingdom struck the gold, silver, clay, and even the iron portions of the statue with pulverizing force, leaving behind a fine dust that was carried away by the breeze. Once the stage was cleared, the stone settled in and grew until it covered the whole earth. Only one kingdom could wield this much power: God's kingdom.

> In the days of these kings the God of heaven will set up a kingdom which shall never be destroyed; and the kingdom shall not be left to other people; it shall break in pieces and consume all these kingdoms, and it shall stand forever. Inasmuch as you saw that the stone was cut out of the mountain without hands, and that it broke in pieces the iron, the bronze, the clay, the silver, and the gold—the great God has made known to the king what will come to pass after this. The dream is certain, and its interpretation is sure (verses 44-45).

Who had ever heard of an eternal kingdom? Empires come and empires go. Nebuchadnezzar's progeny would soon find that out. Only deity could accomplish this great everlasting feat. But which deity? Obviously not Marduk or Aku or Nabu. Otherwise, there would have been no "after" in Daniel's interpretation. Only the God of heaven has the power to not only establish a global kingdom, but to sustain it for eternity.

The Allegorical Stone?

I find it very interesting that there are many who will say, "The head is literal Babylon. The chest and arms are literal Medo-Persia. The belly and thighs are literal Greece. The feet are literal Rome.

But the stone is an allegorical representation of Jesus establishing His spiritual kingdom with the advent of the church." Wait, what? One group who holds to this view is preterists, who say that all of Daniel's prophecies were completed up through the time Jesus walked the earth, although some extend the fulfillment to the end of the Roman Empire. They also believe that the Olivet Discourse in Matthew 24–25 and most of the book of Revelation were fulfilled by AD 70.

What rule of interpretation demands that we pivot from literal to spiritual? The only reason I can think of to make this shift is personal presupposition. Presupposition says that when you are looking at a portion of Scripture that doesn't agree with your already-established doctrine, you must allegorize the passage so that you can mold it into your beliefs.

God has promised throughout the Scriptures that there will come a time when He will set up a literal kingdom over which Jesus will rule from Jerusalem. The psalmist spoke of the Messiah reigning from Zion when he wrote:

> He who sits in the heavens shall laugh;
> the Lord shall hold them in derision.
> Then He shall speak to them in His wrath,
> and distress them in His deep displeasure:
> "Yet I have set My King
> on My holy hill of Zion" (Psalm 2:4-6).

Where is Zion? It is in Jerusalem. God's King, the Messiah, will sit on that throne. And it won't just be Jews honoring Him. Gentiles, too, will seek Him out and follow Him.

> In that day there shall be a Root of Jesse,
> who shall stand as a banner to the people;

for the Gentiles shall seek Him,
and His resting place shall be glorious (Isaiah 11:10).

Notice it says "the" Gentiles, not just "some" Gentiles. This is a global kingdom with a global rule, which will last for 1,000 years.

> Then I saw souls of those who had been beheaded for their witness to Jesus and for the word of God, who had not worshiped the beast or his image, and had not received his mark on their foreheads or on their hands. And they lived and reigned with Christ for a thousand years. But the rest of the dead did not live again until the thousand years were finished. This is the first resurrection. Blessed and holy is he who has part in the first resurrection. Over such the second death has no power, but they shall be priests of God and of Christ, and shall reign with Him a thousand years (Revelation 20:4-6).

Now for those of you who are ready to pounce on me, you can keep your "A-ha" in your A-ha box. In these passages from both the Old and New Testaments, we are not experiencing the eternal state. Earth still exists. Jerusalem is still in the Middle East. The only difference from now is that rather than the Knesset meeting in the city, there's a throne with a king on it. Jesus' thousand-year reign will be the beginning of the eternal kingdom. When Satan and his evil hordes are once and for all defeated at the end of the millennium, a new heaven and new earth will be created. It is from there that our ruling Savior will continue His kingship for eternity.

> There shall be no more curse, but the throne of God and of the Lamb shall be in it, and His servants shall serve Him. They shall see His face, and His name shall be on their

foreheads. There shall be no night there: They need no lamp nor light of the sun, for the Lord God gives them light. And they shall reign forever and ever (Revelation 22:3-5).

A Prostrated King

Nebuchadnezzar's reaction was astounding. Understandable, but astounding.

> Then King Nebuchadnezzar fell on his face, prostrate before Daniel, and commanded that they should present an offering and incense to him. The king answered Daniel, and said, "Truly your God is the God of gods, the Lord of kings, and a revealer of secrets, since you could reveal this secret" (Daniel 2:46-47).

Can you imagine the jaws hitting the floor when the most powerful king in the world prostrated himself in front of a teenage court eunuch? Not only had Daniel just pulled off the impossible by recounting the dream, but he followed it up with a powerful prophetic interpretation that was filled with truth and power. But even though he was laid out before his court servant, the king knew the true source of the dream and its meaning. Daniel's God was the revealer of secrets. Marduk failed. Nabu was a no-show. Aku was off waxing or waning. It was the "God of gods, the Lord of kings" who had stepped up.

Do we see a converted king at this time? Was this his "credited to him as righteousness" moment? Likely not. This was more of an acknowledgment of the God of heaven than it was a conversion. It becomes obvious a couple chapters from now that Nebuchadnezzar was not quite ready to surrender his life to the Lord, if he ever actually did.

What follows takes us back once again to that Egyptian throne room where Joseph had interpreted Pharaoh's dream:

Pharaoh said to Joseph, "Inasmuch as God has shown you all this, there is no one as discerning and wise as you. You shall be over my house, and all my people shall be ruled according to your word; only in regard to the throne will I be greater than you." And Pharaoh said to Joseph, "See, I have set you over all the land of Egypt" (Genesis 41:39-41).

Joseph proved his faithfulness to God, giving Him all the credit and praise. God rewarded him with power and position. Daniel, too, ensured that Nebuchadnezzar knew that he was just the spokesperson. Thus, his divine reward was forthcoming.

Then the king promoted Daniel and gave him many great gifts; and he made him ruler over the whole province of Babylon, and chief administrator over all the wise men of Babylon. Also Daniel petitioned the king, and he set Shadrach, Meshach, and Abed-Nego over the affairs of the province of Babylon; but Daniel sat in the gate of the king (Daniel 2:48-49).

Three of Daniel's character traits are highlighted in this story. First, he was humble, ensuring that God got all the credit from the king. Second, Daniel showed love for people whether they loved God or not. After he had received the dream and its interpretation from the Lord, his first words to Arioch, captain of the king's guard, were "Do not destroy the wise men of Babylon" (verse 24). These were magicians, sorcerers, and astrologers who sought divine wisdom using so many methods that the Mosaic law forbade. Still, rather than leaving these sinners to their fate, Daniel spoke up for them. In the same way, we need to remember to love and reach out to those whose beliefs and lifestyles are very different from our own. Finally, he didn't forget his friends. If Daniel was being promoted, he was bringing his buddies with him.

Unfortunately, it was these buddies who soon found themselves in Nebuchadnezzar's crosshairs.

CHAPTER 3

FAITH
UNDER FIRE

DANIEL 3

As the distribution of my books expands, the number of languages that they are translated into grows. This excites me for many reasons. The truth of God's perfect plans for the end times is breaking into more and more places. The hope that comes from a personal relationship with Jesus the Messiah is reaching a greater number of people.

One more benefit that especially excites me is that the backgrounds and life situations of those reading these books is becoming more diverse. When they were being published solely in English, I could expect that most every reader had a Western mindset. They were American and European, along with my dear friends in South Africa and Down Under.

But now as *Revealing Revelation, Israel and the Church*, and others are translated into languages of Eastern Europe, South America, India, and Eastern Asia, the people who make up my readership include those who think differently culturally. I must keep that in mind as I write. They may also experience a greater hostility from their governments toward evangelical Christianity. In other words, faith, for a greater number of my readers, can be dangerous for them.

That's not to say there is no risk for Christians in the Western world. It's just that what's at stake is different. Relationships, employment, and societal acceptance can all be in jeopardy when believers in the West stand for truth amid social and moral decay. But rejection and persecution are to be expected. Jesus told His disciples,

> If the world hates you, you know that it hated Me before it hated you. If you were of the world, the world would love its own. Yet because you are not of the world, but I chose you out of the world, therefore the world hates you (John 15:18-19).

There are occupational hazards when it comes to following Christ. Chief among them is being despised by the world. But the dangers of faith are nothing new, going back much farther even from the time that the Messiah walked the earth. In this chapter, we'll see how the die-hard commitment of three young men nearly led to them dying a very painful death.

A Really Big Statue

One day, whether encouraged by his priests and wise men or maybe just on a personal whim, King Nebuchadnezzar decided that it would be a good idea to erect a massive golden image. Because the Hebrew word for "image" in Daniel 3:1 implies a human figure, it is possible that Nebuchadnezzar's statue dream years earlier had sparked a little inspiration. After it had gestated for a while, he determined that a giant statue of gold would be just what Babylon needed. But unlike the previous figure, he would make sure that he was more than just the golden head on this one. This enormous idol would be the king from head to foot.

Again, that is just a possibility. The text doesn't tell us whether this was a statue of the king, or Marduk (Bel), or some other god. In fact, Daniel was a little sparse on the details, likely because the statue was not the point of this story. What took center stage here was a to-the-death confrontation between the king and Daniel's three friends.

The prophet is good enough to give us some background so that we can better visualize the scenario. First, we may have a date for the event. While the Hebrew text has no time reference, the Septuagint, the third-century BC Greek translation of the Hebrew Scriptures, begins the chapter with "in the eighteenth year of Nebuchadnezzar." Whether this is based on oral tradition or because one of the 72 translators thought a random time stamp was necessary, we can't say for sure.

Second, we know the location, kind of. The golden image was set up on the plain of Dura. Unfortunately, *Dura* is a common location name. Imagine trying to pin down one specific town named Washington in the United States or San José in Central and South America. We do have a good candidate for the location, however. Nineteenth-century archaeologist Jules Oppert discovered a massive brick square about six miles southeast of Babylon that would have been large enough to support the golden image. The nearness of this location to the capital city would not have made gatherings for worship overly difficult for its population.

Third, we know the size of this monstrosity. Nebuchadnezzar's idol stood 90 feet from top to toe. That's the size of a nine-story building. What makes the image so unusual is that it is only nine feet wide. This 10-to-1 height-to-width ratio was the standard amongst ancient Egyptian obelisks.[4] While perfect for a thin tower, it would have distorted typical human features. So we likely have a tall, quite svelte representation of either Nebuchadnezzar or one of his gods.

Finally, whether solid or plated, we know that it was made of gold. If we were to go with the solid gold theory, we would be talking about wealth that would make even Elon Musk blush. A statue 90 feet tall by 9 feet deep and 9 feet wide has a volume of 7,290 cubic feet. A cubic foot of gold weighs 1,188.6 pounds.[5] Doing the math, we're looking at a total weight of 8,664,894 pounds (3,930,330 kg). And, because you're dying to know, based on the $1,890.84 per ounce[6] price of gold on the day I am writing this, we're looking at a total cost of $262,142,850,735.36. That's a lot of money, even for the king. The other option that looks just as pretty and doesn't involve getting a second mortgage on greater Mesopotamia is that it was built of wood and overlaid with gold. I lean toward Option B.

It's All About Me

Nebuchadnezzar was a flawed man. Chief among those faults was pride, as we'll see even more clearly in the next chapter. Whether this image was of the king or a god, or simply a giant obelisk, it was still a tangible representation of Nebuchadnezzar's power and majesty. There is nothing so personal as someone's belief system. So whether he was the object of worship or he was controlling the nation's worship, it was still him telling the people, "I have the power to tell you what to believe."

This same sin of pride will lead a future leader to erect an image of worship within the temple of God, as we will see later in Daniel's book. That leader, the Antichrist, will force people to show their loyalty to him by worshipping him and receiving a mark identifying themselves with him:

> [The false prophet] was granted power to give breath to the image of the beast, that the image of the beast should both speak and cause as many as would not worship the image of the beast to be killed. He causes all, both small and great, rich and poor, free and slave, to receive a mark on their right hand or on their foreheads, and that no one

may buy or sell except one who has the mark or the name of
the beast, or the number of his name (Revelation 13:15-17).

The beast whose image is referred to is that same Antichrist. A
statue of him is made animated and empowered by the second beast,
or false prophet. The population will then be forced to worship the
genuine article. The penalty for resistance to this idol worship is the
same that our young heroes will face in this chapter: death.

Man's desire to be worshipped by others is part of the sin nature
that we have inherited from Adam. There are some countries that
you can visit in which you'll find giant pictures of those nations' rulers. Murals of Ayatollahs Khomeini and Khamenei cover the sides
of many buildings in Iran. In North Korea, every home is required
to hang portraits of Kim Il-Sung, Kim Jong-Il, Kim Jong-Un, and
Kim Jong-Suk, and to keep them completely free of dust.[7] This dic-
tatorial self-aggrandizement is not surprising. After all, pride is the
sin that caused the fall of the great enemy himself.

> How you are fallen from heaven,
> O Lucifer, son of the morning!
> *How* you are cut down to the ground,
> you who weakened the nations!
> For you have said in your heart:
> "I will ascend into heaven,
> I will exalt my throne above the stars of God;
> I will also sit on the mount of the congregation
> on the farthest sides of the north;
> I will ascend above the heights of the clouds,
> I will be like the Most High" (Isaiah 14:12-14).

Like the devil, much of mankind has replaced the God of the
Bible with a god in their own image—one they can control, one

who makes them comfortable and happy, one who will give them the freedom to be who or what they choose to be. It is only kings and dictators who have the power to force worship of their own personified god onto others.

Stop, Drop, and Worship

Once the image was erected, King Nebuchadnezzar laid out his plan:

> King Nebuchadnezzar sent word to gather together the satraps, the administrators, the governors, the counselors, the treasurers, the judges, the magistrates, and all the officials of the provinces, to come to the dedication of the image which King Nebuchadnezzar had set up. So the satraps, the administrators, the governors, the counselors, the treasurers, the judges, the magistrates, and all the officials of the provinces gathered together for the dedication of the image that King Nebuchadnezzar had set up; and they stood before the image that Nebuchadnezzar had set up (Daniel 3:2-3).

The list of invitees was thorough and detailed, and Daniel made sure the reader knew that everyone attended. To these leaders was made known the king's order:

> The herald proclaimed aloud, "You are commanded, O peoples, nations, and languages, that when you hear the sound of the horn, pipe, lyre, trigon, harp, bagpipe, and every kind of music, you are to fall down and worship the golden image that King Nebuchadnezzar has set up. And whoever does not fall down and worship shall immediately be cast into a burning fiery furnace" (verses 4-6 ESV).

Just as Daniel was determined that every reader know each category of official who attended the announcement, he was just as resolute that we know the full makeup of the orchestra. I switched from the New King James Version to the English Standard Version for the above passage because, in an interesting translation choice, the NKJV pared the worship band down to only five instruments. I can't fault any translation choice because there are some obscure musical terms used in the verse. This is evidenced in the varying lists among the different translations. The NIV substitutes a flute and zither for the pipe and lyre. The Holman Christian Standard Bible finds a place for a drum, and the NASB includes a psaltery. The KJV is the most intriguing, including in their list the cornet and the curiously named sackbut. But whatever the makeup of the band, the king's order was clear. When they started playing, everyone was required to drop and worship.

Once the command had been fully disseminated across the kingdom, the time came for the first run. The orchestra leader tapped the music stand with his baton, lifted his hands, and the band began to play. Instantly, across the land, the population fell to their knees and worshipped. As the music continued to ring out, there was a vocal rumble as the masses uttered their words of praise and honor to the image and to the king. Nebuchadnezzar swelled with pride as he stood there and drank it all in.

But there was a problem. Some of the Chaldeans, who apparently were allowed to peek during worship time, noticed three men who were standing. They wouldn't have been hard to spot, being the only ones still vertical. But what made their disregard of the order doubly outrageous is that they were government officials, men who had been given authority to lead the people on behalf of the king. The Chaldeans were livid. How dare these men defy the order of their master! They waited for the music to end, then ran to go see the king.

"But If Not" Faith

Once in Nebuchadnezzar's presence, the Chaldeans leveled their accusations. They reiterated the king's demand that everyone, at the sound of the music, fall to the ground and worship the image he had constructed. The fiery furnace, they reminded him, was the destiny for all who refused to obey. Then they laid out the charge:

> There are certain Jews whom you have set over the affairs of the province of Babylon: Shadrach, Meshach, and Abed-Nego; these men, O king, have not paid due regard to you. They do not serve your gods or worship the gold image which you have set up (verse 12).

You can almost hear the disdain in their voices when they uttered the word *Jews*. These were people who were notorious for setting themselves apart from the rest. Despite their captivity, they still held an air of being different, loyal to an authority and a law that rose above the king and his decrees. And what had to be most aggravating was that they had been rewarded with positions that seemed to affirm their beliefs of being a cut above. This professional jealousy, combined with a misperceived conception of a superiority complex, made the four Jewish exiles hated by the courtiers in the king's court.

The Chaldeans were thrilled to report the disobedience of Shadrach, Meshach, and Abednego. The king's response was just what they had hoped for. Nebuchadnezzar raged. Who dared to defy his order? Immediately, these young rebels were sent for.

When they arrived, the king recognized them. His anger began to calm a little. He liked these guys and knew them by name. These were loyal servants of his who had done wonders through their administration of the province of Babylon. Maybe they had misunderstood the order. Maybe they just needed a reminder of the dire consequences of disobedience. Quite probably, all it would take was hearing the words from his mouth, an order directly from the great Nebuchadnezzar, to set them straight about who the ultimate power was in this kingdom. He said,

> Is it true, Shadrach, Meshach, and Abed-Nego, that you do not serve my gods or worship the gold image which I have set up? Now if you are ready at the time you hear the sound of the horn, flute, harp, lyre, and psaltery, in symphony with all kinds of music, and you fall down and worship the image which I have made, good! But if you do not worship, you shall be cast immediately into the midst of a burning fiery furnace. And who is the god who will deliver you from my hands? (verses 14-15).

This was a truly amazing statement of power mixed with grace. Nebuchadnezzar was giving them a second chance, something likely quite rare in his court. They had a simple choice: life or death. Worship me or burn. These guys may think that their God is special, but this was Nebuchadnezzar's turf. This was his kingdom, his rules. If they defied him, he would say the word and a contingent of guards would bind them up and toss them into the furnace. What god could save anyone from that fate?

To this day, after reading it so many times, the response of the three Jews still gets to me. It is so simple, yet so incredibly profound. It is the perfect statement of faith in God seen through the lens of eternity.

> Shadrach, Meshach, and Abed-Nego answered and said to the king, "O Nebuchadnezzar, we have no need to answer you in this matter. If that is the case, our God whom we serve is able to deliver us from the burning fiery furnace, and He will deliver us from your hand, O king. But if not, let it be known to you, O king, that we do not serve

your gods, nor will we worship the gold image which you
have set up" (verses 16-18).

This is a powerful statement of respectful, logical defiance. First,
we see the three men disregarding Nebuchadnezzar as the ultimate
authority. Had this monarch ever before heard the words, "We have
no need to answer you"? He was a king and the son of a king. Likely,
all he had ever heard in his life was "Yes, sir!" But Shadrach, Meshach,
and Abednego told him, "We don't need to explain ourselves to you.
If you feel the need to throw us into the fiery furnace, so be it. But
we will not obey you."

The three men also defied Nebuchadnezzar's power. By a word, he
had authority over life and death. He could invade nations, destroy
cities, and wipe out populations if he so desired. As a result, he was
used to fear in his presence. Everyone was paranoid that a misspoken
word or a perceived slight could result in their elimination. These
Jews, though, said to him, "You feel you need to kill us? Give it your
best shot. Just know that there is One more powerful than you here,
and He has the final say as to whether we live or die."

Finally, they defied his sense of victory. No matter what happened to these three men, Nebuchadnezzar would still come out
the loser. The trio's words "But if not" are not a statement of
doubt. They are not saying that maybe God can't save them from
a fiery death. Those three powerful words are Shadrach, Meshach,
and Abednego declaring their absolute acceptance of God's perfect plan. "God, if You save us, great! But if You let us burn in the
fiery furnace, also great! We trust that either way, we are safe with
You, and we know that whether we live or die, it will go to accomplish Your purpose."

There are many who are afraid of the idea of "But if not" when
they pray. They worry that those words will set them at odds against
James's declaration:

If any of you lacks wisdom, let him ask of God, who gives to all liberally and without reproach, and it will be given to him. But let him ask in faith, with no doubting, for he who doubts is like a wave of the sea driven and tossed by the wind. For let not that man suppose that he will receive anything from the Lord; he is a double-minded man, unstable in all his ways (James 1:5-8).

But as we see with Shadrach, Meshach, and Abednego, "But if not" doesn't constitute a lack of faith. Rather, it is a declaration of faith. "This is what I desire, Lord. But if You choose differently, I trust that Your ways are better than my ways. Do with me whatever You desire."

In the spring of 2023, Dr. Rick's wife, Linda, was diagnosed with cancer. Together, they prayed that the Lord would remove it from her and restore her health. But along with that prayer for healing they added, "But Your will be done." The cancer moved rapidly through Linda's body, and by July, Rick's beloved wife of 63 years was with her Savior. They asked of God, and He answered, saying, "I've got something else planned." And together, Rick and Linda said, "Blessed be the name of the Lord."

Do not be afraid of "But if not." Ask your heart's desire, because your Father wants to hear it. But let God be God. While the temporal results could bring pain and sorrow, God's eternal plan for His children will ultimately result in joy and happiness.

God with Us

Shadrach, Meshach, and Abednego didn't have the opportunity to explain to the king the larger perspective of "But if not" faith because Nebuchadnezzar went ballistic. Daniel tells us that the king was "full of fury, and the expression on his face changed toward Shadrach, Meshach, and Abed-Nego" (verse 19). These were his boys, his loyal posse. They were supposed to be the guys that he didn't have to worry about. If you close your eyes, you can visualize the king's face change from hopeful that it is all a misunderstanding to violent rage as he recognized that the loyalty of these men belonged not to him, but to someone else. This wasn't just a broken law; this was personal betrayal. His heart broken and his ego offended, he ordered that "they heat the furnace seven times more than it was usually heated" (verse 19).

Without taking time to have the three men stripped down or beaten or flogged, the king demanded that they be bound and thrown into the fire. So, still wearing their official court clothes, they were tied up and tossed in. As they fell, the flames, which were stoked beyond what the furnace could contain, consumed the guards who had carried them up. This is a beautiful detail added to prove that these were no Hollywood movie flames. They were the real deal, impossible for anyone to survive.

Nebuchadnezzar's wounded pride didn't have long to heal. As he looked to ensure that his erstwhile golden boys had met their deaths, his breath left him in a gasp. He leapt to his feet, and, pointing at the furnace, asked, "Did we not cast three men bound into the midst of the fire?" (verse 24). Those around him, experiencing the same astonishment, confirmed the fact to be true.

The king tried to formulate the words that would allow him to describe the supernatural sight that he was witnessing. Shakily, he finally said, "But I see four men unbound, walking in the midst of the fire, and they are not hurt; and the appearance of the fourth is like a son of the gods" (verse 25 ESV).

The ropes that had bound Shadrach, Meshach, and Abednego were gone. The men had gotten to their feet, adjusted their clothing, reset their turbans, and were gathering in a group to meet this new guy who had shown up.

You can almost hear the wonderment in Nebuchadnezzar's voice as he uttered the last few words of verse 25. The fourth man—what did he look like? What was it that made the king identify him as a son of the gods? Sadly, we get no further description beyond Nebuchadnezzar's awestricken words. Nor do we learn from Daniel definitively who he is. But we can surmise that the king's guess was closer than he realized.

This new member of the fire crew was not a son of the gods, but was likely the Son of the God. Whenever there is a theophany, or an appearance of God in the flesh, it is typically the preincarnate Lord Jesus Christ. He is the only person of the triune Godhead who appears in such a way. On one occasion, when three men appeared to Abraham, we are told that two of them were angels and the third was "the LORD" (Genesis 18:1). When Joshua was about to go into the Land of Promise, he was confronted by a man in battle array known as the Commander of the Lord's Army (Joshua 5:14-15). As this man spoke, we are told that it was "the LORD" who was addressing Joshua (6:2). There are times when God works unseen. There are times when He sends His angels to intervene. Then there are those special few instances when God decides that the occasion deserves a personal, in-the-flesh visit. The fiery furnace was one of those times.

Nebuchadnezzar recognized immediately that he had overstepped into something that was much bigger than himself. He quickly sought to remedy the situation.

> Then Nebuchadnezzar went near the mouth of the burning fiery furnace and spoke, saying, "Shadrach, Meshach, and Abed-Nego, servants of the Most High God, come out, and come here." Then Shadrach, Meshach, and Abed-Nego came from the midst of the fire. And the satraps, administrators, governors, and the king's counselors gathered together, and they saw these men on whose bodies the fire had no power; the hair of their head was

not singed nor were their garments affected, and the smell
of fire was not on them (Daniel 3:26-27).

Isn't it interesting that God didn't act to prevent them from being
thrown into the furnace? Instead, He waited for the time when He
could rescue them out of the fire. Why would He allow His faithful
servants to go through such an ordeal? First, it is within the fires of
life that our faith is proven and grows stronger. Shadrach, Meshach,
and Abednego had great faith before. But after this trial by fire, their
trust in God elevated to furnace-level faith. If you are in the fire right
now, just know that you are not walking it alone. And, as you depend
upon God, trusting in His plan, you are building your own faith up
to furnace level. His words spoken through Isaiah are a great comfort when you are in the flames:

> When you pass through the waters, I will be with you;
> and through the rivers, they shall not overflow you.
> When you walk through the fire, you shall not be burned,
> nor shall the flame scorch you (Isaiah 43:2).

The second reason these three men had to go through this ordeal
was so that God could show Himself to the king. Nebuchadnezzar was clouded with his own self-importance, and it would require
something huge, something supernatural, for the light of reality to
break through. Four guys walking around in a fiery inferno seemed
to do the trick.

> Nebuchadnezzar spoke, saying, "Blessed be the God of
> Shadrach, Meshach, and Abed-Nego, who sent His Angel
> and delivered His servants who trusted in Him, and they
> have frustrated the king's word, and yielded their bodies,
> that they should not serve nor worship any god except

their own God! Therefore I make a decree that any people, nation, or language which speaks anything amiss against the God of Shadrach, Meshach, and Abed-Nego shall be cut in pieces, and their houses shall be made an ash heap; because there is no other God who can deliver like this" (Daniel 3:28-29).

This was the second time that King Nebuchadnezzar had been confronted with the God of heaven. Earlier, the Lord had shown His power over the inner workings of mankind by giving the king a dream, then providing its interpretation. Now He showed His sovereignty over the external, physical makeup of humanity not just by sparing these three young men, but by joining them within the conflagration. The message was clear to the king. There is one God who is over all others, because "there is no other God who can deliver like this."

But the king still wasn't ready to give himself to this one true God. Nebuchadnezzar's declaration was simply a recognition of the great faith of Shadrach, Meshach, and Abednego, and an acknowledgment of the power of their God. There were no words of submission or worship. There was no bowing of the head or bending of the knee. In fact, rather than putting himself under the authority of the Almighty God, the king presumptuously said he would put the Lord under his own protection. "Don't worry, God of Shadrach, Meshach, and Abednego, I've got Your back. I'll make sure nobody speaks badly about you."

This reminds me of Peter seeking to protect Jesus from Himself. When the Messiah began speaking of His eventual and necessary death, the brash disciple would have none of it. "Peter took Him aside and began to rebuke Him, saying, 'Far be it from You, Lord; this shall not happen to You!'" (Matthew 16:22). Immediately, Jesus reproached His disciple, saying, "Get behind Me, Satan! You are an offense to Me, for you are not mindful of the things of God, but the things of men" (verse 23). Why was Jesus' answer so harsh?

It came down to Peter's pride. Rather than submit himself to the will of the Father, the disciple had told his Master how it was going to be. "I know You're worried about the people who want to hurt You, Lord. But rest easy, I'll look out for You." In the same way, Nebuchadnezzar perceived that the Creator God could now breathe a sigh of relief because the great Babylonian king would take Him under his care. In the next chapter of Daniel, Nebuchadnezzar will finally learn who is really in charge.

Our chapter wraps up in a similar manner as the last. The faithful young men are rewarded, and the king promotes them to a higher position within the leadership of the province of Babylon. When we are obedient to God, He rewards us 100 percent of the time. When you're discouraged as you're driving home from church because you've just taught children's Sunday school for the forty-third straight week because no one else is volunteering, and you feel like a failure because the kids weren't listening and the pastor went long and the parents were grumpy and the vacuum jammed on a crayon and no one said, "Thank you," just know that you have been blessed by God. You may not see your reward, but God has seen you. He knows every crumbled cracker ground into the carpet and every spilled cup of Kool-Aid. He's seen you at home studying the lessons and preparing the crafts. He's smiled when you help out the new girl and take a caring interest in the boy whose parents are divorcing. God is watching, and He is storing up your rewards, the treasures in heaven that are so much more valuable than anything you might receive here on earth.

God rewards faith. He rewards the day-to-day faith that expresses itself in obedience and righteous living. He rewards the sacrificial faith that is demonstrated through service and outreach. He rewards the dangerous faith that doesn't compromise, even when the consequences may be harsh. Shadrach, Meshach, and Abednego knew that a life submitted to the one true God was the only worthwhile way to live. Nebuchadnezzar didn't understand that quite yet, but he was about to learn.

CHAPTER 4

LEARNING
THE HARD WAY

DANIEL 4

It's been a nightmare of a morning. The sibling rivalry between your two sons has been at its worst. They whined over who had the bigger waffle at breakfast. They fought over who got to pack which Hot Wheels car in their backpacks. They wrestled over which one got to sit in the back seat behind mom and who got stuck with no leg space behind dad. Their constant bickering and punching and just plain selfishness was getting on your last nerve.

The worst part was that this should have been a fun morning of anticipation. You, your wife, and your boys were on your way to an amusement park 45 minutes from your house. You had intended for this to be a family day filled with joy and great memories. Instead, your wife is now sitting next to you, steaming at the kids' behavior. Your boys are punching each other over a purposeful incursion that breached the imaginary border that separated the back seat into two halves.

"Knock it off," you demand. But you are ignored.

"Stop it, you two, or I will turn this car around." Still, the battle behind you rages.

You look at your wife and shrug. She nods her head. You flick on the blinker and take the next exit off the freeway. Gradually, the boys catch on to the turn of events.

"Dad, why did we turn around?" asks one.

"Dad, why are we going back toward the house?" cries the other.

You answer, "I told you that if you didn't stop, I would turn the car around. You kept going, and now we're headed home."

The questions to you become pleas to their mom. But she makes it clear she's having none of it. Soon, their appeals turn to tears, and the sobs continue after you arrive back home and the boys are banished to their rooms. The rest of the morning passes with no sound from upstairs. But as lunchtime nears, you hear rustling sounds from the bedrooms. Five minutes later, two contrite children come walking down the stairs, their heads lowered, their eyes still a little red.

"Mom, Dad, we're sorry for fighting. We should have stopped when you told us to."

After a mandatory mini lecture, because that's what dads do, you open your arms and the boys come running to you. Your wife leans over and joins the family hug. Soon, you are down at the neighborhood park hitting a ball around. Later that night, it is pizza and a movie. The lesson has been learned, and the sense of family is restored.

Daniel 4 is, in essence, a story about God warning Nebuchadnezzar to stop what he was doing, turning the car around when the king ignored Him, then restoring him to his throne when he finally came to his senses and repented. And not surprisingly, as happened in the previous chapters, this story begins with a dream and an image of the king.

Dreams as Communication

Daniel is a book of dreams and visions. To the Western mindset, the idea of God communicating in this subconscious or spiritual way may seem quite foreign. Yet in the Middle East and other parts of the world, such things are not uncommon. Many Muslims who live in countries where the gospel is prohibited, like Iran, have come to faith in Jesus Christ through dreams and visions. A common story told among new believers is of a man coming to the foot of the bed and telling them about the hope that can be found in Yasu, the name for Jesus used by many Arabic Christians. When people do not have the Word of God available to them, the Lord still finds ways to make Himself known to those who desire to discover the truth of the Creator God.

In the book of Job, after Job's three friends fail to convince him of his sin, Job was verbally accosted by the young upstart, Elihu. During his rebuke, he reminded his elder that God has many ways to speak to mankind.

> In a dream, in a vision of the night,
> when deep sleep falls upon men,
> while slumbering on their beds,
> then He opens the ears of men,
> and seals their instruction.
> In order to turn man from his deed,
> and conceal pride from man,
> He keeps back his soul from the Pit,
> and his life from perishing by the sword (Job 33:15-18).

Elihu's words would have been much more appropriate for Nebuchadnezzar than they were for Job. Pride was the exact issue that the king needed to deal with or tuck away for good. If he wasn't going to do it himself, then God was more than happy to lend a hand.

The other key element in the events of Daniel 4 is that of an image. Unlike the statues of chapters 2 and 3, the representative component in Nebuchadnezzar's new dream is not man-made. Instead, it is a product of nature—a tree. Yet the symbolism conveyed by both the statues and the tree is the same. They characterize the pride of mankind and his glory. And in all three stories, God proves Himself to be more powerful than any person or thing in this created universe. With the statue, God hurled a rock that brought it down. With the golden image, God thwarted the will of the king by saving the three men. With the tree, we'll see that despite its glory, God can and will cut it down. There is only one who is sovereign in this universe, and He wasn't sitting on a throne in Babylon.

A Message for All the People

This chapter is unique in Scripture. It is the one time that a Gentile monarch narrates a story. In the first half of Daniel 4, we read the words of Nebuchadnezzar himself as he sets up the events. Daniel then picks up the narrative for 15 verses before the king comes back and wraps it all up. Once again, this is our prophet using his literary chops to creatively tell a very important story.

King Nebuchadnezzar began with a salutation:

> Nebuchadnezzar the king,
> To all peoples, nations, and languages that dwell
>   in all the earth:
> Peace be multiplied to you (Daniel 4:1).

Because this story was to be sent throughout the realm of Babylon, it was written in proclamation form. Nebuchadnezzar introduced the sender as himself. He then identified the recipients as everyone else who was not him. This story was to be read in every province, city, and village of the empire. Wherever Babylon had influence, the tale would be told. This is fascinating because it is in no way flattering of the king. But as we saw when Nebuchadnezzar prostrated himself in front of Daniel in chapter 2, he was not afraid to humble himself when confronted with power greater than his own.

How relieved the people must have been when they heard this was a message of peace. Imagine a father leading his firstborn to the town square. Word had been spread that the king had a proclamation to be read. Rarely was that good. His wife had stayed home with the younger ones in case the message was about a coming war, higher taxes, a military conscription, or some other bad news. A crowd had already formed by the time they arrived in the town center. After a few minutes, a rustle ran through the crowd. A man dressed in the clothing of a court herald ascended a platform. As he cleared his throat, the father drew his son close to his side.

"From the king to all the people—peace."

An audible sigh of relief passed through the crowd as the dad lifted his arm from his son's shoulders. No new war. No new taxes. This proclamation was to be purely informational. A smile crossed the man's face, but it soon turned to bewilderment as the herald continued:

> I thought it good to declare the signs and wonders that
> the Most High God has worked for me.
>
> > How great are His signs,
> > and how mighty His wonders!
> > His kingdom is an everlasting kingdom,
> > and His dominion is from generation to generation
> > (verses 2-3).

You can imagine the wonder that went through much of the gathered crowd in that town and throughout the empire. Who is this new "Most High God"? Is he more powerful than Marduk or Nabu? Is he more deserving of worship than that giant golden idol the king made us bow down to every time we heard the orchestra?

But there was one group of people who would not have been bewildered. They would instead have been amazed. After years as an exiled minority in a huge empire, for the Jews to hear their God, the one true God, being acknowledged by the king for special recognition and praise must have sent their hearts soaring. I wonder if this was the moment when those God-rejecting, idol-worshipping rebels who had originally been carted off from Jerusalem began to turn their hearts back to their heavenly Father.

The Story of a Tree

The introduction over, Nebuchadnezzar began his tale. To no one's surprise, it was about another dream:

> I, Nebuchadnezzar, was at rest in my house, and flourishing in my palace. I saw a dream which made me afraid, and the thoughts on my bed and the visions of my head troubled me. Therefore I issued a decree to bring in all the wise men of Babylon before me, that they might make known to me the interpretation of the dream. Then the magicians, the astrologers, the Chaldeans, and the soothsayers came in, and I told them the dream; but they did not make known to me its interpretation (verses 4-7).

At this point, some of the listeners may have been thinking, *Haven't we heard this one before? The king dreams. The wise men fail to interpret. Then there was that guy who stepped up and figured it all out. What was his name again?* The answer to their internal query was given as the herald proceeded:

> At last Daniel came before me (his name is Belteshazzar, according to the name of my god; in him is the Spirit of the Holy God), and I told the dream before him, saying: "Belteshazzar, chief of the magicians, because I know that the Spirit of the Holy God is in you, and no secret troubles

you, explain to me the visions of my dream that I have
seen, and its interpretation" (verses 8-9).

Daniel was back. The name would have rung a bell with many in
the empire. He was a very high muckety-muck in the king's court. Just
like those in the province of Babylon would have known the names
of Shadrach, Meshach, and Abednego because of their high positions,
Daniel's name would be recognized throughout the nations of the
empire because of proclamations, visitations, major projects, court
gossip, and a plethora of other ways that people learn of their leaders.

As is often true of prophetic dreams, it begins with the good news:

> These were the visions of my head while on my bed:
>
>> I was looking, and behold,
>> a tree in the midst of the earth,
>> and its height was great.
>> The tree grew and became strong;
>> its height reached to the heavens,
>> and it could be seen to the ends of all the earth.
>> Its leaves were lovely,
>> its fruit abundant,
>> and in it was food for all.
>> The beasts of the field found shade under it,
>> the birds of the heavens dwelt in its branches,
>> and all flesh was fed from it (verses 10-12).

If the dream could have finished then with "and they lived hap-
pily ever after, frolicking under the tree," the listeners would have
been quite content. But there was a problem. There was a sickness
within the tree, and if it was allowed to fester and spread, this idyllic
scene would soon fall apart. The tree had to come down.

I saw in the visions of my head while on my bed, and there was a watcher, a holy one, coming down from heaven. He cried aloud and said thus:

> "Chop down the tree and cut off its branches,
>   strip off its leaves and scatter its fruit.
> Let the beasts get out from under it,
>   and the birds from its branches.
> Nevertheless leave the stump and roots in the earth,
>   bound with a band of iron and bronze,
>   in the tender grass of the field.
> Let it be wet with the dew of heaven,
>   and let him graze with the beasts
>   on the grass of the earth.
> Let his heart be changed from that of a man,
>   let him be given the heart of a beast,
>   and let seven times pass over him" (verses 13-16).

As Nebuchadnezzar watched, a figure came down from heaven. The king referred to this personage as "a watcher, a holy one." The Aramaic word translated "watcher" refers to an angel or a messenger of God. This relates perfectly with the biblical picture of these spiritual servants of the Lord. The four angelic creatures seen by John hovering around the throne of God had "six wings, [and] were full of eyes around and within" (Revelation 4:8). Some of their eyes they put on the Lord, and some they put on His creation. On His cue, they were ready to fly away on those six wings to do His bidding because serving was what they were created for. As David wrote:

> Bless the Lord, you His angels,
> who excel in strength, who do His word,
> heeding the voice of His word.

Bless the LORD, all you His hosts,
you ministers of His, who do His pleasure
(Psalm 103:20-21).

The announcement the watcher brought was a tragic one. This immense tree, beautiful in appearance, beneficial and generous to all that sought food and shelter, was destined for the axe. Not only would it be taken to the ground, but its branches would be stripped and its fruit scattered. There it would lie, exposed to the elements, helpless and worthless.

But there was a glimmer of hope. The stump would not be ground down or cut to pieces. It would remain, and with it, the root system below. True, it would be bound with a band of iron and bronze so that it could not grow. But there would still be life.

This is so typical of God's punishments. They can be harsh and devastating, because that is often what is needed to wake us up to our sin. Yet if we look hard into the darkness of our struggles, we'll see a flicker of light. That is where mercy waits. That is where we will find forgiveness, reconciliation, and, once again, joy.

For Nebuchadnezzar the tree, hope was far off from where he was. And yes, it was now clear that this was about him because the announcement of the watcher shifted its focus from a tree to a person. And there was little doubt who that person was.

The news was not good. Nebuchadnezzar was about to lose his senses. He would go into the wild, be drenched with the dew of the morning, and dine on the grass of the fields along with the livestock and feral animals. Seven times would pass while he was trapped in this condition.

We don't know for sure the length of the "seven times." Were they days, months, or years? In biblical interpretation, context is our best friend, so let's look around. Daniel used the word "times" later in his book to refer to years when he spoke of "a time and times and half a time" (7:25; see also 12:7). Not surprisingly, because it's in Daniel, we also find it in Revelation. In Revelation 12:14 we find the same phrase, again referring to years. Thus, we can safely assume that Nebuchadnezzar was due for a seven-year departure from reality.

Why would the king have to endure this? The dream concluded with a purpose statement, spoken by the watcher:

> This decision is by the decree of the watchers,
> and the sentence by the word of the holy ones,
> in order that the living may know
> that the Most High rules in the kingdom of men,
> gives it to whomever He will,
> and sets over it the lowest of men (Daniel 4:17).

This theme was very much on God's agenda during this time. He wanted to ensure that the king knew who He was, the Jews knew who He was, and the Gentiles of all nations knew who He was. Seventy-two times in the Bible, God uses the words "then they will know that I am the LORD," or ones similar. Of that number, 58 are found in the writings of Daniel's contemporary, the exilic prophet Ezekiel. A key theme in Ezekiel was that God was bringing judgment on His people so that the Jews would know that He is the Lord. But God would later restore the Jews to their homeland so that the world would know that He is the Lord. Time after time in Ezekiel, the reason God gives for His present and future judgments and His present and future restorations was so that all people could see Him for who He is. He's not just another god. He's the King of kings and the Lord of lords.

It is the King of kings portion of that formula that Nebuchadnezzar is about to get schooled on.

Surprising Compassion

The king had told his dream to Daniel, and now he was ready to hear its interpretation, whatever it may be:

> "This dream I, King Nebuchadnezzar, have seen. Now you, Belteshazzar, declare its interpretation, since all the wise men of my kingdom are not able to make known to me the interpretation; but you are able, for the Spirit of the Holy God is in you."
>
> Then Daniel, whose name was Belteshazzar, was astonished for a time, and his thoughts troubled him. So the king spoke, and said, "Belteshazzar, do not let the dream or its interpretation trouble you."
>
> Belteshazzar answered and said, "My lord, may the dream concern those who hate you, and its interpretation concern your enemies!" (verses 18-19).

Daniel's response to the dream is so interesting. The punishment that was about to come upon the king was troubling to him. Remember, Nebuchadnezzar was the man who had kidnapped him from his land, emasculated him, and forced him to serve in his own court. This was also the man who was responsible for the destruction of the holy city of Jerusalem, the razing of the temple, and the slaughter of so many of Daniel's fellow countrymen. But there was no gloating on the prophet's part. There was no joy at the soon downfall of the king. Instead, you can almost picture Daniel walking toward a chair and collapsing in it, or pacing in the wings of the throne room trying to gather his words.

It seems a genuine affection had grown between king and wise man. Daniel had accepted that the Lord had placed him in this position, and he was striving to do his job to the best of his abilities.

This reminds me of a letter that Jeremiah sent to the exiles in Babylon. He told them,

> Build houses and dwell in them; plant gardens and eat their fruit. Take wives and beget sons and daughters; and take wives for your sons and give your daughters to husbands, so that they may bear sons and daughters—that you may be increased there, and not diminished. And seek the peace of the city where I have caused you to be carried away captive, and pray to the LORD for it; for in its peace you will have peace (Jeremiah 29:5-7).

Daniel knew that as the king went, so went the kingdom. And as the kingdom went, so went the living conditions for his fellow exiles. So he served his king wholeheartedly. It is difficult to serve anyone with your whole heart if your heart is against them. Thus, Daniel's heart was now with the king. Did he agree with all that his sovereign did? Likely not. But he truly desired what was best for the man.

True followers of Christ know that this world is not our home. We are exiles here waiting until the day the Lord brings us home. While He tarries, we must follow Jeremiah's directive. We must live our lives, seek the best for our nations, and pray for and seek the welfare of others. To do this, we must ensure that our hearts are with those around us.

The society we live in is polarized, and the hate culture is very strong. Unfortunately, this is true in the church as well as the world. The vitriol that Christians unleash against one another and, even worse, against unbelievers who are lost and are ignorant of the path to salvation is appalling. As God shakes His head at our judgmentalism and petty bickering, the enemy laughs because his strategy for an ineffective and irrelevant church is playing out just as he had planned.

When John wrote, "Do not love the world or the things in the world" (1 John 2:15), he was speaking of the world's system, not the people in the world. As Jesus told the Pharisees when He was dining in the home of the newly reformed notorious sinner Matthew, the tax collector, "Those who are well have no need of a physician, but those who are sick. I did not come to call the righteous, but sinners, to repentance" (Mark 2:17). Like Daniel, we are here to love and show the truth of God's salvation to all sinners, great and small. This includes those who vote differently, who are hostile to the church, who self-identify in ways that don't mesh with Scripture, and who live only for themselves. I'm not saying we agree with their views or accept their sin. I'm saying that we love them with everything we have, because that's how God loved us when we were lost in our own sins.

"You Are the Tree"

Daniel began his interpretation of the king's dream with a recap. Partway through, he made a revelation that Nebuchadnezzar probably already knew. "It is you, O king" (Daniel 4:22), the prophet told him, identifying the tree. He completed the summary with a reminder of the cutting down of the tree, binding of the stump, and the grazing in the fields. You can almost hear Daniel inhale deeply before he continued with what the dream meant for Nebuchadnezzar:

> They shall drive you from men, your dwelling shall be with the beasts of the field, and they shall make you eat grass like oxen. They shall wet you with the dew of heaven, and seven times shall pass over you, till you know that the Most High rules in the kingdom of men, and gives it to whomever He chooses.
>
> And inasmuch as they gave the command to leave the stump and roots of the tree, your kingdom shall be assured to you,

after you come to know that Heaven rules. Therefore, O king, let my advice be acceptable to you; break off your sins by being righteous, and your iniquities by showing mercy to the poor. Perhaps there may be a lengthening of your prosperity (verses 24-27).

Those listening to the herald's pronouncement of these facts very well may have been expecting the next words to be, "So I had Belteshazzar beaten, stripped of his position, and impaled on a very long pole. Let this be a lesson to all that no one speaks to the king as Belteshazzar did!" But they didn't understand the relationship between these two men. Nebuchadnezzar trusted Daniel, and the prophet held a godly love for the king. Daniel's pleading at the end of his interpretation is enough to demonstrate this. "Change your ways, king. Humble yourself, live righteously, show mercy to the poor; maybe that will be enough to keep you from seven years of insanity and humiliation."

But as much as Nebuchadnezzar respected Daniel, he was not prepared to listen to him. Apparently the price was too high, or maybe the judgment was too obscure. It's possible that the dream and its interpretation put a temporary scare into the king. Maybe he changed his ways for a time. Maybe he doled out a special ration of bread to the poor. Maybe he even commuted a few death sentences. But as the weeks and months went by, he slipped back into his old ways. Soon, everything was business as usual.

Nebuchadnezzar's Pride Exceeds God's Patience

How do we know there was no permanent change in Nebuchadnezzar? Because the next words from the herald were, "All this came upon King Nebuchadnezzar" (verse 28). Once again, a gasp would have spread amongst the listeners. This "Most High God," whoever He was, not only predicted their great king's downfall, but He actually made it come to pass. The herald detailed the event:

At the end of the twelve months he was walking about the royal palace of Babylon. The king spoke, saying, "Is not this great Babylon, that I have built for a royal dwelling by my mighty power and for the honor of my majesty?"

While the word was still in the king's mouth, a voice fell from heaven: "King Nebuchadnezzar, to you it is spoken: the kingdom has departed from you! And they shall drive you from men, and your dwelling shall be with the beasts of the field. They shall make you eat grass like oxen; and seven times shall pass over you, until you know that the Most High rules in the kingdom of men, and gives it to whomever He chooses."

That very hour the word was fulfilled concerning Nebuchadnezzar; he was driven from men and ate grass like oxen; his body was wet with the dew of heaven till his hair had grown like eagles' feathers and his nails like birds' claws (verses 29-33).

Nebuchadnezzar was strolling around his rooftop, feeling pretty good about himself. He wasn't thinking about cryptic warnings. Righteous living and mercy on the poor were the furthest things from his mind. Instead, he was dwelling on his favorite subject— himself. "Look what I've built! Has any other king ever created something so amazing? Is there anyone on earth with even half my power? And I did it all with my own two hands! Yeah, I really am kind of a big deal!"

Suddenly, a voice interrupted his personal praise session. It was probably one that he recognized. He had heard it a year earlier in a dream. Dread fell over him. "You were warned. Now your kingdom is taken from you, along with your sanity. Seven years are going to pass until you finally realize that God is God and you are just a man." Immediately, the king's mind left him. His raving was so bad and his lunacy so great that he was driven from the palace and out the city gates.

God's patience is great. But it is not unending. For the unbelieving world, there will come a time when sin becomes so great that His forbearance will end. Just like in the days of Noah, He will pour out His wrath upon His creation. But also, just as He saved the righteous Noah and his family by lifting them above the punishment by means of an ark, He will save His righteous children from His coming wrath by lifting them above the tribulation by means of the rapture. While the believers of the church enjoy their rewards with the Savior, the rest of humanity will endure seven years of suffering.

Seven years. At the end of the seven years of his insanity, the king would recognize who God is. At the end of the seven years of Jacob's trouble, or the tribulation, Israel will recognize Jesus, the One they pierced, as the Messiah and will find salvation. And at the end of those same seven years of God's wrath, the unbelieving world will recognize the sovereignty of the God they rejected. But for them, it will be too late.

Believers also need to realize that God's patience with them has a limit. When we ignore the prompting of the Holy Spirit toward repentance from whatever sin is plaguing us, our heavenly Father will reach a point when He sees that change will come only with some tough love discipline. That is why, when hard times come to God's children, we should always prayerfully evaluate whether there is any modification we need to make in the way we live. Whether the origin of our struggle is the disciplinary hand of God or just the fact that we are living in corruptible bodies in a fallen world, we can always learn from and grow through the pain.

Did Nebuchadnezzar receive punishment or discipline? Was it retributive or reformative? The king's time of insanity is clearly the latter. First, there was a time limit given to it. He would be under this sentence for seven years, and then it was expected that the lesson would be learned. Second, there was a definite purpose to this ordeal. Nebuchadnezzar would suffer his indignity until he truly grasped "that the Most High rules in the kingdom of men, [and] gives it to whomever He will." Once the king understood this truth of God's ultimate sovereignty over all things, then the discipline would end.

That is exactly what happened. At the end of the ordained period, God cleared Nebuchadnezzar's mind enough to allow him an epiphany.

> At the end of the time I, Nebuchadnezzar, lifted my eyes
> to heaven, and my understanding returned to me; and
> I blessed the Most High and praised and honored Him
> who lives forever:
>
>> For His dominion is an everlasting dominion,
>> and His kingdom is from generation to generation.
>> All the inhabitants of the earth are reputed as nothing;
>> He does according to His will in the army of heaven
>> and among the inhabitants of the earth.
>> No one can restrain His hand
>> or say to Him, "What have You done?" (verses 34-35).

It's interesting that with verse 34, Nebuchadnezzar once again picks up the storyline. From verses 19-33, a narrator told the story. Maybe the king didn't want to personally relate the details of his judgment and fall, or maybe it would have been unseemly for a monarch to do so. What is evident by him taking back over the narrative is that Nebuchadnezzar wanted to make sure that all heard about his repentance from his own mouth. "I lifted my eyes to heaven. I blessed the Most High. I praised and honored Him who lives forever." Before, he said, "I have built this kingdom." Afterward, he said, "I finally recognize that God is in control. He put me in this position, and He can take me out of it. Glorify His name!"

Mission accomplished. God sought to humble this mighty king, and the mighty king was humbled. Now the monarch's perspective was one that the Lord could more effectively use to accomplish His purposes. So God gave the kingdom back to Nebuchadnezzar.

> At the same time my reason returned to me, and for the glory of my kingdom, my honor and splendor returned to me. My counselors and nobles resorted to me, I was restored to my kingdom, and excellent majesty was added to me. Now I, Nebuchadnezzar, praise and extol and honor the King of heaven, all of whose works are truth, and His ways justice. And those who walk in pride He is able to put down (verses 36-37).

The king learned his lesson, and this resulted in five blessings. First, his reason returned to him. Second, his honor and splendor returned to him. Third, his counselors and nobles respected him once again and came to him. Chances are that no member of his court was more thrilled at his restoration than Daniel. Fourth, Nebuchadnezzar was restored to his kingdom, regaining his position as sovereign of the empire. Fifth, "excellent majesty" was added to him. This means that as great as he was before, he now became even greater.

Did King Nebuchadnezzar fall back into his old habits? We don't know for sure, because this is the last we hear of this mighty ruler. We do know that he finally understood that although he was the great king of the empire, there is a greater King of heaven. This begs the question: Will we see King Nebuchadnezzar in heaven? That's difficult to know. He certainly had a life-changing experience with the merciful God. But we can never know the true state of his heart. Did he recognize the Lord as the one true God, or did he just shift

Him to the top of his Top Ten Deities list, bumping himself down to number two? There is coming a time when we'll know for sure. I, for one, hope to meet him one day in eternity.

CHAPTER 5

THE END OF AN EMPIRE

DANIEL 5

It was the summer of AD 64. The strength of Rome was at its height and the empire spread from the Atlantic Ocean to well beyond the eastern shores of the Mediterranean. The city itself was the center of power and culture. It was wealthy, decadent, and packed with wooden structures. So when the chariot-racing stadium, Circus Maximus, caught fire, it didn't take much for the embers to fly to the next building, and the next. Soon, the city was ablaze and was burning hotter than, I don't know, a fiery furnace maybe?

The city burned. Day after day, more buildings were razed to the ground. Thousands of citizens were caught in the conflagration, while hundreds of thousands saw their homes and all their possessions fall victim to the flames. People wondered why nobody was helping to put out the fire. Where was Emperor Nero? He was certainly not well loved and people's expectations of him were low. But, still, you'd think that he would do something to stop the capital of his empire from burning to the ground.

At the end of six days, the fire finally burned itself out. Of the 14 districts in Rome, ten were destroyed. The city was in ruins. And people wanted answers. How could this happen? Looking for a scapegoat, Nero blamed the Christians, and many were quick to join him in this explanation. His accusation led to a brutal persecution of first-century believers during which they were arrested, tortured, and executed by crucifixion, burning, or being fed to wild animals in an arena.

More discerning eyes, however, turned toward the emperor. Did he purposely start the fire to clear room for a few of his building projects, only to have the flames get out of control? Or was he looking for an excuse to persecute that new religious sect that followed some king, god, or man? Even back then, everyone loved a conspiracy theory, and who better to theorize against than an unpopular emperor? Truth be known, the fire that destroyed Rome was likely just an accident in a city that, as it was haphazardly constructed over time, became a tinderbox.

But once a conspiracy theory springs into existence, getting rid of it is harder than loosening the jaws of a German Shepherd from the pant leg of a scrap metal thief. Over the decades and centuries to follow, Nero was not only blamed for starting the fire but for not caring as the death toll rose rapidly. Eventually the adage "Rome burned while Nero fiddled" was born, and it has stuck ever since. Never mind that when the fire began the emperor was 35 miles away at his villa in Antium, or that the fiddle wouldn't be invented for another thousand years.

Even though the saying may be incorrect, it is still appropriate for our story in Daniel 5. The crown prince of Babylon was having a party, a wild bacchanalia of epic proportions. Meanwhile, the enemy was at the gates and the city was hours away from collapsing. But on this fateful occasion in 539 BC, the last night of the great empire's existence, "Babylon burned while Belshazzar fiddled."

A Royal Discovery

The first thing we need to do as we approach this new story is to get ourselves situated properly in history. Between the last punctuation mark of chapter 4 and the first capital letter of chapter 5, some 30-plus years passed. Since the death of Nebuchadnezzar in 561 BC, the empire had been declining. The giant statue the monarch dreamed of in chapter 2 could easily have applied to his own descendants. He was the head of gold, then each succeeding section of the statue declined in quality and worth.

Theologian Clarence Larkin, in his classic commentary *The Book of Daniel*, laid out the history:

> Nebuchadnezzar was succeeded at his death, B.C. 561, by his son Evil-Merodach, who at once liberated Jehoiachin, king of Judah, from prison and fed him from his own table (2 Kings 25:27-30; Jeremiah 52:31-34). After a reign of two years Evil-Merodach was put to death by conspirators, headed by Neriglissar, his brother-in-law, who ascended the throne and reigned for about four years, being killed in battle in the year B.C. 556. His son, and successor, Laborosoarchod, an imbecile child, was king for less than a year, when he was beaten to death, and the throne was seized by a usurper, Nabonidus (or Nabonnaid), another son-in-law of Nebuchadnezzar, who had married the widow of Neriglissar, and who reigned from B.C. 555 to the Fall of Babylon in B.C. 538.[8]

"Uh, Amir, I hate to mention it, but you did see that there is no Belshazzar on this list, right?" Good catch! And that was a difficulty for theologians for many years. Skeptical historians were quick to point out the missing king as evidence of the Bible's fallibility. In response, biblical scholars would squirm a little bit and say, "He's out there somewhere. We just haven't found him yet." But there should be no squirming with an explanation like that, because with biblical archaeology it is the perfect justification for any lack of evidence.

"But isn't that a cop-out, Amir? Couldn't you also say that the earth was first populated by tiny blue men who came from a distant planet and crashed to earth in their rocket ship, but we just haven't found the evidence yet?" I could, but I wouldn't. The difference is twofold. First, there is a massive amount of archaeological evidence that proves the truthfulness of the Bible. Not only that, but there is new evidence being uncovered all the time. The second difference is that there has never been any archaeological find that has contradicted the Bible in any way. So if asked about Belshazzar, an early nineteenth-century theologian could have confidently said, "Unless you can show me archaeological evidence that there never was a Belshazzar, then I'll just wait for the confirmation of his existence to be discovered."

He wouldn't have had to wait long.

In 1854, Sir Austen Henry Layard was leading an archaeological dig in the ancient city of Ur. As they uncovered layer after layer, they came across four small clay cylinders from the mid-sixth century BC. On one of these cylinders were written in the Babylonian language and in cuneiform script 31 lines divided into two columns.[9] Later known as one of the Nabonidus Cylinders, this amazing find included a prayer to the moon god, Aku, from Nabonidus, the last of the Babylonian kings, for "Belshazzar, the eldest son—my offspring."

The discoveries didn't end there. Almost three decades later, in 1882, the *Nabonidus Chronicle* was published. This ancient cuneiform text talks about the king being away from his throne for 10 of his 17 years, leaving his "crown prince" Belshazzar in charge.[10] Since then, several more mentions of Belshazzar have been uncovered. When it comes to biblical archaeology, the rule is "If it's not there yet, just wait; it'll come."

A City Primed for a Fall

Now that we've found where we are in Babylonian history, we need to understand the city itself. When we read the words "Babylon the Great" in Scripture, there is a good reason for that appellation. Babylon was huge—15 miles on each side. Surrounding the city was a massive brick wall that was 87 feet thick and 350 feet tall. This wall included 250 towers from which the army could defend the city. It was said that six chariots could drive on top of the defensive wall side by side. For added protection, a moat surrounded the city, with drawbridges leading to great bronze gates.

Dividing the city into two parts was the Euphrates River. But lest anyone think an enemy could use the water as their entrance point to attack, thick bronze gates blocked that pathway too. These mighty defenses were the reason that, on the night of our story, Crown Prince Belshazzar was feeling so comfortable in his palace. This was despite King Cyrus and his massive Medo-Persian army being camped right outside the city's walls. After all, no one could get through Babylon's defenses. Right?

Maybe Belshazzar would have been better served studying the Hebrew Scriptures rather than the palace's wine-tasting menu. If he had, he may have come across words written more than a century before. The prophet Isaiah had written about this very night:

> Thus says the LORD to His anointed,
> to Cyrus, whose right hand I have held—
> to subdue nations before him
> and loose the armor of kings,
> to open before him the double doors,
> so that the gates will not be shut:
> "I will go before you
> and make the crooked places straight;
> I will break in pieces the gates of bronze

and cut the bars of iron.
I will give you the treasures of darkness
and hidden riches of secret places,
that you may know that I, the LORD,
who call you by your name,
am the God of Israel" (Isaiah 45:1-3).

For huge bronze gates to effectively block the water entrance to a great city, two things must be true: First, the water must be deep. Second, the gates must be closed. Unfortunately, for Belshazzar, on the night of Saturday, October 12, 539 BC, if he had taken time away from his party to stroll by the water defenses, he would have found that neither of these necessities was the case.

How could such a failure happen? Once Cyrus the Persian had gotten all his troops into position, he signaled a vast team located along the Euphrates far upstream. They began digging, eventually diverting the river from its course so that it went around the city rather than through it. You would think that someone would have noticed the water level flowing into Babylon rapidly decreasing, but it's hard to catch these kinds of details when everyone is drunk. And why was everyone drunk? Because Belshazzar's shindig was essentially a citywide block party. He had his inner circle guzzling wine inside the palace, while outside in the streets the drunkenness and debauchery continued.

This is also how, on that particular night at the river entrance through the walls, the nearly impenetrable bronze gates with their deadly spikes sticking menacingly out the top stood wide open.

"Hey, Earl, did you remember to close the gates?"

"Shut up and hand me another beer."

When the water was low enough, Cyrus's army simply walked in. Look again at Isaiah 45:1-3. More than 100 years before it happened, God named Babylon's conqueror and how he would breach the city's defenses. Amazing!

A Party Gets Out of Hand

Daniel 5 opens with a feast. "Belshazzar the king made a great feast for a thousand of his lords, and drank wine in the presence of the thousand" (verse 1). This was probably not unusual for Babylon's interim leader. As we'll see when the story progresses, Belshazzar would not be considered a man of great character.

For the young and spoiled, everyday depravity can grow old and tiresome. There is often a need for bigger and better stimulation, or lower and nastier, depending on how you define it. The crown prince came up with an idea that had just the right edge of danger and sacrilege to it. The Jews had a reputation, as did their God. Stories had been around for centuries about plagues in Egypt and miraculous military victories. Even his grandfather, the great Nebuchadnezzar, had fallen under the spell of this so-called Most High God. Wouldn't it be a hoot if they brought in the sacred cups that had been taken from the Jerusalem temple to drink a few toasts?

> While he tasted the wine, Belshazzar gave the command to bring the gold and silver vessels which his father Nebuchadnezzar had taken from the temple which had been in Jerusalem, that the king and his lords, his wives, and his concubines might drink from them. Then they brought the gold vessels that had been taken from the temple of the house of God which had been in Jerusalem; and the king and his lords, his wives, and his concubines drank from them. They drank wine, and praised the gods of gold and silver, bronze and iron, wood and stone (verses 2-4).

Belshazzar made three great mistakes. First, he took sacred vessels and used them for a common purpose. Second, instead of worshipping the God of heaven as he drank from them, he praised the gods of silver and gold. Finally, and most significantly, he took for himself that which belonged to God.

When the Israelites began moving into the Promised Land, their first stop was the city of Jericho. Because it was the firstfruits of all the cities they were to conquer, it belonged to God. Therefore, everything was to be destroyed with the exception that "all the silver and gold, and vessels of bronze and iron, are consecrated to the LORD; they shall come into the treasury of the LORD" (Joshua 6:19). On the seventh day of Israel's siege of Jericho, the Israelites marched around the city's borders seven times, and the walls tumbled to the ground. The soldiers went in and destroyed everyone and everything in the city—mostly.

A man named Achan looked at all the spoils and saw "a beautiful Babylonian garment, two hundred shekels of silver, and a wedge of gold weighing fifty shekels" (7:21). He wanted them for himself, so he took them and buried them in the ground in his tent. But God saw what he had done. And because of his sin, when the Hebrews attacked the next city, they were soundly defeated. It was only when the sacred property belonging to the Lord was returned to Him that He again began blessing the people of Israel.

If God's discipline for His own children was so great, there was no way He was going to let some heathen crown prince debauch His sacred temple vessels. The Lord decided that Belshazzar needed a visitation. He had to be taught that it was not the gods of silver and gold that determined who sat on the throne. It was the Most High God who made those decisions. By the end of that night, as Ezekiel was so fond of repeating, the crown prince and everyone else would "know that I am the LORD."

A Hand Gets into the Party

The more everyone drank, the more raucous the party became. Then a cry rang out. This was followed by a protracted gasp as one person after another realized what was taking place at the front of the banquet hall. "In the same hour the fingers of a man's hand appeared and wrote opposite the lampstand on the plaster of the wall of the king's palace; and the king saw the part of the hand that wrote" (Daniel 5:5). I'm not fully content with the New King James Version's translation of the first part of this verse. It misses the punch of the ESV ("immediately") and the NIV ("suddenly"). People were drinking, dancing, and doing other things best not mentioned, when—BOOM—everything changed. Suddenly there was an interloper in their midst. Someone had crashed the party. Actually, it wasn't even a full someone—just part of a someone.

I love that word "suddenly" when I find it in Scripture. It always signifies an abrupt and usually unexpected turn of events. You find it in the prophets:

> I have declared the former things from the beginning; they
> went forth from My mouth, and I caused them to hear it.
> Suddenly I did them, and they came to pass (Isaiah 48:3).

God kept warning the people. He ensured that they heard His words. But they kept doing what they were doing, thinking that God was making empty threats. Then, suddenly, He acted, and all His promises of punishment were carried out.

This word "suddenly" is one that gives great hope to the church, while also encouraging believers to continue in their diligent service. Jesus was on the Mount of Olives, telling His disciples about His future return at the rapture, when He said,

> Of that day and hour no one knows, not even the angels
> in heaven, nor the Son, but only the Father...Watch
> therefore, for you do not know when the master of the
> house is coming—in the evening, at midnight, at the

crowing of the rooster, or in the morning—lest, coming
suddenly, he find you sleeping (Mark 13:32, 35-36).

We don't know the time or date of His return. He will come suddenly. We don't want to be caught up in sin and immorality at that
fateful moment, as Belshazzar and his cadre were. We want to be about
the Father's business so we can anxiously await that sudden moment
when we will be snatched up to be with our Messiah.

A large, disembodied hand writing on a wall would tend to shift
the mood in any room. It would definitely be the ultimate buzzkill to
any wild party. When Belshazzar saw the hand, he sobered up immediately, his drunk high turning to abject fear. He stared, his mouth agape,
as the hand wrote four words on the wall in a script he didn't understand. Then, as suddenly as it had appeared, the hand vanished, leaving
behind a message etched into the plastered wall. Belshazzar dropped.

> The king's countenance changed, and his thoughts troubled
> him, so that the joints of his hips were loosened and
> his knees knocked against each other. The king cried
> aloud to bring in the astrologers, the Chaldeans, and the
> soothsayers. The king spoke, saying to the wise men of
> Babylon, "Whoever reads this writing, and tells me its
> interpretation, shall be clothed with purple and have a
> chain of gold around his neck; and he shall be the third
> ruler in the kingdom." Now all the king's wise men came,
> but they could not read the writing, or make known to
> the king its interpretation. Then King Belshazzar was
> greatly troubled, his countenance was changed, and his
> lords were astonished (Daniel 5:6-9).

Daniel gives a wonderful physical description of the king's terror.
Essentially, the interim sovereign lost his ability to stand and couldn't

control his shaking. Four words were written on the wall in some language he didn't know. But there was one thing he clearly did understand: that message was for him.

So he did what it seems every Babylonian monarch did when they lacked understanding. He called in the magi. And all these wise men did what they seemed to always do whenever they were called to solve a mystery. They choked. They were utterly useless for interpreting the message, as were the gods they served. Belshazzar was at a loss, but then the queen stepped in. Word had gotten around the palace of the mysterious hand and its cryptic message. Then news of the unsurprising failure of the wise men and the king's despair reached the queen's chambers. She hurried to help.

> The queen, because of the words of the king and his lords, came to the banquet hall. The queen spoke, saying, "O king, live forever! Do not let your thoughts trouble you, nor let your countenance change. There is a man in your kingdom in whom is the Spirit of the Holy God. And in the days of your father, light and understanding and wisdom, like the wisdom of the gods, were found in him; and King Nebuchadnezzar your father—your father the king—made him chief of the magicians, astrologers, Chaldeans, and soothsayers. Inasmuch as an excellent spirit, knowledge, understanding, interpreting dreams, solving riddles, and explaining enigmas were found in this Daniel, whom the king named Belteshazzar, now let Daniel be called, and he will give the interpretation" (verses 10-12).

If Daniel was ever in need of a reference for his résumé, the queen should be number one on his list. It seems that after Belshazzar's grandfather, Nebuchadnezzar (named as his "father" in the passage, meaning his ancestor), had left the scene, Daniel had been gradually shuffled to the side. As the depravity of the royal courts grew, there would have been less and less of a desire to have some old, do-gooder eunuch looking over one's shoulder. Stories of Nebuchadnezzar's reign would have been passed down through the years, so the names of Belteshazzar, Shadrach, Meshach, and Abednego would have been known. But they belonged to a previous generation, which is why Daniel hadn't come to Belshazzar's mind.

But now that Belshazzar had been reminded of this servant of the Most High, there was a glimmer of hope. "Maybe he'll interpret these words for me like he interpreted the dreams of my grandfather!" He sent for the old prophet.

> Then Daniel was brought in before the king. The king spoke, and said to Daniel, "Are you that Daniel who is one of the captives from Judah, whom my father the king brought from Judah? I have heard of you, that the Spirit of God is in you, and that light and understanding and excellent wisdom are found in you. Now the wise men, the astrologers, have been brought in before me, that they should read this writing and make known to me its interpretation, but they could not give the interpretation of the thing. And I have heard of you, that you can give interpretations and explain enigmas. Now if you can read the writing and make known to me its interpretation, you shall be clothed with purple and have a chain of gold around your neck, and shall be the third ruler in the kingdom" (verses 13-16).

Belshazzar pleaded with Daniel for help. He called out Daniel's relationship with Nebuchadnezzar, who had brought him from Judah. The wise men had failed, he told Daniel, and he promised the old court servant great reward if he would help him out.

The Old Man Sets the Kids Straight

When Daniel spoke, he was unable to hide the disdain he held for the man who sat in front of him. He began by telling him that he didn't want any of his rewards. Not only would they mean nothing to him, but he also knew what was about to happen later that night when Cyrus came a-calling. Then, with all the authority that age, wisdom, and a righteous life provide, Daniel proceeded to scold the crown prince like he was a naughty schoolboy.

In the 1988 US presidential election, a vice-presidential candidate debate took place between Republican Senator Dan Quayle and Democrat Senator Lloyd Bentsen. Quayle, 41, who was constantly on the defensive because of his youth, at one point compared his experience to that of John F. Kennedy when that man ran for president. The much older Bentsen retorted, "Senator, I served with Jack Kennedy. I knew Jack Kennedy. Jack Kennedy was a friend of mine. Senator, you're no Jack Kennedy."

In verses 18-23, old Daniel essentially gave the young, upstart interim king the same treatment. "Belshazzar, I served Nebuchadnezzar. I knew Nebuchadnezzar. Nebuchadnezzar was a friend of mine. Belshazzar, you're no Nebuchadnezzar." Your grandfather was a great man, he told the crown prince. He recognized that the Most High God was in charge. And when he forgot, God reminded him, and Nebuchadnezzar learned his lesson.

Then, pointing his bony finger at the young man, Daniel said,

> But you his son, Belshazzar, have not humbled your heart, although you knew all this. And you have lifted yourself up against the Lord of heaven. They have brought the vessels of His house before you, and you and your lords, your wives and your concubines, have drunk wine from them. And you have praised the gods of silver and gold, bronze and iron, wood and stone, which do not see or

hear or know; and the God who holds your breath in His hand and owns all your ways, you have not glorified (verses 22-23).

These words sent another round of gasps through the banquet room. Who talked to the king that way? But Belshazzar sat there and took it. First, because he didn't have a strong enough character to stand up against this old man. Second, he knew Daniel's words were the truth. Third, he needed to know what the message meant, and this man in front of him was the only one who could tell him.

This Daniel proceeded to do:

> The fingers of the hand were sent from [God], and this writing was written.

> And this is the inscription that was written:

> MENE, MENE, TEKEL, UPHARSIN.

> This is the interpretation of each word. MENE: God has numbered your kingdom, and finished it; TEKEL: You have been weighed in the balances, and found wanting; PERES: Your kingdom has been divided, and given to the Medes and Persians (verses 24-28).

As you read the old prophet's words, you can picture in your mind a shifting of the scene. The banquet counter disappeared, replaced by a long table. By the wall, in front of the supernatural writing, a large judge's bench rose. Sitting behind this formidable desk was the Judge. He was the Most High God who had brought the young king into His courtroom, where he was shaking in fear.

The charges had already been announced by Daniel: "You have not humbled your heart. You have lifted yourself up against the Lord of heaven. You have misused God's temple vessels to worship false deities. You have not glorified the One who holds your very breath in His hand."

There was no question about the verdict. It was already written on the wall behind the Judge. Guilty on all charges!

"MENE: God has numbered your kingdom, and finished it." The Most High can do what He wants with the people of the earth, be they royal or peasant. Nebuchadnezzar learned this lesson, declaring, "[God] does according to His will in the army of heaven and among the inhabitants of the earth. No one can restrain His hand or say to Him, 'What have You done?'" (4:35). The Lord evaluated Belshazzar's Babylon, declared it unworthy of existence, and would now destroy it.

"TEKEL: You have been weighed in the balances, and found wanting." Not only was the kingdom unworthy, so was its king. There will come a day when another judgment seat is erected. John speaks of it as a

> great white throne and Him who sat on it, from whose face the earth and the heaven fled away. And there was found no place for them. And I saw the dead, small and great, standing before God, and books were opened. And another book was opened, which is the Book of Life. And the dead were judged according to their works, by the things which were written in the books...And anyone not found written in the Book of Life was cast into the lake of fire (Revelation 20:11-12, 15).

I've got news for you: There is no one on this earth whose works would be worthy enough to gain them a "not guilty" verdict before that throne. All manmade efforts will be found wanting. But we don't have to depend upon our own efforts. Peter, the disciple, wrote, "Christ also suffered once for sins, the just for the unjust, that He might bring us to God" (1 Peter 3:18). Our works will never measure up, but Jesus' work on the cross measured up so ours don't have to. When we receive Jesus as our Lord and Savior, we don't need to worry about that final judgment seat. In fact, we won't even stand to be judged then, having been taken up before in the rapture to be with our Messiah forever. All it takes is believing Jesus is who He said He is and making Him number one in our lives.

"PERES: Your kingdom has been divided, and given to the Medes and Persians." The enemy is at the gate, and they're coming in.

In response, Belshazzar showered Daniel with gifts and promoted him to third in the kingdom, which is akin to the captain of the Titanic proclaiming a mid-Atlantic promotion of his first officer to staff captain. All that was declared by God through Daniel came to pass. It was inevitable because, quite literally, the handwriting was on the wall. By the way, this story is the origin of that often-used phrase. Daniel wrapped up the tale by telling the readers, "That very night Belshazzar, king of the Chaldeans, was slain. And Darius the Mede received the kingdom, being about sixty-two years old" (Daniel 5:30-31).

Lessons of Leadership Failure

There are two important lessons that I see in this sad story of leadership failure:

Stewardship Requires Faithfulness

The Bible speaks frequently about the importance of stewardship. By this I mean the giving of a responsibility to one person by another who is in authority. When given, quite naturally, the one in authority expects the steward to faithfully carry out his directives.

Belshazzar's stewardship was the people of Babylon. However, he neglected them and refused to be responsible to the One who gave him that stewardship. Not only did he not want to be responsible to the Most High, but Belshazzar also totally rejected the God of heaven, who gave him his very breath to breathe. When the time came for the true Master to ask for an accounting of this king's stewardship, he was weighed in the balance and found wanting. In other words, Belshazzar did not measure up to the expectations of a faithful steward.

The apostle Paul spoke of stewardship, writing, "It is required in stewards that one be found faithful" (1 Corinthians 4:2). Stewards have one major responsibility: They are to be faithful or reliable to their master.

I love the Hebrew word for faithfulness. It is אֱמֶת (*emet*), and it conveys firmness and reliability. When Joshua fought the Amalekites, Moses held up his hands as he stood on top of a hill and watched the battle between Israel and the enemy. Israel kept winning as long as Moses' hands were held high. But when the octogenarian leader grew tired and lowered his arms, the battle would sway to the Amalekites. So Aaron, Moses' brother, and Hur provided a stone for the old leader to sit on while they held up his arms. The Bible tells us the day ended with victory for Israel because Moses' "hands were steady [*emet*] until the going down of the sun" (Exodus 17:12). This wouldn't have happened without Aaron and Hur faithfully carrying out their duties.

A faithful steward is one who is "steady" in their stewardship or responsibilities. When you take on a role in your church or you commit to reaching out to a coworker, God expects you to carry out your mission to the best of your abilities. Even when you are discouraged or tired or unappreciated, keep about the Father's business. He sees you, and nothing you do for Him goes unacknowledged.

Faithfulness in a Few Things Results in More Opportunities to Honor God and Bless Others

Jesus, in one of His many parables, told the story about two faithful stewards and their rewards. When the master returned from a long journey to discover that his servants had doubled the money he had left them, he said, "Well done, good and faithful servant; you have been faithful over a few things, I will make you ruler over many things. Enter into the joy of your lord" (Matthew 25:21, 23). I like the approach the New Living Translation takes with the same passage:

> The master said, "Well done, my good and faithful servant. You have been faithful in handling this small amount, so now I will give you many more responsibilities. Let's celebrate together!" (verse 23).

The picture of the master and servants celebrating together is beautiful. It perfectly expresses the joy the Lord has when we follow through and do His will to the best of our abilities. His promise is that when we show we can be trusted with a little, He will open wide doors of ministry for us that will blow our socks off.

King Belshazzar refused to be a faithful steward. As a result, even what he had was taken away from him. His failure to trust God and follow His will stands in stark contrast to the faithful-no-matter-what story we're about to read in the next chapter.

CHAPTER 6

OPEN MOUTHS, CLOSED MOUTHS

DANIEL 6

When you reach the top in your profession or your organization or your sport or whatever group you might find yourself part of, you will soon realize that there are others who want to be there with you. Or, more likely, without you.

This was the situation that Daniel found himself in. He was King Darius's leader of leaders, and many of his junior leaders hated him for it. Daniel had three dynamics going against him. First, he had reached the very top of his profession and was exalted above all others who did what he did. Second, he had earned his lofty position because he was far better at it than anyone else. Third, he was an outsider, a Jew, one of those taken from Jerusalem by the previous and now-defeated empire.

> It pleased Darius to set over the kingdom one hundred and twenty satraps, to be over the whole kingdom; and over these, three governors, of whom Daniel was one, that the satraps might give account to them, so that the king

would suffer no loss. Then this Daniel distinguished himself above the governors and satraps, because an excellent spirit was in him; and the king gave thought to setting him over the whole realm (Daniel 6:1-3).

King Darius the Mede looked at his leadership corps and chose 120 of the best on whom he would bestow authority over his kingdom. He then evaluated these 120 and chose three to be governors over the rest. They would be the leaders of leaders. Daniel, the old, Jewish eunuch taken into exile, was one of those given this exalted position. He may have survived the jealousy and ruthlessness of the backstabbers and court climbers if he hadn't been so darn good at his job.

As time went on, Darius looked at his trio of governors and decided that he needed to do one more corporate reshuffle. One of his "leaders of leaders" far outshone the other two. Before the others of the leadership crew knew what was happening, old Daniel was promoted to the leader of the leaders of leaders. He was now the top banana, the head honcho, court guy numero uno.

That was a step too far. There was no way all these Persians and Medes, who by birth deserved to be in that position, were going to let this holdover foreigner from the previous administration be their boss. He didn't look like them. He didn't act like them. He worshipped his own god while shunning their idols. And he was so straitlaced! There was no skimming with Daniel in charge. No building your own secret nest egg or overcharging the tributes of the districts to pad your own pockets. Daniel was a rules guy, a Goody Two-sandals who didn't know or didn't care how the real game was played.

A Terribly Brilliant Plan

The elderly Jew had to go. But how? The king loved him. The old monarch thought he was the best thing since sliced naan. What fault could they possibly find to bring this man down?

So the governors and satraps sought to find some charge against Daniel concerning the kingdom; but they could find no charge or fault, because he was faithful; nor was there any error or fault found in him. Then these men said, "We shall not find any charge against this Daniel unless we find it against him concerning the law of his God" (verses 4-5).

Their idea was really quite brilliant. If you can't attack a man for his faults, find a way to take him out using his strengths. Even more than his loyalty to the king, Daniel was loyal to his God. If there was a way to use what was, in their minds, an out-of-sync hierarchy, it would be sure to bring the old Jew down.

They sat down and thought. They conspired. They plotted. They schemed. Then, to paraphrase a certain brilliant author, "Then they got an idea. An awful idea. The governors and satraps had a wonderful, awful idea."[11]

These governors and satraps thronged before the king, and said thus to him: "King Darius, live forever! All the governors of the kingdom, the administrators and satraps, the counselors and advisors, have consulted together to establish a royal statute and to make a firm decree, that whoever petitions any god or man for thirty days, except you, O king, shall be cast into the den of lions. Now, O king, establish the decree and sign the writing, so that it cannot be changed, according to the law of the Medes and Persians, which does not alter." Therefore King Darius signed the written decree (verses 6-9).

Because we know all the behind-the-scenes motivations, we're able to see right through these royal shysters. But Darius didn't know the backstory, so we can't blame him for being taken in by this well-concocted plan. First, the officials appealed to the king's trust, while telling him a huge lie. They reported to the king that *all of the officials* had gathered together and agreed to the royal statue they were about to present. If Darius had stopped to consider the petition once he had heard what it involved, he would have known that there was no way his chief administrator would have gone along with it. But these were his leaders and leaders of leaders. Would they really lie to him? Besides, he was a busy man. He didn't have time to break down and analyze every decree that came across his desk.

Second, the officials played to the king's vanity. "Darius, you are so great, so mighty, so powerful, that it's silly that any of your subjects should be asking for help from any god or human other than you. In fact, it's kind of disrespectful, maybe even a bit treasonous, if you think about it." I'm guessing that I would only need both hands and maybe one foot to count the number of kings throughout history who would respond to that kind of flattery with, "Oh, come on, guys. I'm not really all *that* great." Darius was like the other kings of his day. If there was an opportunity to give himself a little more glory, he was all in.

Finally, the officials deftly used the royal law. They made sure to remind Darius that once a law was signed, it could not be undone. When they reminded the king of that legally binding statute, he probably waved his hand dismissively and said, "Yada, yada, yada, I know that. Now, where's the paper?" It was a brilliant play. The officials were laying the trap so that when they brought in Daniel, Darius couldn't say, "You tricked me," or "I had forgotten about that rule." He knew when he signed the decree that the next 30 days would be King Darius Month, and anyone who broke the rules would be lion food.

The trap was laid, and, without knowing it, King Darius had just set the triggering mechanism. Now all that was left was for the officials to wait for Daniel to step in. They knew they would not have to wait long.

The Power of Everyday Faith

What would you do if you were in Daniel's situation? Would you take a hiatus from your faith, figuring that God would understand the danger in which you found yourself? Or would you hide your faith, praying from inside your closet or tucked away down in your basement? Daniel was never a "hide in the basement" kind of guy. Like his three friends who, when the music had been played, had defiantly remained vertical while everyone else in the kingdom was horizontal, Daniel refused to put safety over boldness, fear over faith, himself over God.

> Now when Daniel knew that the writing was signed, he went home. And in his upper room, with his windows open toward Jerusalem, he knelt down on his knees three times that day, and prayed and gave thanks before his God, as was his custom since early days (verse 10).

Why did Daniel have to be so visible in his faith? Would it have been a sin if he had kept his windows closed and his prayers to himself? For Daniel, the answer was yes. It would have amounted to a break in his customary worship routine due to a lack of faith in God's protection. The old prophet was in the habit of praying in a manner prescribed by King Solomon at the dedication of the temple. With hands lifted to the God of heaven, the great king had prayed,

> When they sin against You (for there is no one who does not sin), and You become angry with them and deliver them to the enemy, and they take them captive to a land far or near; yet when they come to themselves in the

land where they were carried captive, and repent, and make supplication to You in the land of their captivity, saying, "We have sinned, we have done wrong, and have committed wickedness"; and when they return to You with all their heart and with all their soul in the land of their captivity, where they have been carried captive, and pray toward their land which You gave to their fathers, the city which You have chosen, and toward the temple which I have built for Your name: then hear from heaven Your dwelling place their prayer and their supplications, and maintain their cause, and forgive Your people who have sinned against You (2 Chronicles 6:36-39).

Daniel was living the words that Solomon had spoken more than 400 years before. Not only that, he was also following the king's remedy for alleviating the punishment. If the exiles who had been carried away as captives were to pray "toward their land" and "toward the temple," Solomon pleaded with God to "hear from heaven," "maintain their cause," and "forgive Your people."

This was not a prayer designed to be spoken from a closet or a basement. A prayer of supplication such as Solomon's should be boldly called out with "windows open toward Jerusalem." Faith that believes in God's future forgiveness, restoration, and return will surely believe in His present-day protection.

"But, Amir, Daniel was a prophet, so he had that prophet kind of faith. He wasn't just a regular guy. Besides, he was old. He knew his time would be over soon anyway." Let me deal with the last assertion first. I don't believe the fear of being torn apart and eaten by wild animals has an age limit. Chances are, whether you are 18 or 80, being thrown into a lions' den ranks right up with being pushed into a piranha pond on the list of ways you don't want to leave this life.

As for the first assertion—that he had some kind of supernatural, prophet-level faith—remember that Daniel's actions here matched who he had always been. From the moment he arrived in Babylon with Shadrach, Meshach, and Abednego, the four pimply faced teenage boys were ready to risk all for God. They were of the "My God will protect me, but even if He doesn't, I'm still going to do what is right" school of faith. There was no inherent difference between those kids and you and me.

James, the brother of Jesus, wrote in his letter of the great prophet Elijah, "Elijah was a man with a nature like ours, and he prayed earnestly that it would not rain; and it did not rain on the land for three years and six months. And he prayed again, and the heaven gave rain, and the earth produced its fruit" (James 5:17-18). Essentially, James was saying that Elijah was simply an ordinary person, just like us. But look at what his faith enabled him to do.

When Jesus' disciples were unable to cast out a demon from a young boy, He told them, "If you have faith as a mustard seed, you will say to this mountain, 'Move from here to there,' and it will move; and nothing will be impossible for you" (Matthew 17:20). Faith is not a matter of genetics or of calling. What counts is how much you trust God.

In your time of trial, even though you don't see a physical manifestation of the Almighty God, do you still believe that He loves you, that He is watching out for you, and that He will always see and reward your righteousness? We live in a highly visual society in which we can see just about anything we desire, either through our televisions or the internet. But God lives beyond the visual, which is why it is so difficult for people to trust Him. Because God is beyond what we can see, faith in Him is also not a visual thing. As the writer of Hebrews put it, "Now faith is the substance of things hoped for, the evidence of things not seen" (Hebrews 11:1).

Is there anything you are not trusting God for? Is there any difficulty you are facing that you can't stop worrying about? Those nights when you are lying awake worrying would be better spent praying. Let God fight your battles. Trust that He loves you. Know that He is there, even if your eyes are not able to make Him out. In those times when the lions' den awaits you, know that you are not entering it alone. As Jesus told the famous doubting disciple, "Thomas, because you have seen Me, you have believed. Blessed are those who have not seen and yet have believed" (John 20:29).

One thing we know for certain about Daniel—he was not dumb. He knew the whole "petition the king" plot was a trap to get rid of him. He would have been in no way surprised to discover his enemies hiding outside his door and waiting for him to launch into one of his thrice-a-day prayers. How they must have exulted when they heard the words of supplication echo from the prophet's living quarters. Immediately, they scurried off to the king.

> They went before the king, and spoke concerning the king's decree: "Have you not signed a decree that every man who petitions any god or man within thirty days, except you, O king, shall be cast into the den of lions?" The king answered and said, "The thing is true, according to the law of the Medes and Persians, which does not alter" (Daniel 6:12).

Once again, these were not dumb men either. They had plotted the perfect crime, and now with the king's repeated affirmation that the law was in place and could not be altered, they prepared to reveal the victim.

What comes next happens so often when people and nations plot against God's people but forget about God. It occurred in 1948, when Israel declared itself to be independent. Five nations attacked the newborn country. The Arab coalition of nations should have won because of their superior numbers and more powerful weapons, but they forgot about God. Instead, they were soundly defeated.

In 1967, five Arab nations, along with supporting troops from a couple others, surrounded Israel with a force more than twice the size of the Jews. Recognizing that an attack was about to take place, the Israeli military launched a preemptive strike. That battle raged, until six days later, the war was over and the Arab forces were sent scampering home. Once again, God had protected His people.

Then in 1973, a coalition force with troops from a dozen countries invaded Israel on the nation's holiest of days, Yom Kippur. Within two-and-a-half weeks, the Arab coalition army was forced back out with more than five times the casualties of the Israeli army. This is what happens when people plot and scheme but fail to take into account the Almighty God who loves and cares for His own.

I could continue with time after time that God has protected my nation, Israel, from the plotting of others. I could do the same with my own life as well, as I've seen the Lord stand with me against the stones and arrows of others. God is faithful. No matter the plots formed against us, we know that God has us taken care of. And even if God chooses not to pull us from the fire, we know that everything will work out for His glory and our reward. That is what He promises; that is what He does.

An Unusual Night with Unexpected Company

The trap was set, the king suckered in, and it was now time for the big reveal. With false concern over Darius's offended majesty, the officials said,

> "That Daniel, who is one of the captives from Judah, does not show due regard for you, O king, or for the decree that you have signed, but makes his petition three times a day." And the king, when he heard these words, was greatly displeased with himself, and set his heart on Daniel to deliver him; and he labored till the going down of the

sun to deliver him. Then these men approached the king,
and said to the king, "Know, O king, that it is the law of
the Medes and Persians that no decree or statute which
the king establishes may be changed" (verses 13-15).

The king realized he had been duped. He spent the rest of the
day trying to figure out a way to save Daniel's life. But it was useless.
As the evening's light began to wane, the officials smugly reminded
Darius, "You can try all you like to save your little pet, O king. But
it can't be done. It's lion time."

In the same way that these wise men hadn't factored a protective
God in their plot, they also hadn't allowed for an offended king. Monarchs tend to get a little miffed when they are conned; they get doubly so when the offenders rub it in. Darius didn't react immediately
to the mocking words of his officials, but neither did he forget them.

Knowing that he was powerless to stop Daniel's fate but hoping
that Daniel's God was not, Darius gave the order. It was quickly carried out.

The king gave the command, and they brought Daniel and
cast him into the den of lions. But the king spoke, saying
to Daniel, "Your God, whom you serve continually, He
will deliver you." Then a stone was brought and laid on
the mouth of the den, and the king sealed it with his own
signet ring and with the signets of his lords, that the purpose
concerning Daniel might not be changed (verses 16-17).

My collaborator on this book, Dr. Rick Yohn, is 86 years old at
the time I'm writing this. That is approximately the age Daniel was
when this incident took place, give or take a few years. Rick would
be quick to point out that God's miraculous intervention didn't begin
with the lions. It began with the casting.

The lions' den was not a cage, but rather, a pit. The word that is translated "cast," or in some translations, "thrown," is used only one other time in Scripture—when Daniel's three friends were cast into the fiery furnace. If anyone is picturing the octogenarian prophet being gently lowered on ropes for a soft landing on the stone floor below, they can put that out of their minds. If it was anything like the casting of Shadrach, Meshach, and Abednego, he would have been given a hard push with no concern about the landing.

But it seems that a soft landing was had after all. The next day, when it was all over, we're given no indications that Daniel was treated for a concussion or that he had to be airlifted to Babylon General Hospital with a broken hip. Instead, we're told he came out with "no injury whatever" (verse 23). But we're getting ahead of ourselves. This is enough to help us realize that God was with Daniel from the moment the ordeal began, and He stayed with him throughout.

If I had to choose to endure one faith trial found in Scripture, I've always felt that this would be the one. Hanging out with a whole pride of temporarily tame lions—how great would that be? But now that I've really processed the incident for this book, I am far less enamored with the idea of facing that experience. Daniel was below ground, so the cool dampness of the den would have been tough on his frail body. The air would have been thick and musty and filled with the stench of wild animals. The rank smells of rotting flesh and fresh excrement, along with the harsh ammonia reek of feline urine, would have made the air almost unbreathable. My hope for Daniel is that the second miracle in the den was God giving Him the same supernatural fresh air that He provided for Jonah that allowed the wayward prophet to survive in the belly of a fish for three days.

After Daniel had quite literally hit rock bottom, a stone was placed over the mouth of the cave. Its purpose was to keep the king from being able to change his mind about Daniel's fate. In one more act of humiliation, he was forced to seal the den with his signet ring. The ledger of royal grievances against the palace courtiers was getting longer.

With the rock in place, it would have been completely dark inside the den. Without the ability to use the sense of sight, the other senses would have heightened. This would include the unfortunate sense of smell, as we've noted, as well as Daniel's hearing. Apart from some possible muted cheering coming from the officials above, he heard a low predatorial rumble. Soft, padded footsteps passed by him, and coarse wisps of hair brushed against his arm. His left leg suddenly buckled after what felt like a rod thwacked into his thigh. A second hit helped him to identify it as an agitated tail swishing side to side.

Despite Daniel's faith, his blood pressure was probably up along with his pulse. That's just natural in a scary situation. People often look at fear as lack of faith. It's not. Fear is a normal emotion that God programmed into us to help us to know when it's time to be very careful. It's what we do with the fear that reflects on our trust of God. If we let our temporary terror turn into long-term anxiety, then we are missing the reality of our protective Father. If fear turns into bitterness or if it leads to questioning the goodness of God, then we are letting the enemy get a foothold of doubt into our lives. But if we use our fear to turn to God, to pray to Him and seek His help, then it is a good thing. And if we let it be the natural warning system it was intended to be, then our emotion of fear is fulfilling its God-created purpose.

Where Daniel was on the spectrum between mild anxiety and a great dread of becoming dinner, we don't know. What we do see is that he trusted God, and as expected, God showed up.

> Now the king went to his palace and spent the night fasting; and no musicians were brought before him. Also his sleep went from him. Then the king arose very early in the morning and went in haste to the den of lions. And

when he came to the den, he cried out with a lamenting voice to Daniel. The king spoke, saying to Daniel, "Daniel, servant of the living God, has your God, whom you serve continually, been able to deliver you from the lions?"

Then Daniel said to the king, "O king, live forever! My God sent His angel and shut the lions' mouths, so that they have not hurt me, because I was found innocent before Him; and also, O king, I have done no wrong before you" (verses 18-22).

What is the only experience more incredible than safely spending the night in a den full of lions? Having an angel show up as the lion tamer. The king had allowed himself no sleep. He had paced back and forth in his chambers, fretting and worrying over his friend. When dawn finally came, he ran to the lions' den. This says something about the genuineness of Daniel's character; Darius actually had hope that the old prophet survived the night in the den. I'm guessing that normally when someone called down into the cave the morning after a tossing, it was a very rare occurrence to have a voice answer back.

But that is exactly what happened that morning. "Daniel, has your God protected you from the lions?" "He sure has. An angel came and made the lions just as nice as can be." Daniel then defended his innocence, which was wholly unnecessary. Darius knew the score. He recognized what this was all about. So he initiated his own little counterplot that he had likely come up with sometime during his nocturnal pacing.

Now the king was exceedingly glad for him, and commanded that they should take Daniel up out of the den. So Daniel was taken up out of the den, and no injury whatever was found on him, because he believed in his God.

> And the king gave the command, and they brought those
> men who had accused Daniel, and they cast them into
> the den of lions—them, their children, and their wives;
> and the lions overpowered them, and broke all their bones
> in pieces before they ever came to the bottom of the den
> (verses 23-24).

The king had been keeping a tab of all the ways his officials had wronged him and his most loyal servant, Daniel, over the past couple days. Now the account was due. In typical monarchical overkill, Darius had the prophet's accusers, along with their wives and children, cast into the den in Daniel's stead. Needless to say, the angelic leonine muzzling had by this time expired.

All Glory Goes to God

Following the example of King Nebuchadnezzar, Darius the Mede wanted everyone in his kingdom to know about the powerful God of Daniel.

> Then King Darius wrote:
>
> To all peoples, nations, and languages that dwell in all
> the earth:
>
> Peace be multiplied to you.
>
> I make a decree that in every dominion of my kingdom
> men must tremble and fear before the God of Daniel.
>
> > For He is the living God,
> > and steadfast forever;
> > His kingdom is the one which shall not be destroyed,
> > and His dominion shall endure to the end.
> > He delivers and rescues,

and He works signs and wonders
in heaven and on earth,
who has delivered Daniel from the power of the lions
(verses 25-27).

There are three elements of this decree to take note of. First, Darius recognized that God is eternal and has an eternal kingdom. Though earthly kingdoms come and go, the kingdom of the God of heaven remains and always will. Second, God delivers and rescues. Every other human thrown into the den of lions was eventually brought out by shovel. Daniel walked out unscathed.

Third, this God works signs and wonders in heaven and on earth. As I mentioned in an earlier chapter, this statement goes against our present-day culture that holds to a universe that is a closed system of cause and effect. If something cannot be proven scientifically, then it has no relevance in our lives. There is no room for a miracle-working God.

Yet we have plenty of evidence that God is alive and well and is carrying out His purpose in governments and individuals throughout the world. The biblically predicted present-day existence of a nation that had disappeared for 2,000 years, but which now has become the eighth strongest world power in only 75 years, is proof positive that God exists and is working in our world. But the nation of Israel is not the only evidence. Every day, on both the national macro level and the individual micro level, our Almighty God and loving Father is supernaturally working in the natural world to bring His plans to fruition.

We have now come to the end of the story time portion of the book of Daniel. Remember, I don't mean story in the fictional sense of the word. But in a world where some people learn better through the recitation of facts and others through the telling of tales, Daniel is the perfect blend of both. So for those of you who have been waiting to get into the predictive history and the apocalyptic visions in Daniel, your time has come. For those who are going to miss the stories, don't worry—there is still more than enough action in the coming chapters to keep you on the edge of your seat.

CHAPTER 7

THE BEGINNING OF VISIONS

DANIEL 7

We live in a time in which we are rarely shocked by the appearance of a creature that exists in the natural world. Instead, the odd and bizarre fill our hearts with amusement and joy. We ooh and aah and sometimes even chuckle as we examine such fantastic creatures as the furry white Venezuelan Poodle Moth, the walrus-nosed Saiga antelope, and the deep-sea blobfish, which, upon being brought to the surface, decompresses to look like a perpetually depressed old man. It hasn't always been like this. It wasn't that many centuries ago when stories of spotted, long-necked, leaf-eating creatures and massive, thick-skinned beasts with noses that reached to the ground would bring wonder, fear, and maybe a little skepticism to Europeans.

Movies, television shows, and video games have jaded us even more to the fantastic. Orcs, Klingons, and creatures from black lagoons have opened the door for many to the possibility of strange beings existing in space, on earth, or even in Middle Earth. As a result of this bar-lowering of the bizarre, today's readers of Scripture likely react with less astonishment than those of the past when they read of the four beasts in Daniel 7. Instead of being amazed that creatures like these exist in the supernatural, their response may be closer to "Oh, that reminds me of those flying things that invaded with the Chitauri fleet when the wormhole opened above Stark Tower in *The Avengers*."

Now that we arrive in the second half of Daniel, we are faced with a major shift in the focus and style of the prophet's writing. We are moving from the incredible to the fantastic. Historical narrative gives way to apocalyptic vision. Daniel shifts from wise dream interpreter to confused vision receiver. We even find a change in the language Daniel writes in. Aside from chapter 1 and a few verses at the beginning of chapter 2, the storytelling first half of the book is all written in Aramaic. With the swing to apocalyptic visions, the second half is all penned in Hebrew, with the sole exception of chapter 7. Why this language swap? Because Daniel's focus is changing. The first half is chiefly concerned with the Gentile world. But now the book is narrowing its focus primarily to the nation of Israel.

In chapter 7, concern is still given to the four Gentile empires of Nebuchadnezzar's statue dream in chapter 2. But here, the emphasis is not on these empires, but on the kingdom of God, which will eventually achieve global domination. Daniel's dream gives us a preview of what is on the world's agenda beginning with his day and reaching far into the future.

This is one of my favorite chapters in the book of Daniel because it not only provides a look into the future that God has laid out for the world, but it also gives us a stunning glimpse of the King of heaven and His wonderous throne room. As does John centuries later in Revelation, Daniel now invites us along to his audience before the Ancient of Days. And it is marvelous!

A Brief Introduction

Because we are leaving the narrative portion of the book, our progressive timeline is no longer necessary. We last left Daniel under the care of King Darius the Mede, around 539 BC. As chapter 7 opens, he has reversed the clock and is back under the authority of the degenerate King Belshazzar, about 11 years earlier.

> In the first year of Belshazzar king of Babylon, Daniel had a dream and visions of his head while on his bed. Then he wrote down the dream, telling the main facts (Daniel 7:1).

Daniel is about to tell of one vision given in three scenes. The first is of four beasts coming up out of the sea. The second is of a courtroom from which judgment is given. The third sees the Son of Man descending to receive His kingdom. The revelation of this vision makes up the first half of the chapter. What I love about Daniel's apocalyptic writing is that he always lets us know what his visions mean. In fact, the entire second half of this chapter provides an explanation of what the bizarre first half means. As one who has a strong history of interpreting other people's dreams and visions, he was not going to leave his readers in a quandary.

A Vision of Four Beasts

As Daniel was lying on his bed, God invaded his sleep. I find this interesting because many of my most powerful sermons and book ideas come to me as I lie on my bed. Sometimes it is when I lay awake that God sparks an idea. Other times, His truth comes to me as I slumber, so that in the morning, I can't wait to get to my computer to write out my thoughts. That's after I get my double espresso, of course.

As Daniel slept, God showed him some very strange images:

> I saw in my vision by night, and behold, the four winds of heaven were stirring up the Great Sea. And four great beasts came up from the sea, each different from the other. The first was like a lion, and had eagle's wings. I watched

till its wings were plucked off; and it was lifted up from the earth and made to stand on two feet like a man, and a man's heart was given to it.

And suddenly another beast, a second, like a bear. It was raised up on one side, and had three ribs in its mouth between its teeth. And they said thus to it: "Arise, devour much flesh!"

After this I looked, and there was another, like a leopard, which had on its back four wings of a bird. The beast also had four heads, and dominion was given to it.

After this I saw in the night visions, and behold, a fourth beast, dreadful and terrible, exceedingly strong. It had huge iron teeth; it was devouring, breaking in pieces, and trampling the residue with its feet. It was different from all the beasts that were before it, and it had ten horns. I was considering the horns, and there was another horn, a little one, coming up among them, before whom three of the first horns were plucked out by the roots. And there, in this horn, were eyes like the eyes of a man, and a mouth speaking pompous words (Daniel 7:2-8).

Weird.

It's hard to know what Daniel was feeling when he saw these images. Was he terrified, or was his mouth hanging open in wonderment as he asked himself, *What in the name of Aaron's gray beard is going on?*

The symbolism of the first creature would have triggered memories for the wise prophet. It was remarkably similar to Nebuchadnezzar's fall from sanity in Daniel 4, only in reverse. In the king's experience, he was a man who stood upright. But then he suddenly became beast-like. He ate grass with the animals of the field and grew out his hair like the feathers of an eagle and his nails like the talons of a bird. The flying lion in the vision began completely animal-like, but eventually lost his wings and, in a precursor to George Orwell's *Animal Farm*, shunned his four legs for two. And while Daniel's vision saw this beast receiving the heart of a man, Nebuchadnezzar had his man's heart traded for that of a beast. This flying lion was Babylon.

More beasts proceeded to exit the sea. Each one we can tie with the kingdoms of Nebuchadnezzar's statue dream of chapter 2. The bear that was devouring the three ribs speaks of the Medo-Persian Empire, which conquered Lydia, Egypt, and Babylon. The leopard with its four wings and four heads was the future kingdom of Greece that would split into four empires following the death of Alexander the Great. Then there's that final, terrible beast with its ten horns and its verbally pompous little horn. For that one, we're going to need a little angelic wisdom. Thankfully, that's just what we're going to get.

This is not the last time that these beasts or this "little horn" visit Daniel's dreams. Daniel chapters 8 and 11 will have return appearances of some or all of these characters. And much later in Scripture, they will return once again to the visions of John the Revelator in the ominous chapter 13 of his apocalyptic letter.

> I stood on the sand of the sea. And I saw a beast rising up out of the sea, having seven heads and ten horns, and on his horns ten crowns, and on his heads a blasphemous name. Now the beast which I saw was like a leopard, his feet were like the feet of a bear, and his mouth like the mouth of a lion (Revelation 13:1-2).

Notice this beast's animal similarities? They are the same as Daniel's, only in reverse order. This is because Daniel was looking into the future, while John looked back into history. Do you again see why Daniel and Revelation should be studied together? They are deeply intertwined. What Daniel predicts, Revelation fulfills.

The Ancient of Days

As each of my older children finished school, they participated in their graduation event. It was always a big production with acting and dancing. My daughter in particular was involved in the performance. When one act would finish, the curtain would close. From off stage, the audience would hear bumping and shuffling as props and equipment were moved around. Eventually, all would quiet down, and the curtain would open for the next act.

This is similar to what happens between verses 8 and 9 of Daniel 7, only without the curtain. With more precision and far less prop dropping, the scene shifts from the sea to a courtroom. Thrones are hustled in from off stage, then the cast enters. Daniel watched as each took their place. But once the star of the show entered, the prophet had no more attention for any of the other players. Taking His place on the throne at center stage sat the Ancient of Days.

It is hard not to shudder in awe as you read Daniel's description. There is astonishment and reverence in his words. He grasps for adjectives to describe the One who is in front of him. He stumbles over numbers trying to define the glorious multitude of those serving the Lord in His court. He does an amazing job at describing the indescribable, but we still need to recognize that we are reading just a glimpse at a fraction of a tiny percentage of what he witnessed.

> I watched till thrones were put in place,
> and the Ancient of Days was seated;
> His garment was white as snow,
> and the hair of His head was like pure wool.
> His throne was a fiery flame,
> its wheels a burning fire;
> a fiery stream issued
> and came forth from before Him.

A thousand thousands ministered to Him;
ten thousand times ten thousand stood before Him.
The court was seated,
and the books were opened (Daniel 7:9-10).

This chapter is the only place in all of Scripture that this wonderful appellation, Ancient of Days, is used of the Lord. It's a majestic title referring to God's eternal existence. While we are creatures of time with a beginning and an ending, God always was, is, and will always be. This reminds me of the description of God's eternal nature given by Moses:

Lord, You have been our dwelling place in all generations.
Before the mountains were brought forth,
or ever You had formed the earth and the world,
even from everlasting to everlasting, You are God
(Psalm 90:1-2).

From eternity past to eternity future, the great "I AM" is. And now, Daniel was staring at Him face to face. The Ancient of Days had taken His place as Judge on a fiery throne that had been rolled in on flaming wheels. Daniel said that a thousand thousands were serving Him. Then he checked himself, knowing that even that huge number wasn't adequate for the entourage of the Ancient of Days. He upped his estimate to ten thousand times ten thousand, probably still feeling that number to be inadequate. Interestingly, this also parallels John as the disciple sought to describe the throne room of God. Once again, though, we see him reversing the order we find in Daniel, ascribing to the throng "ten thousand times ten thousand, and thousands of thousands" (Revelation 5:11).

Once everything is in place, the court comes to order. But very quickly, Daniel learns that he is not there to witness a trial. He is at a sentencing.

Crime and Punishment

The time of the first three beasts came and went in Daniel's vision. What was left, if you'll recall, was a final beast with an obnoxious little horn that just can't seem to shut its mouth. It was speaking "pompous words" when we left it before the introduction to the Ancient of Days. And now that we've returned to it, it is still running its mouth. Despite the arrogant rantings, the books are opened, the sentence is passed, and the punishment is immediately carried out:

> I watched then because of the sound of the pompous words which the horn was speaking; I watched till the beast was slain, and its body destroyed and given to the burning flame. As for the rest of the beasts, they had their dominion taken away, yet their lives were prolonged for a season and a time (Daniel 7:11-12).

What books were opened? We can't know for sure. Likely they contained the works of the beasts/nations and of the little horn. The first three creatures were spared destruction, although their power was taken away. The final beast was given to the burning flame.

This idea of a beast being tossed to the fire may be familiar to those of you who read my book *Revealing Revelation*. In John's vision, the Antichrist is described as a beast, as is his prophet. Like in Daniel's dream, their fate is also the flames.

> Then the beast was captured, and with him the false prophet who worked signs in his presence, by which he deceived those who received the mark of the beast and those who worshiped his image. These two were cast alive into the lake of fire burning with brimstone (Revelation 19:20).

Daniel and John are both describing the same event. A day will come when Jesus will return to rule from His throne in Jerusalem. At this second coming, the Antichrist and his false prophet will be the first to receive the eternal judgment of being cast into the lake of fire. Tragically, they will not be the last.

The Son of Man

Daniel's up-and-down roller-coaster vision now reaches another high point. A new person is about to enter the scene. While the prophet may not have known exactly who He was, those of us who have been blessed with hindsight have His identity pegged from the get-go.

> I was watching in the night visions,
> and behold, One like the Son of Man,
> coming with the clouds of heaven!
> He came to the Ancient of Days,
> and they brought Him near before Him.
> Then to Him was given dominion and glory and a kingdom,
> that all peoples, nations, and languages should serve Him.
> His dominion is an everlasting dominion,
> which shall not pass away,
> and His kingdom the one
> which shall not be destroyed (Daniel 7:13-14).

If you'll remember in Nebuchadnezzar's statue dream, there was a fifth kingdom that rolled into the picture in the form of a great stone. When it struck the multilayered figure, the rock brought it crashing to the ground. What Daniel was now witnessing was the coming of that Rock with His kingdom in tow.

This is not the only time we will see the Son of Man being brought into the presence of the Ancient of Days. I'll give you three guesses who else saw the two united in a vision, but I bet you'll only need one. That's right—it was the disciple John who described the emotional scene when Jesus the Messiah stepped forward as the only one worthy to open the scroll:

> I looked, and behold, in the midst of the throne and of the four living creatures, and in the midst of the elders, stood a Lamb as though it had been slain, having seven horns and seven eyes, which are the seven Spirits of God sent out into all the earth. Then He came and took the scroll out of the right hand of Him who sat on the throne (Revelation 5:6-7).

"But, Amir, how do we know that this Son of Man is the same as the Lamb? If He was, wouldn't He be called the Son of God instead?" Fair point. Let's dig a little deeper into this title, because this is one of the key moments in the entire book.

First, we need to recall that chapter 7 is the hinge chapter of the entire book. Again, Daniel is making two shifts. One is from narrative to visions. The second is from Aramaic to Hebrew. Chapter 7 is the anomaly that contains both Aramaic and a vision. It is the transition point, and thus, the key.

Not long ago, I was talking about this chapter with a very good friend of mine, Dr. Seth Postell, academic dean of Israel College of the Bible in Netanya. He said that the theme of the narrative chapters is Daniel and his friends being tested to worship things that are not God. The Aramaic word used for "worship" is *palach* (פְּלַח), which is similar to the Hebrew *pulhane* (פּוּלְחָן), meaning "ritual, worship." All through the first part of Daniel's book, the friends are willing to die rather than give *palach* to anything but the one true God.

Then we come to verses 13-14 and the Son of Man descending with the clouds to the Ancient of Days. When the Son of Man was brought before the Lord on His throne, the Almighty God bestowed upon Him "dominion and glory and a kingdom." Why? "That all peoples, nations, and languages should serve Him." In the Aramaic, the word translated "serve" is *palach*—"to worship"! Suddenly, we see that all tribes, tongues, and nations are worshipping the Son of Man.

The Son of Man must be deity—otherwise, chapter 7 of Daniel would contradict the rest of the book. When Jesus stood before Caiaphas, the high priest asked Him if He was "the Christ, the Son of the Blessed" (Mark 14:61). Jesus' response caused the high priest and the chief priests, elders, and scribes to cry blasphemy. Quoting from Daniel 7, He said, "I am. And you will see the Son of Man sitting at the right hand of the Power, and coming with the clouds of heaven" (verse 62). Jesus claimed to be the Son of Man from Daniel's vision, thereby making Himself worthy of the *palach* of all people, including the high priest and all Jesus' other accusers.

"But, Amir, if Son of Man refers to someone who deserves to be worshipped, then why does God call Ezekiel by that name?" Very fair question. The phrases "son of man" and "Son of Man" are used nearly 200 times in the original languages of Scripture. The prophet Ezekiel and the Gospels are responsible for the vast majority, with their usage being 93 times and 84 times, respectively. In the Old Testament, the phrase is most often seen as referring to one's humanity—i.e., a son of the human race. It is in this context that God chose "son of man" to be His nickname for Ezekiel.

When we look at the wording in Daniel 7, we can see that his usage of the phrase follows the normal Old Testament pattern. "Son of Man" in verse 13 is referring to a male human being. Now, wait before you jump to any conclusions. I still believe that it was the Jesus the Messiah that Daniel saw in his vision, as we just got through proving. In Aramaic, there is a one-letter preposition that is normally translated as "like." Daniel uses that word in this context. So what he is saying is that he saw someone like a son of man. In other words, he saw a person who, by all appearances, was actually a person.

This person descended on the clouds. Upon touching down, He was ushered before the Ancient of Days, at which time He was given all authority over the eternal kingdom of God and was deemed worthy of the worship of all mankind. Again, this is how we know that the figure descending was the 100 percent God and 100 percent man, Jesus Christ. It is not the phrase "Son of Man" that confirms His identity.

In the New Testament, the use of that three-word title changed. Jesus Himself in the Gospels co-opted "Son of Man" as a personal label. He used it to refer to Himself (John 1:51; 6:53), to describe His authority and earthly ministry (Mark 2:10, 28), to anticipate His suffering and death (Matthew 26:45; John 3:14), and to predict His future exaltation and glory (Matthew 13:41-42; 26:64).

The apostle John heard Jesus often speak of Himself as the Son of Man. This is why, when the Savior visited him on the island of Patmos, he was able to follow Jesus' pattern of using the definite article *the*:

> I turned to see the voice that spoke with me. And having turned I saw seven golden lampstands, and in the midst of the seven lampstands One like the Son of Man, clothed with a garment down to the feet and girded about the chest with a golden band. His head and hair were white like wool, as white as snow, and His eyes like a flame of fire (Revelation 1:12-14).

John could see the features of Jesus in this white-haired, flame-eyed figure in front of him. He looked very different, but still quite the same. So while Daniel saw someone like *a* son of man, John saw someone like *the* Son of Man.

In Daniel's vision, Jesus was descending to receive His kingdom. This is the fifth kingdom in Nebuchadnezzar's statue dream of chapter 2. When that occurs, the people of Israel will once again live securely in their land, and the Gentile nations will come to worship Jesus in Jerusalem.

> Arise, shine;
> for your light has come!
> And the glory of the LORD is risen upon you.
> For behold, the darkness shall cover the earth,
> and deep darkness the people;
> but the LORD will arise over you,
> and His glory will be seen upon you.
> The Gentiles shall come to your light,
> and kings to the brightness of your rising.
>
> Lift up your eyes all around, and see:
> They all gather together, they come to you;
> your sons shall come from afar,
> and your daughters shall be nursed at your side.
> Then you shall see and become radiant,
> and your heart shall swell with joy;
> because the abundance of the sea shall be turned to you,
> the wealth of the Gentiles shall come to you
> (Isaiah 60:1-5).

The dominion of the Son of Man is everlasting. However, His reign in Jerusalem does have a 1,000-year time limit. After that, we will be ushered into a new heaven and a new earth, where we will serve the One who gave Himself for us that we might enjoy eternity with Him.

The Dream Interpreter Receives an Interpretation

Daniel was shaken up. He reported to his readers, "I, Daniel, was grieved in my spirit within my body, and the visions of my head troubled me" (Daniel 7:15). This was understandable. Even in his dream state, he knew he was receiving no ordinary message. This was a vision from God, and it was extremely important. The problem was that he had no idea what it meant. Here he was, the guy who was known for interpreting the dreams of others, and now he found himself in desperate need of some interpretation of his own. Looking around, he spotted someone nearby, and went to him for help.

> I came near to one of those who stood by, and asked him the truth of all this. So he told me and made known to me the interpretation of these things: "Those great beasts, which are four, are four kings which arise out of the earth. But the saints of the Most High shall receive the kingdom, and possess the kingdom forever, even forever and ever" (verses 16-18).

We don't know from whom or from what Daniel sought help. But, as usual, the narrative is remarkably similar to John's experience in Revelation. A vast multitude of white-robed people were waving palm branches and worshipping the Lord on His throne. John wanted to know who they were. A nearby elder came to help him out, saying, "These are the ones who come out of the great tribulation, and washed their robes and made them white in the blood of the Lamb. Therefore they are before the throne of God, and serve Him day and night in His temple. And He who sits on the throne will dwell among them" (Revelation 7:14-15). This help from a nearby messenger happens numerous times throughout the disciple's apocalyptic vision.

As we saw earlier through James's words, when we need wisdom about a situation, God is there to give it. "If any of you lacks wisdom, let him ask of God, who gives to all liberally and without reproach, and it will be given to him" (James 1:5). That wisdom could come through a pastor or a friend or a book or a multitude of other sources.

God wants to impart His wisdom and knowledge to you. If you ask, it will be given.

Whether this was an angel or an elder or someone else who helped Daniel, we don't know. What is clear, though, is that Daniel picked the right source from whom to get answers. In explaining the vision, this personage said,

> Those great beasts, which are four, are four kings which
> arise out of the earth. But the saints of the Most High
> shall receive the kingdom, and possess the kingdom forever,
> even forever and ever (Daniel 7:17-18).

This made sense to Daniel. It fit with Nebuchadnezzar's dream. What didn't make sense was the fourth beast with its horns. That was a new twist. Daniel pushed for an answer: "So there was a fourth terrible beast too. It chomped on and trampled all that was around it. There were ten horns on its head, but there was also that little one. It was the one that spoke pompously and persecuted the saints. But then the Ancient of Days came to the rescue, judged the horn guilty and the saints innocent, and gave the saints the kingdom. So, like, what was up with that?"

Daniel's First Question Answered

Daniel's information source took the questions one at a time. The prophet had said he "wished to know the truth about the fourth beast" (verse 19). The messenger answered:

> The fourth beast shall be
> a fourth kingdom on earth,
> which shall be different from all other kingdoms,
> and shall devour the whole earth,
> trample it and break it in pieces (verse 23).

The first three kingdoms, Babylon, Medo-Persia, and Greece, would be limited in scope. The fourth kingdom, however, would have control over the entire earth. It would be violent and overshadowing as it sought its one-kingdom world domination. Remember, at the time of this vision, Daniel was at the tail end of Babylon's power. He had likely heard of the Medes and the Persians who lived to the east of Babylon. But Greece wasn't even on the horizon, nor was that fourth kingdom, the Roman Empire. To think that there would be a future kingdom that was so much more powerful than even the former glory of Nebuchadnezzar's Babylon must have been awe-inspiring.

Daniel's Second Question Answered

The second aspect Daniel had asked about was "the ten horns that were on [the beast's] head" (verse 20). As we saw earlier, this was a clear shift from Nebuchadnezzar's statue. The reply was that "the ten horns are ten kings who shall arise from this kingdom" (verse 24). Unfortunately, Daniel's source doesn't elaborate beyond that somewhat unsatisfying answer. This is when we go back to our favorite interpretation word, *context*, and to our favorite Daniel companion book, Revelation.

If you happened to have read *Revealing Revelation*, your Spidey-senses likely began tingling from the first moment you read about the ten horns. Maybe your hand has been raised this whole time as you called out, "Amir, pick me! Pick me!"

As you may remember from Revelation, the disciple John stood on a sandy shore. From there he saw "a beast rising up out of the sea, having seven heads and ten horns, and on his horns ten crowns, and on his heads a blasphemous name" (13:1). Later, when John was carried away in the Spirit by an angel into the wilderness, he saw "a woman sitting on a scarlet beast which was full of names of blasphemy, having seven heads and ten horns" (17:3).

You may still be thinking, *Great, Amir, it's nice to know that John mentions them. But that still doesn't tell us what they are.* Keep reading in Revelation. We need to look just a little further into the wilderness account to get an explanation from John's transporting angel:

> The ten horns which you saw are ten kings who have received no kingdom as yet, but they receive authority for one hour as kings with the beast. These are of one mind, and they will give their power and authority to the beast. These will make war with the Lamb, and the Lamb will overcome them, for He is Lord of lords and King of kings; and those who are with Him are called, chosen, and faithful (verses 12-14).

The ten horns are ten kings, and out of these ten kings will arise one more king, the "little horn." You've probably got a good idea of who this is, but let's look at what the messenger says, just to make sure.

Daniel's Third Question Answered

The third part to Daniel's query focused on the "other horn" (Daniel 7:20) that had risen to prominence over the ten and had spoken so haughtily. This is the one that had the prophet troubled because he saw the harm it would do to God's people. The messenger replied:

> Another shall rise after them;
> he shall be different from the first ones,
> and shall subdue three kings.
> He shall speak pompous words against the Most High,
> shall persecute the saints of the Most High,
> and shall intend to change times and law.
> Then the saints shall be given into his hand
> for a time and times and half a time (verses 24-25).

Essentially, Daniel's information source repeats back what the prophet had just said to him. But this isn't only a reiteration. There are three key pieces of new information. First, he clarifies that the horn is another king or ruler. In his arrogance, this ruler will place himself over all the others, ushering in a one-world government. We know this horn as the beast and the Antichrist.

Initially, all will give their allegiance to the beast. This includes the Jews who will be thrilled at this man who can finally bring them peace. There is one group of people, however, that won't buy into the deception of the Antichrist and his prophet. And that is the second tidbit of information the messenger gives. These people are identified as "the saints," who will refuse to follow the beast or receive his mark. As a result, they will come under severe persecution. Who are these saints? Once again, we turn to Revelation.

John watched as 144,000 servants of the Most High were sent out to act as witnesses of the true God. Immediately following this commissioning, he spotted a great multitude of people from all over the globe. These were the white-robed masses we read about earlier in this chapter. When John admitted ignorance about their identity, his elder guide told him:

> These are the ones who come out of the great tribulation, and washed their robes and made them white in the blood of the Lamb. Therefore they are before the throne of God, and serve Him day and night in His temple. And He who sits on the throne will dwell among them. They shall neither hunger anymore nor thirst anymore; the sun shall not strike them, nor any heat; for the Lamb who is in the midst of the throne will shepherd them and lead them to living fountains of waters. And God will wipe away every tear from their eyes (Revelation 7:14-17).

There are many on this earth who are content to live for themselves now. They see no reason to submit themselves to the "confines" of God's lordship. They figure that there will be enough time to get right with God before they die, or in the event of the rapture, during the tribulation. But they are incredibly foolhardy to count on either eventuality. First, there is no telling whether there will be time to repent before one dies. Besides, repentance is a heart issue, not just a matter of words or rites. A last-minute fire insurance commitment is not a commitment at all. In contrast, a truly repentant heart can discover salvation even at one's very last breath.

The second reason this is foolhardy is that only a fool would willingly risk the possibility of going through the tribulation. It will be a horrible time during which the vast majority of the world's population will die terrible deaths due to violence, disaster, or scarcity. And for those who give their lives to the Lord after the church is taken in the rapture, the tribulation will be that much worse. Not only will you face all the horrors that will come upon the natural world, but the godless society governed by the beast will be out to get you also. That enormous mass of people that John saw in Revelation 7 were tribulation martyrs. That means every one of them was violently slaughtered for their faith.

The torment of the saints on earth will be bad, but it will get even worse for "a time and times and half a time." Here is where we find the third bit of information given by the messenger. There is a time frame to the suffering of the tribulation saints.

If you'll recall, in chapter 4, we discussed the length of Nebuchadnezzar's departure from sanity. He was to be cast away from civilization for "seven times" (verse 16). Because of the greater biblical context, we determined that this meant seven years. It is that same wider context that lets us see that here the messenger is speaking of a period of three-and-a-half years—time (1) + times (2) + half a time (½). Later in this book, we will come back to this unique phrasing and how it relates to the seven years of the tribulation.

The persecution of the saints will be dreadful to behold. But it will end. For most, they will be rescued from the persecution by death, at which time they will be ushered into the presence of the Holy God. But for those who manage to stay alive, the final buzzer will sound at the end of the second three-and-a-half years of the tribulation. That is when judgment will come. The messenger told Daniel:

> The court shall be seated,
>   and they shall take away his dominion,
>   to consume and destroy it forever.
> Then the kingdom and dominion,
>   and the greatness of the kingdoms under the whole heaven,
>   shall be given to the people, the saints of the Most High.
> His kingdom is an everlasting kingdom,
>   and all dominions shall serve and obey Him
> (Daniel 7:26-27).

What the Antichrist will not realize is that he has been given power only for a time. When his period comes to an end, he will be brought before the courtroom that will be presided over by the Ancient of Days. According to Daniel's vision, the court will pronounce judgment on the Antichrist, and he will be thrown into the lake of fire along with his false prophet.

This is the justice that the tribulation martyrs were calling for during the fifth seal judgment. From under the altar, they pleaded with God, who was on His throne, crying out to Him, "How long, O Lord, holy and true, until You judge and avenge our blood on those who dwell on the earth?" (Revelation 6:10). The "how long" question is answered in Daniel 7. At the time of Jesus' second coming, He will bring the punishment of the court on the satanic enemies of God's people. The tribulation martyrs who experienced such violence and bloodshed need never worry about them again.

The beast and false prophet will finally be dealt with, but there will still be one other who needs to be put out of action.

> Then I saw an angel coming down from heaven, having the key to the bottomless pit and a great chain in his hand. He laid hold of the dragon, that serpent of old, who is the Devil and Satan, and bound him for a thousand years; and he cast him into the bottomless pit, and shut him up, and set a seal on him, so that he should deceive the nations no more till the thousand years were finished (Revelation 20:1-3).

Satan will be bound for 1,000 years. During that time, the world will be under new management. The kingdom and dominion of the world will "be given to the people, the saints of the Most High" (Daniel 7:27). The King of kings will be the new landlord. He will set up a new world order—a theocracy. This is the fifth kingdom that Nebuchadnezzar saw. It is a kingdom so perfect and so glorious that it will cause other nations to rush to Jerusalem to worship the One who is on the throne of David.

Despite the happy ending of the messenger's interpretation, Daniel did not have a sense of peace. He concluded by admitting that "my thoughts greatly troubled me, and my countenance changed; but I kept the matter in my heart" (verse 28). There was a lot of ugly to get through before God's people reached the beauty of the millennial kingdom, when the Messiah would reign from Jerusalem.

If Daniel had known what was coming next, he likely would have relished the relative tameness of this first vision. Two years later, he would have a second vision that would leave him physically sick for days.

THE RAM AND THE GOAT

DANIEL 8

If you are not an animal lover, you may well be tiring of Daniel's visions. So far, we've had a lion, a bear, and a leopard—oh my! Then there was that fourth beast, which seemed like an angry escapee from *The Island of Dr. Moreau*. And now that we have come to chapter 8, sure enough, we find more animals. At least these are more of the petting zoo variety. Down by a waterway, Daniel sees a sheep and a goat. Fluffy, docile, and more than a little cute, maybe the prophet is taming things down for a children's story time.

It doesn't take long, though, to realize that if you put this sheep and this goat into your petting zoo, there will be no end to the lawsuits. These are two very angry animals. Quickly, the bodies start flying. The Lord has brought these two creatures out of the barn because He wants to show Daniel two more nations. They are powerful, they are violent, and out of one of them will arise a person who will be a forerunner of the future beast.

Battle by the Ulai River

Two years have passed since Daniel's first vision. When God wanted to communicate to him this time, He bypassed His throne room and took Daniel to a river.

> In the third year of the reign of King Belshazzar a vision appeared to me—to me, Daniel—after the one that appeared to me the first time. I saw in the vision, and it so happened while I was looking, that I was in Shushan, the citadel, which is in the province of Elam; and I saw in the vision that I was by the River Ulai (Daniel 8:1-2).

Two-hundred-and-twenty-five miles to the east of Babylon was the city of Shushan, or Susa. Over its multimillennial history, this city had its ups and downs as far as power and influence. At the time of Daniel's vision, it was in one of its down periods. But that was soon to change. After being conquered by Cyrus the Great in the mid-sixth century BC, the city would grow to be a Persian capital within the Achaemenid Empire. Shushan was the home base of Nehemiah, from which he carried out his role as a cupbearer to the king. It is also the city where a young Jewish girl, Hadassah, rose up to become Queen Esther, wife of the great King Ahasuerus.

But Daniel's vision journey took place well before those glory days. He was transported to the city and came to rest by the Ulai River. Once he got his bearings and looked around, he spotted a ram—a very angry ram.

> I lifted my eyes and saw, and there, standing beside the river, was a ram which had two horns, and the two horns were high; but one was higher than the other, and the higher one came up last. I saw the ram pushing westward, northward, and southward, so that no animal could withstand him;

nor was there any that could deliver from his hand, but
he did according to his will and became great (verses 3-4).

There was nothing particularly remarkable about this ram. He had
two horns, just like most rams, although one of them rose higher than
the other. What set him apart from other ovines was this sheep's attitude. He was mad, and he was spoiling for a fight.

Trotting in from the east, he trampled any animals that got in
his way. Turning to the right, he crushed the animals to the north of
him. Spinning back around, he stomped on any who got in his way
to the south. He was invincible. Life was great for this ram, mighty
among the sheep.

But then to the west, a little dot appeared. As it drew nearer, it
grew larger. Two facts quickly became evident about this new visi-
tor: Whatever was coming wasn't stopping, and it was moving fast.

As I was considering, suddenly a male goat came from
the west, across the surface of the whole earth, without
touching the ground; and the goat had a notable horn
between his eyes. Then he came to the ram that had two
horns, which I had seen standing beside the river, and ran
at him with furious power. And I saw him confronting
the ram; he was moved with rage against him, attacked
the ram, and broke his two horns. There was no power
in the ram to withstand him, but he cast him down to
the ground and trampled him; and there was no one that
could deliver the ram from his hand (verses 5-7).

A tough guy is only as strong as his competition. The powerful ram became quite sheepish once he was hit by the hard-charging
goat. The angry newcomer was relentless. He knocked the ram to the
ground, broke off his horns, then danced a four-step on him just to

make sure that he never got up again. Even if someone had wanted to help the former bully, no one could.

And then things got really weird.

The goat had a horn, but once his power had grown, the horn broke off. In its place grew four new horns, flowering out so that each one faced a different direction. And, as if we didn't have enough horns already, a new one grew up out of one of the four. It was a little one, and we see that it exalted itself with its words.

Hit the brakes! If you're reading Scripture and you suddenly come across something that seems familiar, that's likely because it is. A little horn appearing and speaking pompously? We've seen that one before. That was the beast, also known as the Antichrist. Daniel's visions are starting to tie together.

This little horn doesn't remain small for long. It grows and grows until it reaches all the way to the "host of heaven; and it cast down some of the host and some of the stars to the ground, and trampled them" (verse 10). He then became so great in his own mind that he arrogantly went up against God Himself, interfering with the sacrifices that were required by the Mosaic law.

Confusion is evident in Daniel's description. He kept his narrative to generalities despite the necessity for details if anyone was to understand what was taking place. As he stood there trying to process what he was witnessing, he overheard a nearby conversation.

> I heard a holy one speaking; and another holy one said to that certain one who was speaking, "How long will the vision be, concerning the daily sacrifices and the transgression of desolation, the giving of both the sanctuary and the host to be trampled underfoot?"

> And he said to me, "For two thousand three hundred days; then the sanctuary shall be cleansed" (verses 13-14).

Then the vision ceased. You can almost picture the old eunuch standing there beside the water. All the action was done. The battles were finished; the pompous, blasphemous words were silenced. Now, Daniel was staring into empty skies, listening to the passing waters of the river, the stillness only occasionally broken by the conversation of two nearby angels. It would be understandable if his mental and physical stability were a touch fragile. Likely, the least provocation could send him crashing to the ground.

A voice from the river was that provocation.

Gabriel—the Angel with the Answers

Someone suddenly appeared next to Daniel.

> Then it happened, when I, Daniel, had seen the vision and was seeking the meaning, that suddenly there stood before me one having the appearance of a man. And I heard a man's voice between the banks of the Ulai, who called, and said, "Gabriel, make this man understand the vision." So he came near where I stood, and when he came I was afraid and fell on my face; but he said to me, "Understand, son of man, that the vision refers to the time of the end" (verses 15-17).

Before Daniel had a chance to wonder who this new person-like being was, a voice made an introduction. This was Gabriel, a messenger angel of God. I hesitate to use the phrase *messenger angel* because the meanings of the original biblical words that we translate as "angel"—both the Hebrew מַלְאָךְ and the Greek ἄγγελος—literally mean "messenger." So essentially, I am calling Gabriel a "messenger messenger." But because of the way we translate it, the phrase *messenger angel* is a good way to describe both Gabriel's being and his function.

This is the first time we meet Gabriel in Scripture. He appears again in Daniel's next vision in chapter 9. Then we see him again in his most famous role as the one who announced to Zechariah the priest that he would be father to John the Baptist (Luke 1:8-20) and to Mary that she would be the mother of Jesus the Messiah (Luke 1:26-38). But just because we haven't heard of him before doesn't mean that Gabriel hasn't been around nor that Daniel didn't know of him.

Remember, the Bible is a very short book when compared to the thousands of years of history that it covers. God has done a lot of work that isn't covered in its pages. It is very possible that in the stories and traditions passed down in the Jewish oral culture that Gabriel was a name known to many. That could be what explains Daniel's reaction when the angel draws near to him. He drops to the ground. Maybe it was because he was in the presence of God's chief messenger. Maybe it was due to the overwhelming nature of what he had just witnessed. Or maybe he fell because he was afraid that what he had seen was about to play out in reality at any moment.

Whatever it was, Daniel's knees buckled, and he went down, even as Gabriel assured him that the latter part of the events he had just witnessed wouldn't happen until the end times. The messenger's words didn't help. The old prophet was out. Both pastor Rick and I have been teaching and preaching for many years. It is not unusual for us to see closed eyes and nodding heads amongst the listeners as we are presenting our biblical messages. What we rarely see are those who fall asleep even before we begin to teach.

This is what Gabriel faced. The voice told him to explain the vision, but his audience was out cold on the ground.

> Now, as he was speaking with me, I was in a deep sleep with my face to the ground; but he touched me, and stood me upright. And he said, "Look, I am making known to you what shall happen in the latter time of the indignation; for at the appointed time the end shall be. The ram which you saw, having the two horns—they are

the kings of Media and Persia. And the male goat is the kingdom of Greece. The large horn that is between its eyes is the first king. As for the broken horn and the four that stood up in its place, four kingdoms shall arise out of that nation, but not with its power" (Daniel 8:18-22).

Undeterred by Daniel's slumbering state, Gabriel woke him and stood him up. Once again, Gabriel told him that the interpretation of the vision refers to the latter time. Let me take a moment to inform you that this is not my interpretation. This is not pastor Rick's interpretation. This is Gabriel's interpretation. Pastor Rick and I just teach the Bible. Gabriel wanted to make sure Daniel knew that even though the vision started off sounding like its fulfillment was coming in the next few hundred years, there would be a later and greater realization of the vision far in the future.

The Near and Far Nature of Bible Prophecy

It is typical of prophecies to have a near and a far fulfillment. Understanding this dual nature of biblical prophecy is essential for proper interpretation. For example, when Jesus was on the Mount of Olives talking to His disciples about the end times, He said, "When you see Jerusalem surrounded by armies, then know that its desolation is near. Then let those who are in Judea flee to the mountains, let those who are in the midst of her depart, and let not those who are in the country enter her" (Luke 21:20-21). Most readers will say that this was fulfilled in AD 70 when Rome levelled the temple and destroyed the city. And they are right. It was a horrible time filled with suffering and death.

However, there are many in the preterist camp who say that this prophecy from Jesus ends with first-century Rome. They say each prophecy gets one fulfillment. The destruction of Jerusalem was so terrible that it covered the hyperbolic and allegorical end-times scenarios painted in the rest of the Olivet Discourse, as well as in Revelation, and even in what we will see in the rest of Daniel.

But if we are to take a literal approach to interpreting Scripture, we know that AD 70 could not possibly be the complete fulfillment of Jesus' words. How can I be so sure? When in doubt, just keep reading the context. You don't have to go far. In the next paragraph, Jesus continued:

> There will be signs in the sun, in the moon, and in the stars; and on the earth distress of nations, with perplexity, the sea and the waves roaring; men's hearts failing them from fear and the expectation of those things which are coming on the earth, for the powers of the heavens will be shaken. Then they will see the Son of Man coming in a cloud with power and great glory. Now when these things begin to happen, look up and lift up your heads, because your redemption draws near (Luke 21:25-28).

The only way to make those words fit with a single-fulfillment interpretation is to spiritualize the entire paragraph. It's in the spiritual world, some people say, that all these terrible things take place in the skies and in the seas and on the earth. As far as the return of the Son of Man, this, too, is a spiritual event. It is Jesus instituting the spiritual kingdom of God into the world. But a spiritual return of Jesus doesn't explain why He tells His listeners to "look up and lift up your heads."

A much simpler and more literal view of Jesus' words says that there was a near fulfillment in AD 70 during which Jerusalem and its temple were destroyed. But there will also be a later and greater fulfillment, when the persecution of the Jews will be to such an extent that they are forced to flee to the mountains and hide. As the remainder of the judgments of the tribulation are carried out upon the earth, the Jews will take sanctuary until they see their Messiah coming to the rescue. It is then they will recognize Him for who He is—the One they rejected, the One they crucified, the One they pierced (Zechariah 12:10). One by one, they will accept Jesus as their Lord and Savior, receiving the redemption that He will bring to them. And so all Israel will be saved, as Paul promised us in Romans 11:26.

A single prophecy with two fulfillments.

As Gabriel began his interpretation, he laid out the near fulfillment of the vision. But along the way, he transitioned to a later and greater realization of the prophetic dream. What he conveyed to Daniel was terrible, and it made clear the horrific reason that the Jews will flee Jerusalem just as Jesus predicted more than five centuries after the old prophet's vision.

When will this later fulfillment take place? We don't know for sure. But what we do know is that God has chosen the time, and that He has done so for a reason. Gabriel made that clear when he began, "Look, I am making known to you what shall happen in the latter time of the indignation; for at the appointed time the end shall be" (verse 19). The phrase "appointed time" is used nearly 20 times in Scripture, varying upon which translation you read. Five of those occurrences are here in Daniel (8:19; 10:1; 11:27, 29, 35). In each usage, you find the idea that God is in control and has set certain times when He is going to accomplish something. God appointed a time when He created the world, and He has appointed a time when He will destroy it and make a new earth. He appointed a time for you to be born and a time when your spirit will leave your body. God's timing may not always agree with our ideas of mercy, logic, justice, and love, but because He is both sovereign and holy, we can be sure that His ways are always best.

The Ram and the Goat ID'd

There is nothing poetic or cryptic in Gabriel's next words. Daniel wasn't left trying to read into the subtext or discover the angel's true meaning. In a refreshing move amongst the Old Testament prophets, Gabriel gave a straightforward interpretation of Daniel's vision:

> The ram which you saw, having the two horns—they are the kings of Media and Persia. And the male goat is the kingdom of Greece. The large horn that is between its eyes is the first king. As for the broken horn and the four that stood up in its place, four kingdoms shall arise out of that nation, but not with its power (Daniel 8:20-22).

As we saw in Daniel 5 with the handwriting on the wall, it would not be long until Daniel himself would be a witness as the ram came trouncing into Babylon. The two-horned tag team of the Medes and the Persians reigned strong for two centuries after that great conquest. But all during that time, a cultural revolution was taking place to the west in Greece. Eventually, the power of that social transformation manifested itself in military strength. The martial powerhouse of Philip of Macedon began conquering from the north the numerous Greek city-states. His goal was to create the Hellenic League that would be powerful enough to take down the Persian Empire. But before he could attain that goal, he was assassinated at the wedding of one of his daughters.

Into his place stepped his 20-year-old son, Alexander, and the course of history was changed. It wasn't until after Alexander's death that he was given the title "the Great," but from the beginning of his military campaigning, all would have thought it appropriate. As the Greatest of All Time, he was both the G.O.A.T. and the goat of Daniel's vision. Alexander and his army raced across Asia Minor and into the Levant. The goat found the ram at the modern-day city of Issus, called Cilicia by the apostle Paul, near the Syrian border. Just as Daniel saw it, the battle, which took place on November 5, 333 BC, was a rout. The army of Darius III was crushed, and the mighty Persian Empire effectively ended.

Alexander was the large horn, and under his authority the Greek Empire continued to expand. But then something unexpected happened. The great horn broke off. At the young age of 32, Alexander died under mysterious circumstances while in the palace of former King Nebuchadnezzar in Babylon. Unfortunately for the empire and all those under its rule, Alexander had not established a succession plan. As a result, the Greek Empire was split into four smaller empires.

Before we leave Alexander behind, I want to note a significant impact his conquests made on the world. As his army drove east, they brought Greek customs and, more importantly, the Greek language with them. As a result, by the end of the fourth century BC, Greek was the lingua franca, or common language, of the civilized world much the way English is today. This linguistic spread is still influencing you and me today. How?

In the third century BC, there was a large population of Jews living in Alexandria, Egypt. As citizens of one of the four empires birthed after the death of Alexander, these Jews spoke Greek rather than Hebrew. This language barrier separated them from their holy writings. So the Jews of Alexandria demanded that their Scriptures, our Old Testament, be translated into words they could understand. Scholars set to work and created a Greek translation known as the Septuagint, or LXX. This was a huge development. Not only did the Septuagint provide these Jews their Scriptures, but for the first time, Gentiles were exposed to the God of Abraham, Isaac, and Jacob.

A couple centuries later, when it came time for the Gospel writers to tell about the life of Jesus, for Paul and others to pen their epistles, and for John to communicate his apocalyptic vision, they too used Greek. Because of the incredible expanse of the Roman Empire, never before in history had so many people from so many diverse backgrounds spoken the same language. It is no surprise that this was God's "appointed time" to send the Messiah to this earth for our redemption.

The Empire Divides

Alexander was gone. Who would now lead the empire? While the emperor had not named a successor, he had appointed four generals to oversee his conquests. Cassander, Lysimachus, Ptolemy, and Seleucus had each been given control over a portion of Alexander's territory. Following the violent turmoil that typically accompanies the sudden death of a ruler, each of these governors finally agreed to take control of their own mini empire. Two centuries after Daniel received his vision, history shows that "the large horn was broken, and in place of it four notable ones came up toward the four winds of heaven" (verse 8). Prophecy perfectly fulfilled.

Of the four new empires, there is only one that the vision now follows. The territory given to Seleucus covered Syria, Mesopotamia, and farther east. It is this region and the Seleucid line of which Gabriel now speaks:

> In the latter time of their kingdom,
> when the transgressors have reached their fullness,
> a king shall arise,
> having fierce features,
> who understands sinister schemes.
> His power shall be mighty, but not by his own power;
> he shall destroy fearfully,
> and shall prosper and thrive;
> he shall destroy the mighty, and also the holy people.
>
> Through his cunning
> he shall cause deceit to prosper under his rule;
> and he shall exalt himself in his heart.
> He shall destroy many in their prosperity.
> He shall even rise against the Prince of princes;
> but he shall be broken without human means.

And the vision of the evenings and mornings
which was told is true;
therefore seal up the vision,
for it refers to many days in the future (verses 23-26).

I realize that is a long quote to try to digest all at once. But I wanted you to feel the power of Gabriel's words. It's no wonder that the vision left Daniel physically ill. Look at the number of times "shall" appears in the passage. We don't see "might" or "could." This was God saying, "I've seen what is coming. I know who this guy is. This is what he is going to do, and it is going to be terrible. But don't worry; I'll deal with him in the end."

Remember, prophecies often have a near view and a far view. The first part of Daniel's vision had only an early fulfillment. That is why Gabriel could be so succinct in his interpretation. "The ram is Medo-Persia and the goat is Greece." Not much wiggle room there.

But with verse 23, the style of the narrative changes. Rather than giving us a name, Gabriel speaks of "a king." Instead of providing a date, he only says it is "in the latter time." This generality opens the door for us to look for a dual fulfillment. But we are careful in doing so. We can only ascribe to this or any other prophecy a near and far fulfillment if the wider context of Scripture backs us up. In this case, it most definitely does.

The Vision's Near Fulfillment—Antiochus IV

The fifth ruler after the founding king of the Seleucid Empire was Antiochus III. Like Alexander a century before, this king was also given the title "the Great" because of his conquests. He was a popular ruler within his empire and had a reputation for fairness. This caught the attention of the Jews in Jerusalem. Located near where the Seleucid Empire and the Egyptian Ptolemaic Empire met, Jerusalem had passed back and forth between the two rival kingdoms. When the leaders within the city looked at their current Egyptian ruler and compared him with Antiochus III, they decided a change would be nice. So, they opened the gates of the city to the Seleucid ruler, who then drove out the Ptolemaic Egyptians. Antiochus III never forgot what the Jews of Jerusalem did for him, and he remained friendly with the city through his long tenure as king.

But as always happens with people, Antiochus III died. His son Seleucus IV Philopator became the new emperor, but 12 years into his rule he was assassinated. Next in line was his ten-year-old son, but he never had a chance to sit on the throne. Seleucus IV's brother, Antiochus IV, had already decided that he should be the next emperor. He drew in a cabal around him and seized the throne, demonstrating his understanding of "sinister schemes" (verse 23) and his "cunning" (verse 25).

Antiochus IV was pure evil. Believing himself to be deity, he christened himself Epiphanes, meaning "God manifest." Those who knew him instead secretly called him Epimenes, meaning "madman." Narcissistic, violent, and cruel, bloodshed followed Antiochus IV wherever he went.

As we saw earlier with both Nebuchadnezzar and Darius, kings with a god complex desire the prayers and worship they feel they deserve. Antiochus IV followed this same pattern. When a decree was sent out demanding the citizens of the empire worship him as a god, all of the Seleucid Empire went along with it. All, that is, except for the Jews. They knew that there was only one God, and that crazy man sitting on the throne was not him.

Antiochus IV blew a gasket. At his command, his army poured into Jerusalem. And with this invading force came violence, torture, and death. Jerusalem was a bloodbath. The priestly class paid a particularly high price. But the Jews were used to suffering and persecution. They knew they would survive this latest onslaught.

Then the emperor took his oppression a step too far. He attempted to stop the Jews from worshipping God. Temple sacrifices were outlawed.

The mandates of Judaic law were forbidden. He ordered pagan sacrifices to be burned on the temple's altar, then he desecrated this holy house of God Almighty by dedicating it instead to Zeus. This desecration of 167 BC, called "the abomination of desolation," is one of our ties to this vision's future reality. Three times it is mentioned in Daniel, all pointing to an end-times fulfillment (9:27; 11:31; 12:11).

The desecration of the temple was too much. You can take away the Jews' lives, but you cannot take away the Jews' God. A man named Judas Maccabeus organized a revolt that, through military genius and divine help, drove Antiochus IV and his army out of Judea. Three years later, the emperor died of an illness, to no one's regret.

The Vision's Far Fulfillment—Antichrist

As terrible as Anitochus IV was, there is another ruler coming who will also exalt himself as an "Epiphanes." Paul wrote of his coming:

> Let no one deceive you by any means; for that Day will not come unless the falling away comes first, and the man of sin is revealed, the son of perdition, who opposes and exalts himself above all that is called God or that is worshiped, so that he sits as God in the temple of God, showing himself that he is God (2 Thessalonians 2:3-4).

That passage could easily have been written about the Seleucid emperor. But Antiochus IV had been dead for more than 200 years when Paul dictated this passage. This is undoubtedly speaking of a future world leader, a future "little horn," a future beast.

When will this beast arrive? Jesus gave us a time frame in Matthew's account of the Olivet Discourse. He told the disciples, "'When you see the 'abomination of desolation,' spoken of by Daniel the prophet, standing in the holy place' (whoever reads, let him understand), 'then let those who are in Judea flee to the mountains'" (24:15-16). The beast or Antichrist will set up the abomination of desolation. Like Paul, Jesus was not looking backward. He was looking to a time of future fulfillment, as we saw in our near/far illustration a few pages back.

Following the example of Antiochus IV, this future tyrant will break a treaty of peace with Israel. Similar to the earlier emperor, he will desecrate the temple. Similar to the earlier emperor, he will severely persecute the Jews. And similar to the earlier emperor, he will blaspheme God, arrogantly claiming that he is the one who is divine. The book of Revelation tells us that the false prophet will have an image made of his boss, the Antichrist. Somehow, the false prophet will animate the idol so "that the image of the beast should both speak and cause as many as would not worship the image of the beast to be killed" (Revelation 13:15). The parallels between the emperor and the beast are many. The main differences between the two are that the former is in the past while the latter is in the future, and for as bad as Antiochus IV was, the Antichrist will be so much worse.

It is no wonder that Daniel reacted the way he did.

> I, Daniel, fainted and was sick for days; afterward I arose
> and went about the king's business. I was astonished by
> the vision, but no one understood it (Daniel 8:27).

Not only were the sights Daniel witnessed in his vision disturbing, but Gabriel's explanation was unsatisfying for him. Yes, he understood the identities of the ram and the goat, but beyond that, the vision was still an incredibly troubling mystery. He was a man of wisdom. He craved understanding. If only Gabriel would come back and fill in some of the blanks that he had left empty.

It took 11 years of waiting, but finally, God's messenger returned to Daniel. While the old prophet was praying, Gabriel swooped down next to him. In the next chapter, we'll discover what he said.

CHAPTER 9a

PROMISES MADE, PROMISES KEPT

DANIEL 9:1-19

Promises made, promises kept." This has been a favorite slogan of politicians for decades. It was plastered on a banner by supporters of Hubert Humphrey at the 1968 Democratic National Convention. Chicago mayor Harold Washington confidently claimed it for himself in the 1980s, while Michigan governor John Engler touted the slogan in the 1990s.[12] Most recently, it was a hallmark phrase of President Donald J. Trump and New York City mayor Bill DeBlasio. Want an instant heated debate? Find someone from the political party opposite your own and compare notes on how well the last two on that list lived up to their catchphrase. I'll grab the popcorn and watch as the tempers flare.

Unfortunately, we live in a time when we don't really believe politicians will keep their promises. We hope they will, but we expect they won't. If you really like the person, you'll make excuses as to why they had to change their mind and compromise. If you don't like the person, you'll tell your spouse or your neighbor, "See, I told you so."

When it comes to marriage and friendships, you hope that the promises-made to promises-kept ratio climbs much higher. But you are also fully aware that real life intervenes. The time your husband promises you that he'll make it to the parent-teacher conference but calls at the last minute to tell you that he just can't get away from work. The time your wife promises that she'll be available for your date night, but then gets called in for an overtime shift. You're disappointed, but you know that when your husband's boss expects him there, then he better be there. You were really looking forward to the evening out, but you know that your wife working an extra shift will do more good for the family budget than spending money on dinner and a movie.

Sometimes promises fail simply because we make dumb mistakes. We forget things. We misplace stuff. Or we come up with lame excuses because we just don't want to follow through with our commitment.

Let's face it: Everyone blows it at some point. You can trust a lot of people most of the time, but can you ever trust anyone all the time? No, because either intentionally or unintentionally, everyone will disappoint somebody sometime.

Or will they? Is there anyone who is dependable 100 percent of the time? The prophet Daniel would answer that question with an emphatic yes. And as we jump into chapter 9 of his book, we see the prophet taking the time to thank God for being a faithful promise keeper, and then reminding God that another one of His commitments is coming due.

Exile Winding Down

Daniel was around 82 years old as chapter 9 unfolded. He probably never imagined that he would live to see this day. He was a young man in his teens when King Nebuchadnezzar invaded Jerusalem and removed him from the city along with 3,000 of his countrymen. They became captives of a pagan king and were forced to learn their new country's language, culture, and gods. Later, when Judah's king rebelled, the prophet heard reports of the horrors of the siege of Jerusalem and the ultimate destruction of the city. Why would Daniel have ever expected that he would live to be an old man in the capital city of an empire that had so much disregard for human life?

But while Daniel may not have expected to survive until the end of the captivity, he knew that the Jewish people would. Before he had been taken from Jerusalem, he would have seen Jeremiah the prophet. He would have heard his warnings and witnessed the way the king and his court disrespectfully treated the old man. After his deportation, Daniel would have read the letter that Jeremiah had sent to the exiles in Babylon. Despite the dire situation, the letter held a message of hope. It promised a future for the Jewish people.

> When seventy years are completed for Babylon, I will visit you, and I will fulfill to you my promise and bring you back to this place. For I know the plans I have for you, declares the LORD, plans for welfare and not for evil, to give you a future and a hope. Then you will call upon me and come and pray to me, and I will hear you. You will seek me and find me, when you seek me with all your heart (Jeremiah 29:10-13 ESV).

This is a prophetic promise directly from God Almighty, in which we once again see a near fulfillment and a far fulfillment. In the short term, after a certain amount of time, the Jews will be allowed to go back home. In the long term, there is a time coming when all Jews will seek the true God. And in that day, they will find Him because they will finally be seeking Him with all their heart. This had to give huge comfort to Daniel. He knew that God is a promise keeper, so there would come a day when all the idolatry and sinfulness would be gone. The Jews would once again be united with God with one heart, one spirit, and one purpose.

In this first half of Daniel 9, the prophet alludes to three promises that had been given by God to the Jews. These divine commitments were incredibly important. Not only do they explain the reason Judah was in its current predicament, they also offer tremendous hope that there was a time limit to their suffering.

Seventy Years, Then Home

Babylon was defeated. The degenerate King Belshazzar was dead, and the Babylonian army was devastated. There was a new king in town, and he was a definite upgrade from the incompetent rabble that had taken the throne after Nebuchadnezzar had left the scene. This transfer of power from the Babylonians to the Medo-Persians was the fulfillment of a promise that God had made to His chosen people. Recognizing this fulfilled prophecy sparked in Daniel's mind another promise from the Almighty:

> In the first year of Darius the son of Ahasuerus, of the lineage of the Medes, who was made king over the realm of the Chaldeans—in the first year of his reign I, Daniel, understood by the books the number of the years specified by the word of the LORD through Jeremiah the prophet, that He would accomplish seventy years in the desolations of Jerusalem.
>
> Then I set my face toward the Lord God to make request by prayer and supplications, with fasting, sackcloth, and ashes. And I prayed to the LORD my God, and made confession (Daniel 9:1-4).

Again, what was the source of Daniel's 70-year assurance? It was the words of the prophet Jeremiah. Jeremiah said, "Seventy years," so Daniel wrote, "Seventy years." He didn't allegorize the number.

He didn't say, "God once said that a day is like a thousand years and a thousand years are like a day, so Jeremiah must have meant… uh, I convert days to years, then multiply by…where did I put that abacus?" This is why we insist on a literal approach to understanding Scripture *unless it is clear* that the author is using allegorical language. When this prophet quoted another prophet, he did so taking the other man at his literal word.

The above passage shows that Daniel saw how God had kept His promise to usher out the Babylonians and bring in the Medes. He also knew that there were more promises that the Lord had made regarding His people Israel. So Daniel began to pray.

There is never a wrong time to pray. Was God faithful? Praise Him through prayer. Realized you've blown it? Pray your heartfelt confession to Him, assured of His forgiveness. Claiming one of His promises? Pray a reminder to Him of His words. You don't do this because you're worried that He has forgotten His commitment. Instead, when you pray His words to Him, you are stating your faith in His faithfulness. These prayers can take place anytime and anywhere, by yourself or with anyone else joining in.

The destruction of Babylon was a momentous occurrence. The closest modern-day equivalent I can think of is how many of my older Eastern European readers must have felt when the Soviet Union collapsed. They had lived their whole life under the oppression of the Communist state. It must have seemed impossible that they would ever experience true freedom. Then the Communist leadership began to tumble in one Soviet Socialist Republic after another. Finally, the Communist state imploded, and the tyranny was no more.

Babylon was the greatest empire of its day. Likely, there were few who could have imagined life without the oppression of their Chaldean overlords. But God said He was going to bring the empire down, and that's exactly what He did. Again, literal fulfillment to prophecy. As Daniel thought about it, he felt humbled, he felt grateful, and he felt painfully aware of his sins and the sins of his people. So he prayed. He confessed personal and national sins, he recognized the righteousness of God's judgment on them, and he asked God to fulfill His promise to return His people to Jerusalem.

It was a bold move when, after recognizing his own sinfulness, Daniel immediately reminded God that He had a promise to fulfill. This is especially true after the Lord had just brought down an empire for him and his people. But God is always ready to hear our petitions to Him when we approach Him with a humble and pure heart and with an attitude of submission to His will. Daniel knew he could remind God of His promises because God has a history of keeping them.

God's Promises to His People
Promise One: Disobedience Would Result in Captivity

A friend of mine told me a story of when he was a young pastor's kid. The youth group was over at their house for a barbecue. My friend, who was about eight years old at the time, had a squirt gun, and he kept shooting water at one of the older youth leaders. The leader told him to knock it off, but the boy kept shooting him. Finally, the youth leader said, "If you shoot me one more time, I'm going to pick you up and throw you fully clothed into the pool."

My friend figured that there was no way this old guy would do that to a child, especially to the pastor's kid. So he called his bluff and shot him. Next thing he knew, he was flying through the air toward the pool. Climbing out of the water, looking like a drowned cat, my now-crying friend had to take the wet walk of shame through about 30 or so teenagers into the house to dry off and change his clothes. As he passed the old youth leader, the man said, "You can't say I didn't warn you."

Actions have consequences. If you do this, I'll do that. This is God's history with His creation. It started all the way back in the Garden. God presented Adam with a lush home filled with every kind of produce a person could ever want. There was only one stipulation given by the Lord: "Of every tree of the garden you may freely eat; but of the tree of the knowledge of good and evil you shall not eat, for in the day that you eat of it you shall surely die" (Genesis 2:16-17). Action and consequence. If you eat from that tree, I'll allow death into this world. You do this; I'll do that. Before we groan at Adam for being such an idiot for breaking the only rule he had, let's stop and think of all the times when we knew the consequences to our sinful actions but we went through with the sins anyway.

When the time came for God to choose one group of people to be His testimony to the nations, He codified proper actions and the consequences for either keeping or disregarding them. Through Moses, the Lord gave the Israelites a detailed game plan for righteous living. If only the nation would follow this law, the consequences would be fabulous. As Moses was giving his last series of messages to the people before his death, he told them,

> Now it shall come to pass, if you diligently obey the voice of the LORD your God, to observe carefully all His commandments which I command you today, that the LORD your God will set you high above all nations of the earth. And all these blessings shall come upon you and overtake you, because you obey the voice of the LORD your God (Deuteronomy 28:1-2).

"All these blessings" are listed in the next 12 verses. "If you do this," God told them, "then I can't wait to do that for you." But the Lord knew the hearts of mankind. He knew it was necessary to include the other side of the obedience coin. Moses told the people, "It shall come to pass, if you do not obey the voice of the LORD your God, to observe carefully all His commandments and His statutes which I command you today, that all these curses will come upon you and overtake you" (verse 15). Then for the next 53 verses, Moses listed out a litany of punishments, each one deserved and each one terrible. The consequences of wrong choices couldn't have been clearer.

As Daniel began his prayer, he knew that the destruction of Jerusalem and the exile were just. God had warned the people time after time with prophet after prophet, but they had refused to stop following other gods. They kept shooting God with the squirt gun, thinking, *Surely He won't do that nasty stuff to us. We're His chosen people. He loves us! Besides, we've gotten away with it for so long, we're not even sure God is still paying attention.*

But God was paying attention. The Jews made the mistake of confusing God's long-suffering patience with weakness or apathy. When He had finally had enough of the northern kingdom, He brought in Assyria to clear the people out of the land. And when His patience had run out with the southern kingdom, He whistled for Nebuchadnezzar, who came rushing in to do the Lord's bidding.

Recognizing that sin was the root of the Jews' difficulties, Daniel humbly approached God. Describing his demeanor at the time, he wrote, "I set my face toward the Lord God to make request by prayer and supplications, with fasting, sackcloth, and ashes" (Daniel 9:3). He didn't just come to God with a "Sorry, Lord, my bad. No hard feelings, right?" Daniel felt the full brunt of his sins and those of the nation. The weight of the wrongdoing wore him down. He refused himself nourishment and adorned himself with the signs of mourning. It was in that heartbroken attitude that he prayed:

> O Lord, great and awesome God, who keeps His covenant
> and mercy with those who love Him, and with those who
> keep His commandments, we have sinned and committed
> iniquity, we have done wickedly and rebelled, even by
> departing from Your precepts and Your judgments. Neither
> have we heeded Your servants the prophets, who spoke in

Your name to our kings and our princes, to our fathers and all the people of the land. O Lord, righteousness belongs to You, but to us shame of face, as it is this day—to the men of Judah, to the inhabitants of Jerusalem and all Israel, those near and those far off in all the countries to which You have driven them, because of the unfaithfulness which they have committed against You (verses 4-7).

The anguish of Daniel is evident. His words are heartrending. And this is just the first third of his prayer of repentance. I encourage you to put down this book, pick up your Bible, and read verses 8-15. Only someone who truly knows God can feel that devastated at offending Him.

Some may wonder why Daniel included himself in this prayer. He seemed to be a good guy, a true servant of the Lord. Whereas the nation was so bad, Daniel stood out for being so good. But Daniel recognized who he was. He was a Jew. It was his people who had offended God. It was his people who had rebelled and worshipped idols. Daniel was not just a "me," he was part of an "us." As such, he felt responsibility for the sins of his nation.

As we pray for our countries, we should do so as citizens. Whether you are British or Brazilian, Taiwanese or American, Italian or Israeli, there is no country that has kept its path with God. We must pray for our countries, asking for God's forgiveness on us, confessing our failure to heed His ways. This is true nationalism at its best.

God will always follow through on His promises for good or for bad. Israel had sinned against the Lord. Therefore, Daniel pleaded for divine forgiveness for the sins of the people so that they might start fresh again.

Promise Two: The Babylonian Captivity Would Last 70 Years

God created mankind to work hard and to rest. Both are needed to provide for one's needs and to make sure that one doesn't collapse due to exhaustion. In His act of creation, the Lord modeled for us what this six-days-on, one-day-off pattern looks like. Then, just to make sure people got the point, He codified it as the fourth commandment in the Mosaic law.

> Observe the Sabbath day, to keep it holy, as the LORD your God commanded you. Six days you shall labor and do all your work, but the seventh day is the Sabbath of the LORD your God (Deuteronomy 5:12-13).

In the same way that God created mankind with a need for rest, he did the same for the land. For farmland to remain healthy, it must intermittently be left fallow so that it can rebuild its nutrients and its moisture. This was God's plan for the land, and because He is a God of order, it is no surprise that the planting/fallow timing looks a lot like the schedule of Sabbaths. God told Moses,

> Speak to the children of Israel, and say to them: "When you come into the land which I give you, then the land shall keep a sabbath to the LORD. Six years you shall sow your field, and six years you shall prune your vineyard, and gather its fruit; but in the seventh year there shall be a sabbath of solemn rest for the land, a sabbath to the LORD. You shall neither sow your field nor prune your vineyard" (Leviticus 25:2-4).

Six years you plant, then one year you don't. Let the land enjoy its Sabbath so that the soil can be refreshed. Because God knows us so well, He nipped the obvious lack-of-faith question in the bud even before it could be asked. He told the Israelites not to worry about how they would eat that seventh year. "I will command My blessing on you in the sixth year, and it will bring forth produce enough for three years" (verse 21). God never gives us a command that is impossible to obey. Logic told the Israelites that they would starve that seventh year. Faith said, "Trust God. He has always provided in the past, and He will provide now too."

Once again, because God knows humanity so well, He knew that the Israelites' faulty logic would win out over their faith. So He warned them against neglecting the land Sabbaths:

> I will bring the land to desolation, and your enemies who dwell in it shall be astonished at it. I will scatter you among the nations and draw out a sword after you; your land shall be desolate and your cities waste. Then the land shall enjoy its sabbaths as long as it lies desolate and you are in your enemies' land; then the land shall rest and enjoy its sabbaths. As long as it lies desolate it shall rest—for the time it did not rest on your sabbaths when you dwelt in it (Leviticus 26:32-35).

It is here that we find the reason for the 70-year Babylonian captivity. Sin led to the exile. The lack of agricultural Sabbaths determined the exile's length. It had been 490 years since Israel had let the farmland remain fallow. How can we be sure of that number? Because we know basic math. Jeremiah said that "this whole land shall be a desolation and an astonishment, and these nations shall serve the king of Babylon seventy years" (Jeremiah 25:11). As we widen our context, we see that Jeremiah's 70 years are directly tied to the land Sabbath:

> Those who escaped from the sword he carried away to Babylon, where they became servants to him and his sons until the rule of the kingdom of Persia, to fulfill the word of the LORD by the mouth of Jeremiah, until the land had

enjoyed her Sabbaths. As long as she lay desolate she kept Sabbath, to fulfill seventy years (2 Chronicles 36:20-21).

If we multiply a Sabbath every seven years by a 70-year span, we arrive at 490 years of agricultural disobedience by the Jews in the land. It was God's promise-keeping nature that allowed the prophet to boldly state, "I, Daniel, understood by the books the number of the years specified by the word of the LORD through Jeremiah the prophet, that He would accomplish seventy years in the desolations of Jerusalem" (Daniel 9:2).

What would happen when the 70 years were up? There would be a homecoming. God never intended for the people of Israel to remain apart from the Promised Land. He had given it to them as an everlasting home. As we saw earlier, through Jeremiah, the Lord promised, "After seventy years are completed at Babylon, I will visit you and perform My good word toward you, and cause you to return to this place. For I know the thoughts that I think toward you, says the LORD, thoughts of peace and not of evil, to give you a future and a hope" (Jeremiah 29:10-11). God's love for Israel never waned. His goal was always to bring the people home. This continued to be His goal when He dispersed the Jews from their land in the first and second centuries AD. For nearly 2,000 years they wandered the earth, until in 1948 He once again established a nation of Israel in the Promised Land. Since that time, millions have returned to their ancestral home.

Promise Three: God Will Punish the Nation That Took the Jews Captive

"Wait a minute, Amir! God needed to discipline Israel. Babylon was kind enough to oblige. And then God punished the Babylonians for doing it? Shouldn't He have thanked them?" Absolutely not. Nebuchadnezzar was a bad guy and an idol worshipper. The conquests he made were not for God but for himself. It is unlikely he ever knew he was being used by God. He was a violent man and a narcissist, and he led an army of brutal thugs who murdered, raped, and pillaged their way through city after city. Those evil actions would never be on the Lord's honey-do list for any world leader.

Instead, what we see God doing is using the sinful actions of mankind to accomplish His will. Babylon was plowing through the Middle East, so the Lord ensured that Nebuchadnezzar's timing and his route would be according to His plan for the discipline of Judah. Did God force the king to kill and destroy? Was Nebuchadnezzar protesting to God, saying, "But Lord, You know that I'm a lover, not a fighter"? No, the conquering king was doing his conquering thing. God just guided his path so some good could come of it.

But you might protest, "Amir, if God could guide Nebuchadnezzar, why couldn't He just stop him? Think of all the lives He could have saved."

Often, what looks like a good thing on the surface is, in reality, the opposite. Just ask Peter, who, when promising to protect Jesus from harm, was told by the Lord, "Get behind Me, Satan! You are an offense to Me, for you are not mindful of the things of God, but the things of men" (Matthew 16:23). I often wonder what was going through Peter's mind immediately following that rebuke. "Uh, Lord, maybe You misunderstood. I was trying to help You."

Discipline had to come to Israel. The land had to get its Sabbath years. If the exile had never happened, the Jews would have continued in their sin, and God would have been shown to be a deity who did not have the wherewithal to follow through on His warnings.

Just as a father feels pain when he disciplines his child, Israel's Father grieved as He watched take place what needed to be done. He mourned the dead and lamented the violence. And He vowed to avenge the sinful way the Babylonians treated His people.

> "Then it will come to pass, when seventy years are completed,
> that I will punish the king of Babylon and that nation, the

land of the Chaldeans, for their iniquity," says the LORD; "and I will make it a perpetual desolation. So I will bring on that land all My words which I have pronounced against it, all that is written in this book, which Jeremiah has prophesied concerning all the nations. (For many nations and great kings shall be served by them also; and I will repay them according to their deeds and according to the works of their own hands)" (Jeremiah 25:12-14).

Again, notice the reason for God's punishment of the Babylonians. They would pay for the evil done through "the works of their own hands." Sin would be punished, Israel would be chastened, and God would remain holy.

Reminding God of His Promises

It is because our Lord is a promise-keeping God that Daniel could speak out boldly the last part of his prayer. Confident in God's character, trusting in His mercy, understanding His purposes, and holding tightly to His words, the man of God cried out:

O Lord, according to all Your righteousness, I pray, let Your anger and Your fury be turned away from Your city Jerusalem, Your holy mountain; because for our sins, and for the iniquities of our fathers, Jerusalem and Your people are a reproach to all those around us. Now therefore, our God, hear the prayer of Your servant, and his supplications, and for the Lord's sake cause Your face to shine on Your sanctuary, which is desolate. O my God, incline Your ear and hear; open Your eyes and see our desolations, and the city which is called by Your name; for we do not present our supplications before You because of our righteous deeds, but because of Your great mercies. O Lord, hear!

> O Lord, forgive! O Lord, listen and act! Do not delay for
> Your own sake, my God, for Your city and Your people
> are called by Your name (Daniel 9:16-19).

God loves it when we trust Him. He loves our dependence on His love and grace. This reminds me of when the Hebrews were ready to leave Mount Sinai. They had exasperated God to the extent that He was ready to be done with them. He told Moses that He would follow through with His promise to give them the Promised Land, but they would do it without Him. He said to His prophet, "Go up to a land flowing with milk and honey; for I will not go up in your midst, lest I consume you on the way, for you are a stiff-necked people" (Exodus 33:3).

The thought of moving forward without God was horrifying to Moses. He pleaded with God to change His mind, saying, "If Your Presence does not go with us, do not bring us up from here" (verse 15). If the choice was wilderness with God or Promised Land without God, Moses was determined they weren't going anywhere. The Lord saw Moses' faith. The prophet's dependence on Him softened His heart toward the people. "So the Lord said to Moses, 'I will also do this thing that you have spoken; for you have found grace in My sight, and I know you by name'" (verse 17).

"I know you by name." Wow! What reassurance! What encouragement! There are many reasons why we may stand out to God, and not all of them are good. Just ask Pharaoh and Saul and Judas. But Moses had found grace in God's eyes. Therefore, God knew him by name. I work as hard as I do so that God will know me that way and for that reason. In fact, I sign all my books with Exodus 33:17. Are you living a life of daily sacrifice focused on what truly matters so that you stand out to God?

It is true worship when we challenge God to act according to His character. It is in those times we are saying, "Lord, I believe You are who You say You are. So I'm praying this fully expecting You to be You." That is faith. That is worship.

The Lord heard Daniel's prayer. In fact, at the very first word the prophet uttered, God sent out an answer. The messenger who brought that answer was someone very familiar.

THE MESSIANIC COUNTDOWN

DANIEL 9:20-24

It's been a surprisingly enjoyable night with some new friends. You and your wife were a little hesitant to visit at first. Despite these being church acquaintances, you really don't know them that well. When they said three other couples were also going to join the get-together, you weren't sure of what to expect. After all, it's a New Year's Eve party. Was this going to turn into a drinking party where you would end up playing designated driver? But as the evening wore on, you realized that you wouldn't have to worry about that. Everyone was having a safe, fun time, and you were really starting to connect with the other couples.

Suddenly, the host of the party came in from the kitchen. She held a tray with ten flutes of sparkling apple cider, and called out, "Okay, everybody! It's time for the countdown!" As you lift your glass, you angle your wrist so that you can see your watch. 11:51 p.m.

You take a quick glance at your wife, who looks as confused as you are. But you both shrug. When in Rome...

With the glasses distributed, your host picks up her own cider, and says, "Okay, here we go! 483, 482, 481…"

Confused, but not wanting to seem rude, you join in with the countdown, trying to keep up the enthusiasm of your host and her husband. But by the time you near the end of the 300s, you and your wife have retaken your seats on the sofa. Somewhere in the lower 100s, your wife nods off with her head on your shoulder, and you have to make a spectacular save to keep the cider in her slowly tipping glass from spilling on the carpet.

When "…3, 2, 1" finally arrives, the "Happy New Year!" wishes are lackluster, and no one has the breath left to sound off any of their paper horns.

To justify a countdown beginning at 483, the payoff when you get to zero needs to be spectacular. A birthday or an anniversary are not big enough. Neither is simply turning the page on a new year. However, in chapter 9 of Daniel, Gabriel the messenger brings with him tidings that, if they had been properly understood, would have kept the Jewish nation on the edge of their seats from 483 all the way down to the cider toasts.

God's Quick Response to Prayer

The incredible paragraph in Daniel 9 that follows the conclusion of Daniel's prayer tells us volumes about who God is, the way He operates, and His love for those who follow Him.

> Now while I was speaking, praying, and confessing my sin and the sin of my people Israel, and presenting my supplication before the LORD my God for the holy mountain of my God, yes, while I was speaking in prayer, the man Gabriel, whom I had seen in the vision at the beginning, being caused to fly swiftly, reached me about the time of the evening offering. And he informed

me, and talked with me, and said, "O Daniel, I have
now come forth to give you skill to understand. At the
beginning of your supplications the command went out,
and I have come to tell you, for you are greatly beloved;
therefore consider the matter, and understand the vision"
(verses 20-23).

Daniel used the phrases "while I was speaking" and "fly swiftly."
Then, again, "Yes, while I was speaking…" Gabriel followed with,
"At the beginning of your supplications…" Daniel had presented to
the Lord a beautiful 16-verse, 4-paragraph prayer of confession and
petition. He concluded it with "O Lord, listen and act," to which
God responded, "You bet! It's already in progress."

"While," "swiftly," and "at the beginning"! That is how God operates. When you are facing a situation that has you pouring out your
heart to God—maybe it's in confession or out of desperate need or
amidst great sorrow—you don't need to wonder whether He is hearing you. You don't have to fret about getting your words just right.
Here's a prayer pro tip: The Lord listens to your heart; the words are
just window dressing.

But when you need God to be near, just know that from before
you even start praying that He understands your need and is already
working out the answer. Remember, you don't need to convince Him
of anything with your fine-sounding, well-thought-out reasoning. You
don't need to share with Him a divided computer screen that dis-
plays on one side the pros of Option A and on the other the pros of
Option B. He's already made the right decision. He's busy working
out the best plan for your life not because of your words but because
of His love and your faith.

"So, Amir, I can ask for anything I want, and God is just itch-
ing to give it to me? Mercedes Benz, here I come!" Slow down, my
friend. That's not quite how it works. The apostle John wrote of this

very thing: "Now this is the confidence that we have in Him, that if we ask anything according to His will, He hears us. And if we know that He hears us, whatever we ask, we know that we have the petitions that we have asked of Him" (1 John 5:14-15). Notice those four words "according to His will." This is where the Faith movement gets it wrong. Health and wealth is not always in God's will for us. In fact, as we saw with Daniel and his friends, it is typically in the hard times when our faith grows.

Imagine a life where God just gives you everything you ask for simply because you believe He can. Essentially, you would be like a baby living in a comfortable little crib. You'd have your little baby faith that tells you that if you cry loud enough, your Father will give you want you want. It would be a cushy little life and you'd be absolutely worthless to everyone.

Daniel's prayer was not for himself. It was for the nation. It was so God would be glorified in His people's restoration. It was for repentance and restoration so that the Jewish people could fulfill their call to be a light to the world. It was "according to [God's] will." That is the kind of prayer that God would never say no to.

Not only did God answer Daniel's prayer, but He did so immediately. What was it about the situation the prophet was facing that caused God to respond so quickly? First, another of His prophecies was about to become a reality. The 70-year exile was nearing its completion, so the occasion of Daniel's request coincided directly with God's purpose and timing. When we are walking in step with the Holy Spirit, He will direct us to pray for things that God has already prepared for us.

Second, Daniel was "greatly beloved" (Daniel 9:23). As we saw at the end of the previous chapter, it is an incredible blessing to be beloved by God and to have Him know our name! The word used here for "beloved" is special. Another way to translate the Hebrew, חֲמוּדוֹת (*chamudot*), is "beloved by the people and God." Daniel was greatly loved because he was one of God's children. Beyond that, he was greatly esteemed by God because of his lifetime of faithfulness in the service of the Lord. That is what matters in life. Not always were the prophets loved by the people. Jesus said of the holy city, "O Jerusalem, Jerusalem, the one who kills the prophets and stones those who are sent to her" (Matthew 23:37). But it is not people's praise that we should live for. I've often said that we serve an audience of One. As long as God is pleased with our lives, then we are doing well. It is that kind of life that Daniel was commended for. What a goal to strive for. We are all loved despite who we are and what we've done. That is simply the depth of the Father's grace and mercy. But how amazing is it when we can also be loved because of who we are and valued and revered because of what we have done. How wonderful it is when we can tangibly demonstrate through our sacrifice and service our passionate love for God that originated in His love for us!

The third reason for the Lord's quick response was that He had a communication agenda. He wanted Daniel to understand His calendar so that he could then relay it to his readers. We are amongst the beneficiaries of this divine purpose.

Seventy Weeks Are Determined

Gabriel began his message to Daniel by saying, "Seventy weeks are determined for your people and for your holy city" (Daniel 9:24). Immediately, we notice two changes in focus. The first is a difference in time frame. Instead of 70 years, Gabriel referenced 70 weeks. Second, rather than looking at Babylon, Medo-Persia, Greece, and Rome, this message is for Jerusalem. The future of Jerusalem and the people of Israel will be determined within a 70-weeks window.

But was the angel really saying that all of Jewish history would be resolved in the next 15 months? For clarity, we need to go back to the original language. The Hebrew word translated as "weeks" is literally "sevens." So what Gabriel told Daniel was that "seventy sevens are determined for your people." Thus, the options that we have are to treat the component parts of these "sevens" as days or as years. Does Gabriel mean a literal week, or is it a "week of years"?

Seven years is a common span in Jewish tradition. If you'll recall, the Sabbath for the land was divided into seven-year increments. In the book of Leviticus, the Jews were to count off seven land Sabbaths, or seven times seven years, which came to 49. That next year, they were to "proclaim liberty throughout all the land to all its inhabitants. It shall be a Jubilee for you; and each of you shall return to his possession, and each of you shall return to his family" (Leviticus 25:10). The slaves would be freed, and the people would have a bonus Sabbath year for the land.

Within the context of our passage here in Daniel 9, only a year interpretation of "sevens" or "weeks" makes logical sense, particularly when we look back on it through the lens of history. Therefore, the period of time Gabriel referred to as "seventy weeks" is 70 times 7 years, or 490 years. That number should be pinging your recognition bells from the previous chapter. Looking backward, that was the number of years that the Jews ignored God's mandate for the land Sabbath. Looking forward, this was also the number of years that God had determined to finally bring His chosen people to a point where they, to a man, woman, and child, would acknowledge the Messiah and receive the free gift of salvation through Jesus' death and resurrection.

As we progress through Gabriel's message, we see that there are four divisions within the 70 weeks. Daniel 9:25 tells us that "there shall be seven weeks and sixty-two weeks." Then in verse 27, we read of "one week" and "the middle of the week." Thus, the time frames we are working with are the first 7 weeks (49 years) and the next 62 weeks (434 years). This is what gave us our New Year's Eve countdown of 483. Two more periods are important in Gabriel's message—the final week (7 years) and the middle of the final week (3.5 years). Those numbers will be essential as we seek to understand the prophecy that the messenger is revealing to Daniel.

But before God's messenger got too far into what will take place during that period, he told us why it all matters. Have you ever been trapped on the receiving end of a seemingly never-ending diatribe? As the person drones on and on, you may have found yourself thinking, *Get to the point!* There is no possibility of us feeling like that with Gabriel's message. He graciously gives us the point before he begins. Laying out a sixfold purpose statement, he begins each new objective with the word "to":

> Seventy weeks are determined
> for your people and for your holy city,
> to finish the transgression,
> to make an end of sins,
> to make reconciliation for iniquity,
> to bring in everlasting righteousness,
> to seal up vision and prophecy,
> and to anoint the Most Holy (verse 24).

Each one of these goals is active and purposeful. There is a sense of finality as he says they are "to finish" and "to make an end" and "to seal up." As we read this list, it also becomes evident that these are not human objectives. Gabriel is not giving Daniel a to-do list; these missions are such that only God can accomplish them.

In studying these purpose statements, another very exciting revelation becomes clear. These weeks are leading up to two incredible events. The first statements point to a time when the Messiah will come to put an end to the eternally destructive ramifications of sin. Then in the second three, we see the return of the Messiah to usher in His kingdom.

The Threefold Purpose of Jesus' First Coming

Purpose One: To Finish the Transgression

Each of these first three steps deals with sin, and in each one, Gabriel uses a different Hebrew word to describe the offense. In this first statement, he uses the word פֶּשַׁע (*pesha*), which means "a crime." When Israel transgressed, they were not doing it out of ignorance. They knew what was right, but like criminals who know they are breaking the law, they purposely decided to act contrary to God's precepts and principles. The psalmist speaks of rulers consciously determining to go "against the LORD and against His Anointed, saying, 'Let us break Their bonds in pieces and cast away Their cords from us'" (Psalm 2:2-3). Those are words of open rebellion rather than accidental sin.

Isn't this the attitude of so many today who say that the Bible binds or restricts their freedom to enjoy the pleasures of life? This is even true in the church, where denominations and individual Christians water down the moral code of Scripture. What used to be considered sin is now acceptable as a personal choice. Progressive Christianity considers itself to be enlightened as its followers focus on the love of God, relegating to the past all the "oppressive rules" of historical Bible interpretation.

If it were just a matter of putting away empty church traditions, I would applaud them. Too much pharisaical legalism has infected the church over the years and smothered the grace, mercy, and love that should be the hallmarks of how we treat the sinful world. Where I part ways with these overly tolerant Christians is when they begin to soften the dos and don'ts that are clearly spelled out in Scripture. Claiming righteous motives, they demand that all people's lifestyle choices be accepted and celebrated. How can people understand the true love of God if His people consider them to be sinners? Scriptural morality, they say, creates an unnecessary and un-Christlike barrier that blocks the path to God.

But an obstruction-free path that avoids the biblical absolutes of holiness does not lead to God—at least, not the real one. Instead, it creates a progressive god of one's own making—a beautiful idol cast in the image of culture rather than the words of the Bible. As Paul said in Romans 1:22, "Professing to be wise, they became fools," and they are leading far too many people into a false sense of spiritual security based on their foolishness.

The message that Gabriel brought would bring to an end Israel's penchant for purposely acting contrary to the statutes of God's covenant. It had taken the people 70 years to pay for their transgressions. But now the slate was clean. The land had its Sabbaths. It was time for the Jews to return to their land, but this time, with the commitment of following God's law.

Purpose Two: To Make an End of Sins

The second word that the messenger uses for sin is חַטָּאת (*chatat*). This means "to miss the mark, to offend." It has the same sense that Paul held when he wrote, "For all have sinned and fall short of the glory of God" (Romans 3:23). Gabriel told Daniel that God was about to put an end to the people's continual falling short of His standard.

Not many generations had to pass after Abram's calling before the people of Israel ceased measuring up to what God had expected from them. He had purposed for them to be a light to the Gentiles. Instead, they preferred the darkness of the surrounding nations.

How could there ever be an end of sin in Israel? Daniel would have had no idea how to answer that question. But Gabriel made it clear that it would happen within that 70 weeks of years. If only Daniel had the benefit of reading the New Testament, the details about the fulfillment of this promise would have been made clear to him. Quoting the words of Isaiah, the apostle Paul gave new insight to them by writing,

I do not desire, brethren, that you should be ignorant of
this mystery, lest you should be wise in your own opinion,
that blindness in part has happened to Israel until the
fullness of the Gentiles has come in. And so all Israel will
be saved, as it is written:

> "The Deliverer will come out of Zion,
>   and He will turn away ungodliness from Jacob;
>   for this is My covenant with them,
>   when I take away their sins" (Romans 11:25-27).

A day was coming when not only would Israel's sins be atoned for,
or covered over, but they would be taken away. All the rebellion and
idol worship and immorality would be forgiven, removed, and cast
away "as far as the east is from the west" (Psalm 103:12). The Son of
Man whom Daniel saw descending in the clouds to the Ancient of
Days would provide the pathway for this total reconciliation through
the sacrifice of Himself on the cross. This was still far beyond the
time of Daniel, but the event would fit perfectly into the prophetic
layout of the 70 weeks.

Purpose Three: To Make Reconciliation for Iniquity

The word the NKJV translates as "reconciliation" in Daniel 9:24
is better understood as "to atone." Gabriel was saying that within these
70 weeks will be found the atonement, or covering over, of iniquity.
The Hebrew word used for sin in this phrase is עָוֺן (*avon*), and it means
"to twist or bend." This is a perfect word to apply to the Jews of Daniel's time because they had been living a bent lifestyle for generations.

When the prophets proclaimed the words of God, the people
would "bend" their pronouncements to suit their personal lifestyles.
Even the religious scholars of their time bent the law to remove the
concepts of mercy and grace, leaving only criticism and judgment.

A time was soon coming, however, when provision would be made for a once-for-all sacrifice for sin. This one act by Jesus on the cross would be the ultimate atonement, opening the door for Israel's reconciliation to the One who had given them so much but had received so little in return.

This perfect and complete atonement would affect not only Israel, but the entire world. While Daniel had to look forward to this event, we need to look 2,000 years backward. The Lamb of God who takes away the sin of the world paid the ultimate sacrifice, putting an end to the power of sin in the lives of those who receive Him as Savior and Lord.

As we move to the next three purposes found in the weeks, we'll quickly realize that the fulfillment of this "end to sin" promise will not come for the Jews until a time that is still future from ours today. They will see their completion when the sacrificial Lamb returns as the Lion of Judah and the great Warrior King of all kings.

The Threefold Purpose of Jesus' Second Coming
Purpose One: To Bring in Everlasting Righteousness

Everlasting righteousness. Where on this spinning globe of ours can you possibly find that? There are flashes here and there of righteous acts. One might even find great shining examples of righteous people. Billy Graham was a man who daily served his Lord. The testimonies of hundreds of thousands of believers include walking forward at one of Graham's crusades to receive Jesus as their Lord and Savior. But if you spoke with Billy's daughter, Anne Graham Lotz, you would likely hear from her that her father was a great man, a godly man, a man after the Lord's own heart. You would not hear from her, however, that he was a perfect man. And that is no knock on Billy Graham. He would have told you the same thing! There is no righteousness in God's creation that can be considered everlasting. Only the righteousness of God Himself is capable of living up to that descriptor.

But today, all around the world, people are attempting to appear righteous before God and man. They go through the rituals, they say the prayers, they run down the checklist of what godliness looks like and they make sure they tick each box—twice. But so many of these people are only expressing a form of godliness while denying its power. Just as Jesus accused the Pharisees of spiritual emptiness, these "look at me" religion followers are "like whitewashed tombs which indeed appear beautiful outwardly, but inside are full of dead men's bones and all uncleanness. Even so you also outwardly appear righteous to men, but inside you are full of hypocrisy and lawlessness" (Matthew 23:27-28).

Today, in Israel, you can still find a culture of empty, it's-all-about-me religiosity. What Jesus said in the first century is still true today. "But all their works they do to be seen by men. They make their phylacteries broad and enlarge the borders of their garments. They love the best places at feasts, the best seats in the synagogues, greetings in the marketplaces, and to be called by men, 'Rabbi, Rabbi'" (verses 5-6). But what God told Daniel through Gabriel is that within the 70-week period, the people of Israel would turn aside from their religiosity and sinful indulgences. Instead, they would desire a true righteousness that is everlasting, and they will receive it.

When will this everlasting righteousness be brought into the world? It will be that day when the One who is everlastingly righteous, from eternity past to eternity future, makes His return to this earth. That is when all humanity will finally see Him for who He is. And that is when the Jews will recognize and mourn for the One "whom they pierced" (Zechariah 12:10). When Jesus the Messiah returns, bringing righteousness to the earth, Jeremiah's great prophetic statement will be fulfilled:

> "Behold, the days are coming," says the LORD,
> "That I will raise to David a Branch of righteousness;

a King shall reign and prosper,

and execute judgment and righteousness in the earth.

In His days Judah will be saved,

and Israel will dwell safely;

now this is His name by which He will be called:

THE LORD OUR RIGHTEOUSNESS"

(Jeremiah 23:5-6).

Purpose Two: To Seal Up Vision and Prophecy

Once the nation of Israel recognizes Jesus as their Messiah, there will be no more need for vision or prophecy. Finally, the Lord's chosen nation will be perfectly fulfilling its role of reflecting the character of God. His love, mercy, grace, forgiveness, long-suffering, justice, and faithfulness will all be expressed in the reality of a formerly rebellious nation once-and-for-all-time reconciled to its Creator.

Does sealing up vision and prophecy mean that there are no more prophecies that will need fulfillment? Definitely not. There will still be a millennial kingdom to enjoy, in which Jesus the Messiah will rule from a throne in Jerusalem. The devil will still need to be released from his 1,000-year lockdown to deceive the nations into rebelling against the King of kings. The final battle must come, which will be followed by the Great White Throne judgment. Once all humanity has been properly sorted out between those with their names in the Book of Life and those not included, God will trigger a demolition of the current heavens and earth to make way for the new model that will be free of all sinful taint.

What is being sealed up is the need for any new prophecy. All that is to come has already been predicted. And, in the millennial kingdom, any questions that need answering can be taken right to the Lord, who will be ruling in Jerusalem. Prophets, priests, and mediators of any kind will be relegated to the unemployment line.

Purpose Three: To Anoint the Most Holy

While this could be referring to Jesus Himself, the phrase "Most Holy" is not typically used of a person. Most likely, this is referring to the fourth temple.

"Woah, woah, woah, Amir! We don't even have a third temple built yet, and you're already talking about a fourth one?" I am, and let me tell you why. The temple is a place that represents God's presence with His people. It is not His home. There are no magical powers hidden within the structure. It is simply the place that God designates to be the center of worship to ensure that everyone is keeping on the religious straight and narrow.

This was essential in the monotheistic world of Israel after the people entered the Promised Land. At that time, the tabernacle represented God's presence with humanity. If instead of one primary place of worship they had 57 of them spread across the country, that's 57 places where theology and worship could go wrong. This was especially true in those times before phones, the internet, and ease of transport. So God had Solomon build the first temple as the center of worship. It served its purpose until the people forgot what the temple was for and began using it to worship idols. Hence, Daniel and his buddies ended up in Babylon and the first temple was destroyed.

After the exile, when the people returned to the land under Persian rule, they built a second temple. This time, they were determined to do it right. No foreign gods, no idols—this was God's home and it would stay that way. Initially, the second temple was small and plain compared to the size and flash of the original, but when King Herod the Great came along, he fancied it up quite a bit.

Unfortunately, by the time of Herod's upgrades, the people had once again forgotten that the temple was to be a place of true sacrificial worship of God. Instead, it had become a center of rules, traditions, and commerce. This was the reason for Jesus' righteous indignation when He overturned the tables of the money changers and the sellers, saying, "It is written, 'My house shall be called a house of prayer,' but you have made it a 'den of thieves'" (Matthew 21:13). Because the people had removed the real God from the temple, God removed the temple from the people. It was destroyed in AD 70 by the Romans.

As we saw in an earlier chapter, in the middle of the seven-year tribulation, the Antichrist will desecrate the temple. I am no great logician, but it seems to me that for the Antichrist to desecrate the temple, there needs to be a temple to desecrate. Hello! Not a tough concept. That is the third temple—the tribulation temple. Why would the Jews, who are notorious for not giving allegiance to anyone not Jewish, possibly make their commitment to some European guy? Let me tell you: The first man who offers to work out a deal to put a temple back on the Temple Mount could run for king of the world and easily take the Jewish vote.

Is this temple the "Most Holy" that Gabriel spoke to Daniel about? It's anything but. It will last only until the end of the tribulation, when an earthquake will demolish much of Jerusalem, including this temple.

But by that time the Messiah will have come, returning to the Mount of Olives with His church in tow. And, once again, we are speaking of a literal return of the physical Jesus standing with real feet on the genuine Mount of Olives. This is not an allegorical event. This is a real event that all will see with their eyes as the feeling of impending doom fills the chests of Jesus' enemies. Jesus will defeat the forces that originally gathered in the valley of Armageddon and marched to Jerusalem. The Antichrist and false prophet will be tossed into the lake of fire, and Satan will be locked away in the abyss. At that point, it will be time for us to settle in for 1,000 years. Ezekiel saw a vision of this coming millennial era, during which he was lifted high up on a mountain. Below him he could see a massive city spreading for miles and miles. Within that city was an enormous temple.

A man joined him on the mountain and said to him, "Son of man, look with your eyes and hear with your ears, and fix your mind on everything I show you; for you were brought here so that I might show them to you. Declare to the house of Israel everything you see" (Ezekiel 40:4). The man had a measuring rod with him, which he then used to conduct a very detailed measurement of this fourth temple. This is the "Most Holy" temple. It is this house of God that will be built and anointed at the end of the 70 weeks. And it is in this holy place that people from all over the world will gather to worship the Savior King who is on the throne in Jerusalem.

Remember this as we seek to piece together the order of the 70 weeks. The millennial temple is the only one that fits the "Most Holy" category. It will not be completed until after the seven years (one week) of the tribulation. Something has to happen that gets us from Daniel's historical time to the millennium's future time.

Now that we understand the *why* of the 70 sevens, Gabriel is ready to explain the *whats*. Up until now, the prophecy has all been straightforward. However, now God's messenger is about to take Daniel and us into some very unexpected places.

SEVENTY WEEKS ALL ACCOUNTED FOR

DANIEL 9:25-27

Several months back, Israeli prime minister Benjamin Netanyahu was interviewed on one of the major news channels. He handled himself very well, despite it being evident that the man asking the questions was not a fan of his. Once the segment concluded, the scene shifted to the studio where a panel awaited the interviewer. As they talked back and forth about the problems of the region and the relationship between Israelis and Palestinians, I realized that their understanding of the geopolitical factors affecting the Middle East was surprisingly limited. This was due to them seeming to have no grasp of the spiritual aspect of the region. They were treating Israel and the surrounding nations as they would any other place on the globe.

But Israel and the Middle East are not like every other region in the world. To truly understand the ins and outs, one must dig deeper. Because we read the Bible, we are allowed that deeper view. We are given access to peek behind the curtain to see what others cannot see and to understand what others lack the capability to comprehend. God has chosen the nation of Israel, and the city of Jerusalem in particular, as the center of all that He has planned for the remainder of this world's existence. This is no surprise to anyone who is a student of God's Word. Jerusalem has been at the center of God's focus ever since He gave the city to the Jews back in the time of King David.

Now Gabriel was about to open Daniel's eyes to God's future plans for Israel, beginning with the first seven weeks.

> Know therefore and understand,
> that from the going forth of the command
> to restore and build Jerusalem
> until Messiah the Prince,
> there shall be seven weeks (Daniel 9:25).

The First Seven Weeks of Years Identified

As opposed to the dates, like that of the rapture, that are kept beyond our reach, the beginning of the initial seven weeks of years is a moment we can accurately pinpoint. At the time of Gabriel's answer to Daniel's prayer, Jerusalem was a mess. The temple was destroyed, the walls were down, the city was leveled. The once-beautiful creation of David and Solomon, admired and visited by dignitaries from far away, was now a heap of ruins.

If you'll recall God's words to the exiles through Jeremiah, He promised, "When seventy years are completed for Babylon, I will visit you, and I will fulfill to you my promise and bring you back to this place" (Jeremiah 29:10 ESV). Some of the older Jews had been in Babylon for the full seven decades. They had taken seriously God's command given through Ezekiel to make a life for themselves there. And now that Darius had gotten rid of the last vestiges of the crumbling Babylonian Empire, their prospects were improving even more.

For these established exiles, leaving their settled lives behind to return to a pile of rubble would have been a hard sell.

This didn't change much even after the rebuilding had begun in Jerusalem. Years later, when Ezra had gathered a volunteer group of exiles to make the difficult return, he "looked among the people and the priests, and found none of the sons of Levi there" (Ezra 8:15). You would think that of any of the Jews who would want to return to Jerusalem and the temple, it would be the Levites, who had responsibility for the worship of God. Ezra was forced to send out a special delegation to convince some of the priestly class to leave what they had in exile and migrate back home.

But the exiles who were homesick were ready to return, despite Jerusalem being in shambles. They just needed the go-ahead.

They got it.

"Perfect, Amir! Now we just need to look for the first time a king commanded them to go home and rebuild Jerusalem, and we've got the timing of Gabriel's message." You're exactly right! Only it's not quite as easy as you think. There were five decrees issued in connection with the return of the exiles and the restoration of Jerusalem. Each has been identified by one scholar or another as the one Gabriel was referencing. But for the timing to be proper, there can only be one correct decree. Thankfully, Gabriel was very specific about this order. The command must be for the restoration and building of Jerusalem.

Here are our options: First, King Cyrus of Persia issued a decree in 538 BC. In it, he wrote, "All the kingdoms of the earth the LORD God of heaven has given me. And He has commanded me to build Him a house at Jerusalem which is in Judah" (Ezra 1:2). That certainly looks promising, until you see what he is looking to build. He is sending the Jews back to build a house for God—a temple. A temple is not a city. Scratch this one off our list.

Second, King Artaxerxes I issued a decree regarding the rebuilding of Jerusalem, which initially sounds promising. The returned exiles were facing opposition from people in the surrounding provinces with regard to the restoration of the temple. These antagonists wrote lies to the king, who bought into their deception. So he issued a decree in which he wrote, "I gave the command, and a search has been made, and it was found that this city in former times has revolted against kings, and rebellion and sedition have been fostered in it...Now give the command to make these men cease, that this city may not be built until the command is given by me" (Ezra 4:19, 21). So yes, this is about the rebuilding of the city. But it is the opposite of what we want. This decree *stopped* the rebuilding of the city, rather than *started* it.

Third, at the prompting of the prophets Haggai and Zechariah, the returned exiles under Zerubbabel and Jeshua defied the Persian monarchs and recommenced construction of the temple. This was around 520 BC. The surrounding governors had fits when they saw the construction begin. Immediately they wrote to the king, who was now Darius I. King Darius had his team do some investigation, and they turned up Cyrus's original decree from nearly two decades back. Rather than backing the bad guys, it fully supported the Jews' activities. The king then wrote to the governors, telling them, "Let the work of this house of God alone; let the governor of the Jews and the elders of the Jews build this house of God on its site" (Ezra 6:7). Then, to add insult to their injury, he ordered that they provide the Jews with whatever they needed for construction and for their sacrifices. It's a beautiful story of those who come against God's people getting what they deserve. But it's not the decree we're looking for. Once again, it's directed toward the temple.

Fourth, when 458 BC arrived, the rebuilt temple had been in operation for more than five decades. That means that this next decree couldn't be about the temple again, right? Wrong. Ezra was about to lead a contingent of people home to Jerusalem. King Artaxerxes was convinced of the great power of the Jewish God, so he wanted to make sure that He was happy with him. What better way to make a god happy than to give him a bunch of stuff. So he sent Ezra off with gold and silver and all sorts of gifts, all of it "given to you for the service of the house of your God, deliver in full before the God of Jerusalem. And whatever more may be needed for the house of your God, which you may have occasion to provide, pay for it from the king's treasury" (Ezra 7:19-20). What an amazing God we serve, who can, as Ezra put it, "put such a thing as this in the king's heart" (verse 27). Sadly, for our purposes, this decree was still all about the temple.

But fear not; we still have a fifth option. About 13 years pass until we find Nehemiah, who was the cupbearer to King Artaxerxes. Nehemiah had a brother named Hanani, who lived in Jerusalem. When his brother came back to the Persian capital city of Shushan, Nehemiah asked about the welfare of Jerusalem. Hanani gave a very negative report, saying, "The survivors who are left from the captivity in the province are there in great distress and reproach. The wall of Jerusalem is also broken down, and its gates are burned with fire" (Nehemiah 1:3). This broke Nehemiah's heart.

The next time Nehemiah went before the king, Artaxerxes noticed his distress. He asked his favored servant what the problem was, and after a quick prayer, Nehemiah answered, "If it pleases the king, and if your servant has found favor in your sight, I ask that you send me to Judah, to the city of my fathers' tombs, that I may rebuild it" (2:5). And there you have it. He didn't want to go to rebuild or resupply the temple. His heart was to rebuild and restore Jerusalem. I find it quite amusing that the one decree we were looking for is the only command that is not written out in the text, but only alluded to.

In 444 BC, King Artaxerxes granted Nehemiah permission to leave his court position, commissioning him to rebuild the city of Jerusalem and its walls. It was now time for the clock to start ticking. Nehemiah took a team to Jerusalem, got the city officials organized to do the work, and miraculously rebuilt the city's wall in only 52 days.

"Wait, Amir! Fifty-two days is not 49 years. What about Gabriel's first seven weeks?" I'm so glad you remembered. The wall was the priority because it gave protection from outside forces. It also gave Jerusalem legitimacy as a real entity. No self-respecting city of that time was without a wall. But then the hard work began. Remember, Jerusalem was a metropolis when Nebuchadnezzar rolled in and levelled it. There was a lot to clean up and rebuild. The people had no bulldozers or debris-removal trucks. Everything had to be broken down by hammer and carted out by foot or by donkey. The restoration and rebuilding of the city of Jerusalem began in 444 BC and was completed in 395 BC.[13] That's 49 years, or seven sets of seven.

The Next 62 Weeks of Years Identified

As many of you likely noticed earlier, I cut short Gabriel's pronouncement about the weeks in Daniel 9:25. The full quote reads:

> Know therefore and understand,
> that from the going forth of the command
> to restore and build Jerusalem
> until Messiah the Prince,
> there shall be seven weeks and sixty-two weeks;
> the street shall be built again, and the wall,
> even in troublesome times.

We've accounted for the first seven weeks. Now we've got to figure out the other 62. For those of you who aren't fans of math, stay with me. As numbers go, these are pretty exciting ones. Once we solve the equation, the payoff is amazing—Messiah the Prince! In other words, looking backward from our modern vantage point, the sum of 7 plus 62 equals Jesus.

Let's check this out. Adding 7 and 62 gives us 69. Then we multiply that 69 times 7 (the number of years in a "week"). Let me get my pencil and some paper. We've got 3, then carry the 6, and add it to the 42. Got it—483 years! So if we add 483 years to our 444 BC starting date when King Artaxerxes commissioned Nehemiah to rebuild the city, we get AD 38.

"Wait, Amir. By the year 38, Jesus had already been gone from the earth for more than half a decade. Please don't tell me we need to go back and look for another decree!"

Relax! It's okay. We've got the right kingly order.

It all comes down to the calendar. If we chart the date using our Gregorian calendar of 365 days per year, then we are going to overshoot the time that Jesus was walking this earth. But the Jews didn't use the Gregorian calendar. They used the lunar calendar, which has only 360 days per year. You may be saying, "Okay, Amir, but that's a difference of only five days a year. You flew past your target date by a full six years." But when you multiply it out, you find that days do turn into years. With the Gregorian calendar, we're looking at 176,295 days. But if we convert it to lunar, then we're looking at 173,880 days.

This is where we're going to have to get a little deeper in the math. To do so, I'm going to bring in a friend of mine, Sir Robert Anderson. Well, maybe not exactly a friend, since he's been dead for more than a century. But I'm betting that if Sir Robert were alive today, we'd both enjoy sitting down and sharing a bowl of hummus.

Sir Robert Anderson was the second Assistant Commissioner (Crime) of the London Metropolitan Police from 1888 to 1901. He was a prolific writer, an intelligence officer, and a theologian. In 1894, Anderson wrote *The Coming Prince*, in which he so graciously worked out our mathematical equation, naming the day the 69 weeks was fulfilled as April 6, AD 32. It was this day "on which the Lord Jesus rode into Jerusalem in fulfillment of the prophecy of Zechariah 9:9; when, for the first and only occasion in all His earthly sojourn, He was acclaimed as 'Messiah the Prince the King, the Son of David.'"[14]

Now if that isn't chills-worthy, I don't know what is. God's words always come to pass. Through Gabriel, He informed the world of when the Savior King would come riding into Jerusalem. Almost half a millennium later to the precise day, He did just that!

Messiah Will Be Cut Off

Gabriel does not leave much time for celebration. The good news has been revealed. Now it's time for him to disclose the bad news:

> After the sixty-two weeks
> Messiah shall be cut off, but not for Himself;
> and the people of the prince who is to come
> shall destroy the city and the sanctuary.
> The end of it shall be with a flood,
> and till the end of the war desolations are determined
> (verse 26).

The Jews were looking for a great warrior Messiah. They were expecting a hero like the one John later described in Revelation 19. This mighty leader would come riding in on a white horse to defeat the oppressive Romans. "Out of His mouth goes a sharp sword, that with it He should strike the nations. And He Himself will rule them with a rod of iron. He Himself treads the winepress of the fierceness and wrath of Almighty God" (verse 15). This was the man they wanted. Under His authority the Jews could not only defeat Rome, but they might even take over the empire.

But instead of Revelation 19, they got Isaiah 53. In place of the mighty warrior, they got the suffering servant. There was no soldier on a white steed. They witnessed instead a rabbi on the foal of a donkey. But they weren't discouraged—at least, not right away. Maybe this was His way of tricking the Romans. Maybe He would pull a rope-a-dope, catching the oppressors off guard when He whipped off His robe to reveal armor and weaponry. But instead of picking up a sword, this Rabbi picked up Scripture. Instead of going after the Gentiles, He used God's words to slice and dice the Pharisees, Sadducees, and teachers of the law.

Then, worst of all, this unaffiliated teacher with no formally sanctioned religious education who had somehow managed to escape rural nowhere Nazareth had the audacity to talk about them like He was one with authority. In a series of seven vicious accusations we can read about in Matthew 23:13-36, He shredded the religious leaders, calling them hypocrites, blind guides, and fools. Then placing Himself in the position of God, He said, "O Jerusalem, Jerusalem, the one who kills the prophets and stones those who are sent to her! How often I wanted to gather your children together, as a hen gathers her chicks under her wings, but you were not willing!" (verse 37).

It's no wonder that the religious establishment wanted to kill Jesus. They didn't have the insight or capacity to understand that when He put Himself in the position of God, He was simply expressing His rightful authority. By midweek, not only were the Jewish leaders hostile, but the people were becoming disillusioned. The more they listened to Jesus' teaching, the less He sounded like a warrior. By all appearances, this miracle-working phenom from Israel's north was going to turn out to be all talk and no action.

Finally, the time came when the religious leaders struck out at this so-called Messiah. The crowds were more than ready to back their play. They had gone all in for Jesus, and He had let them down. "Crucify Him," cried the Pharisees. "Crucify Him," cried the Sadducees. "Crucify Him," cried the teachers of the law. "Crucify Him," agreed the people. The word Gabriel used that is translated "cut off" means "to exterminate." That is what the Jews of that time did to their Messiah:

> He has borne our griefs
> and carried our sorrows;

yet we esteemed Him stricken,
smitten by God, and afflicted.
He was wounded for our transgressions,
He was bruised for our iniquities;
the chastisement for our peace was upon Him,
and by His stripes we are healed.
All we like sheep have gone astray;
we have turned, every one, to his own way;
and the LORD has laid on Him the iniquity of us all
(Isaiah 53:4-6).

Jerusalem Will Be Destroyed

The Messiah had come. Then the Messiah had gone. Gabriel continued with a warning about what would happen soon after Jerusalem's mistreatment of the Chosen One. A "prince who is to come" would bring his army in and destroy both the city of Jerusalem and the temple.

Less than four decades after Jerusalem exterminated the Messiah, God exterminated Jerusalem. Titus, the princely son of Roman emperor Vespasian, besieged Jerusalem. Four months later, his army breached the walls, massacred the people, leveled much of the city, and destroyed the second temple. Prophecy given, prophecy fulfilled.

The Seventieth Week of Years Identified

Some of my favorite words in Scripture seem rather common and innocuous. But when you see them in context, they can be momentous. Earlier, I mentioned one of those words—"but." For instance, "The wages of sin is death, but the gift of God is eternal life in Christ Jesus our Lord" (Romans 6:23). Our future is hopeless because our sin has earned us death. But the gift of God! Everything changes with that one little conjunction. "For" gives us reasons, "so that" leads to purpose, and "therefore" offers application.

Now we come to another huge little word. Gabriel said, "Then he shall confirm a covenant with many for one week" (Daniel 9:27). There is a whole lot wrapped up in the temporal adverb "then." In fact, up until today, it's been nearly 2,000 years of "then" in that little word.

It is often difficult to nail down the timeline of biblical prophecy. There are certainly those times when God makes it clear, like when Gabriel told Daniel that the ram would be Medo-Persia and the goat would be Greece. But often, looking forward to the fulfillment of prophecy is like looking at a mountain range. Dr. Rick, my collaborator on this book, lives near Denver at the foot of the majestic Rockies. He is an avid photographer and often hikes in the mountains to find his shots. There have been many times when he has seen what looks like back-to-back rises or peaks. But upon reaching the top of the near one, he is surprised to find that the second peak is actually miles away.

That is what we find hidden in Gabriel's "then." We assume a short time frame to the word because that is its most common usage. However, when we look at the context, we quickly discover that the next peak must be a long way off. This is evident when we hold back on our urge to focus on the words "one week" and instead consider the confirming of the covenant. Who is the "he" of Gabriel's words, and what is the "covenant"? Those words do not at all fit the context of AD 70 and Titus's destruction of Jerusalem. In fact, there is no time, even during the brutal reign of Antiochus IV, that this description fits. Therefore, we must accept that it is yet to come.

The Ruler Confirms a Covenant for Seven Years

So who is the "he" in this passage? To understand this, let's look at the full text of the verse:

> Then he shall confirm a covenant with many for
> one week;

but in the middle of the week
he shall bring an end to sacrifice and offering.
And on the wing of abominations shall be one who
    makes desolate,
even until the consummation, which is determined,
is poured out on the desolate (verse 27).

Remember, the context of Gabriel's words is a message for the Jewish people. The fact that there is sacrifice going on tells us two things: First, Jerusalem has been reestablished and is inhabited by Jews. Second, as we saw earlier, the temple has been rebuilt. The former has been true for just over 75 years, formally beginning in 1948. The latter has yet to occur. Because of what we've already learned about the beasts and the temples, it is no big leap to recognize that the "he" is speaking of the Antichrist. He will make a covenant with the Jews at the beginning of the tribulation that will include the rebuilding of the temple.

When Daniel 9:27 speaks of "covenant," we come to another amazing word. The word that the prophet uses here is הִגְבִּיר, *hegbir*, which means "to increase, enhance, amplify." If I were to ask my son to turn up the volume on the television, I would use the word *hegbir*. What this tells us is that this is not an ordinary covenant. It is not just a promise of peace, or a commitment to the normalization of relationships with other countries. What the Antichrist will offer to Israel is something much bigger than that. It will be so turned up that the Jewish people can't help but sign on the dotted line. What is it that could be that momentous? A temple.

When the beast paves the way for the temple to be reestablished, the Jews will join the rest of the world in celebrating him. After the incredible instability following the mysterious disappearance of all the followers of Jesus in the rapture and an unsuccessful attack on Israel by Russia, Iran, Turkey, and others during the Ezekiel 38 War, a man of peace who can bring stability and unity to the globe will immediately garner the allegiance of most nations.

The Ruler Sets Himself Up as God for the Final Half-Week

The peace and harmony brought by the Antichrist will last only for so long—three-and-a-half years, to be precise. Gabriel warns, "In the middle of the week he shall bring an end to sacrifice and offering" (verse 27). The Antichrist will tire of playing the kumbaya game. His true agenda will be enacted. Satan has always wanted the worship of mankind. Now he has his opportunity by empowering the Antichrist so that the world will worship him through his proxy. The Antichrist will go along with it, believing he deserves humanity's adoration. Most of the world will jump on board the worship of this man, but, as we've seen before, the Jews just can't seem to let go of their monotheism. Like Antiochus IV before him, the Antichrist will unleash terror on the Jews and will profane the temple by making it a place to worship him. Sacrifices and offerings to God will cease, and the beast will place an image of himself in the Holy of Holies to be worshipped.

As we saw in an earlier chapter, the Antichrist will be aided in this endeavor by the false prophet, who will insist that everyone worship his master. This servant of Satan will ensure that loyalty to the Antichrist is demonstrated by causing all people "both small and great, rich and poor, free and slave, to receive a mark on their right hand or on their foreheads, and that no one may buy or sell except one who has the mark or the name of the beast, or the number of his name" (Revelation 13:16-17). What is that number? 666.

Jesus spoke of this violent time to His disciples, saying, "'When you see the "abomination of desolation," spoken of by Daniel the prophet, standing in the holy place' (whoever reads, let him understand), 'then let those who are in Judea flee to the mountains'" (Matthew 24:15-16). Paul said that the Antichrist's action will be unexpected, taking people off guard. He wrote in warning, "When they say, 'Peace and safety!' then sudden destruction comes upon them, as labor pains upon a pregnant woman. And they shall not escape" (1 Thessalonians 5:3).

Praise the Lord that those who have given their lives to Jesus will not be around for the insanity of the tribulation. Remember, even as all this political intrigue is taking place, natural disasters ordained through the judgments of God are wiping out hundreds of millions of people. But there is even more going on than that. In the spiritual realm, there are battles being fought. And that is where Daniel's next vision takes us.

CHAPTER 10

THE UNSEEN WARFARE

DANIEL 10

A young computer programmer is working in his cubicle. His attention is drawn to someone stepping into his workspace. It's the FedEx man with an envelope. The programmer, Thomas Anderson, signs for his package, opens it, and finds a phone. Immediately, the device rings, startling Anderson. Nervously, he answers. On the other end is a voice he recognizes.

"Morpheus?"

This brief phone encounter launches a series of events that ultimately lead the programmer into the presence of the mystery man from the phone call. As they talk, Morpheus offers Anderson a choice in the form of two pills. If the young man chooses the red pill, all will be revealed of what Morpheus calls the Matrix. The blue pill, however, will erase Anderson's memory, allowing him to go back to his former life, blissfully ignorant of reality. Anderson chooses the red pill, which is the beginning of his transformation into the sci-fi hero Neo, and how Hollywood has managed to make well in excess of $3 billion in worldwide sales from the four-movie Matrix franchise.

I couldn't help but think of this movie as I approached Daniel 10. In *The Matrix*, people live their lives quite normally, contentedly ignorant that there is so much more to reality than what meets the eye. What they think is their day-to-day life is simply a computer program designed to keep them distracted while an intelligent computer system feeds off humanity as an energy food source. In other words, they think they know reality, but there is so much more to this world than what their five senses can pick up.

This is not far from the truth. While there is no Matrix, there is a whole world surrounding us that most people are completely unaware of.

"Wait, Amir, how can you be sure there is no Matrix? Have you ever taken the red pill?" No, I haven't, and based on your question, I would highly recommend you cancel your Netflix subscription because it doesn't seem to be doing you any favors. And while I haven't taken the red pill, I have read the red letters of Jesus' words in my Bible. In fact, I've read all the black-lettered words too. And what they tell me is that there is a spiritual world surrounding us in which angelic and demonic forces are doing battle. God's Word also makes it clear that what happens in the spiritual realm can often have great ramifications in our natural world.

The Enemy and His Army

How do we account for all the chaos in the world? If God created everything perfectly, why is there so much anger, hatred, deception, and misery, and why does it all seem to continuously be getting worse? People may blame a person or a culture, a government or a legal system. But to do so would be to focus on the symptom rather than the disease. There is one entity in creation who has done everything in his power to lead the nations into sin, to destroy the people of Israel, and to turn humanity away from God. He is the one who Paul calls "the god of this age" (2 Corinthians 4:4), and who Jesus refers to as "a liar and the father of lies" (John 8:44 ESV).

We have heard him referred to by many names: Lucifer, Satan, the devil, the enemy, and others. But despite him being "the god of this age," he is neither omniscient (all-knowing), omnipresent (everywhere at once), nor omnipotent (all-powerful). Those qualities belong to the God of all ages, the one true God, alone. But that doesn't mean that we should underestimate Satan. He is powerful and clever, and Jude compared those who arrogantly go up against Satan and his minions to irrational "brute beasts" (Jude 10). Still, our enemy is a created being. As with all that is created, he is less than his Creator. He is less powerful and less wise, and he is subject to the One who formed him and gave him life.

The devil is not alone in his work. He has an army of minions who, like him, have fallen from their exalted position as servants of the Almighty. And in their role as lackeys of the enemy, they are committed to carrying out his unholy purposes. Their goal is to suppress the truth of God, to exchange that truth for a lie, and to deny all that God says is best. Chief amongst their targets is the salvation that is found in Jesus the Messiah. They seek to suppress the knowledge of the hope that God offers so that the devil can take with him as many as possible to eternal separation from the Lord. Why would he do that? Because he knows that God "desires all men to be saved and to come to the knowledge of the truth" (1 Timothy 2:4). It hurts God to see His creation making choices that will have negative eternal consequences. Causing that sorrow is all the power that vanquished foe still has.

It is in this intersection between the supernatural and the natural that spiritual warfare takes place. Satan has his spiritual horde constantly influencing decisions and actions in the natural world, while God allows His angels to fight those actions on the side of good. This is the battlefield that Paul referred to when he wrote:

> Put on the whole armor of God, that you may be able
> to stand against the wiles of the devil. For we do not

wrestle against flesh and blood, but against principalities,
against powers, against the rulers of the darkness of this
age, against spiritual hosts of wickedness in the heavenly
places. Therefore take up the whole armor of God, that
you may be able to withstand in the evil day, and having
done all, to stand (Ephesians 6:11-13).

The heavenly places are those spiritual realms where the battles
between good and evil forces are continuously taking place. The
effects of those skirmishes influence governments, corporations, social
media platforms, religious groups, the press, and each one of us. In
his fourth vision beginning in chapter 10, Daniel is confronted with
the world beyond touch, taste, smell, sight, and hearing. Then for
the final three chapters of his book, he will walk us through what he
witnesses in the unseen realm of this final vision.

The Time of the Vision

Daniel began by situating his next vision. He wanted to ensure
his readers knew the timing of the event and the strange circumstances leading up to the revelation. He began by writing, "In the
third year of Cyrus king of Persia a message was revealed to Daniel,
whose name was called Belteshazzar" (Daniel 10:1).

The year was 536 BC, and it had been less than three years since
Cyrus had put an end to stand-in King Belshazzar and the much-
weakened Babylonian Empire. It had also been just a couple of years
since the Persian king had issued a decree announcing God's command to him "to build Him a house at Jerusalem which is in Judah"
(2 Chronicles 36:23). Included in that decree was an invitation for
any of the Jews who wanted to return to Jerusalem from their exile
to feel free to do so.

This occurred in a time of transition and upheaval for the Jews.
There would have been great optimism in the air, and possibly some

division between those who chose to risk all by going back to their decimated capital city and those who decided to stay in the land of exile. Daniel likely had little choice in what he would do. Whether by divine will or royal fiat, the old prophet and court-wise man remained where he could best serve his God and his king.

The Prophet Is Shaken

We now come to another place where I am forced to wonder what the translators of the King James and the New King James Versions were doing. I am a big fan of the NKJV and I use it for all my teaching, but there are a number of places in Daniel where I disagree with their decisions. The second part of verse 1 reads this way in the NKJV:

> The message was true, but the appointed time was long;
> and he understood the message, and had understanding
> of the vision.

The problem here is that the phrase "the appointed time was long" is not in the Hebrew text. Instead, you will find the Hebrew word צָבָא (*tsava*), which means "military service or military campaign." As a result, the ESV translates the phrase, "The word was true, and it was a great conflict." The NIV words it, "Its message was true and it concerned a great war." Both of these options much better communicate what the text is actually saying.

The revelation to Daniel of a great conflict of some kind was very disturbing. It shook the prophet to such an extent that he went into a three-week period of mourning. "I ate no pleasant food, no meat or wine came into my mouth, nor did I anoint myself at all, till three whole weeks were fulfilled" (verse 3). Because of the source of the vision, Daniel had no doubt as to its truthfulness. He also understood that it had to do with great amounts of warfare. What he didn't know was its meaning. Who were the actors in this great military drama? When would this take place? How do the Jews fit into this vision?

He mourned. He prayed. He waited.

In His time, God answered.

The Messenger Arrives

It had been three weeks since the vision. Three weeks of Daniel expecting God to show up. But after 21 days of anticipation, the great interpreter of other people's dreams had nada when it came to his own. Following the wisdom of "When all else fails, take a walk," Daniel cleaned himself up and headed outdoors.

Because of his age and position, it isn't surprising that he had an entourage around him. Those of you who live by a river know that there are few places more beautiful to enjoy God's creation than by the water's edge. Thus, it was as Daniel strolled along the banks of the great Tigris with his assistants nearby that the Lord's messenger arrived.

> Now on the twenty-fourth day of the first month, as I was by the side of the great river, that is, the Tigris, I lifted my eyes and looked, and behold, a certain man clothed in linen, whose waist was girded with gold of Uphaz! His body was like beryl, his face like the appearance of lightning, his eyes like torches of fire, his arms and feet like burnished bronze in color, and the sound of his words like the voice of a multitude (verses 4-6).

Notice the number of times Daniel used the word "like." I feel for him. He was doing his best to describe the indescribable. This is a hallmark of apocalyptic literature. In Daniel, "like" is found 28 times. In Revelation, John used it 63 times. But the king of "like" is poor Ezekiel, who needed 92 uses of the word to describe the four creatures, the wheels, the seraphim, and all the other elements of his visions.

Daniel saw this incredible personage coming toward him, but the men who were with him saw nothing. However, they felt something:

> I, Daniel, alone saw the vision, for the men who were with me did not see the vision; but a great terror fell upon them, so that they fled to hide themselves. Therefore I was left alone when I saw this great vision, and no strength remained in me; for my vigor was turned to frailty in me, and I retained no strength. Yet I heard the sound of his words; and while I heard the sound of his words I was in a deep sleep on my face, with my face to the ground (verses 7-9).

Imagine standing by a river with some friends, when suddenly someone in your group jumps up and stares at the sky. At first you think it's a joke, but then you see the fear in his eyes. What would you do? We know what Daniel's companions did. They ran.

Daniel remained, but his body was incapacitated. He couldn't have joined the flight of his friends even if he wanted to. He dropped to his knees, then all fours, before finally stretching flat out with his face to the ground. He slipped into a strange world of slumber in which his body slept, but his mind was still able to register the words being spoken around him.

A similar collapse took place with John on the Isle of Patmos. When confronted with the man who had appeared to him, the disciple "fell at His feet as dead" (Revelation 1:17). What roused him? Exactly what brought Daniel back to his feet. It was a touch.

John felt the hand of the man upon whom he had leaned at the Last Supper. It was his friend, his teacher, his Savior. For Daniel, however, the voice that accompanied the touch he felt was not that of God, but of a messenger who was bringing God's words to him.

> Suddenly, a hand touched me, which made me tremble on my knees and on the palms of my hands. And he said to me, "O Daniel, man greatly beloved, understand the words that I speak to you, and stand upright, for I have now been sent to you." While he was speaking this word to me, I stood trembling (Daniel 10:10-11).

"Man greatly beloved"! I get a little misty when I read those words. Here was this old man who had lived a long life of servitude. He had done his best to do the right thing. When opportunities arose for him to make a stand for God, he had done so, even at the risk of his own life. He was probably fairly confident that he was okay with the Lord, but you just never know for sure.

Then came those words: "O Daniel, man greatly beloved." What I wouldn't give to someday hear "O Amir, man greatly beloved." I hope I will, particularly at the bema seat judgment when those in the church receive their reward. But Satan has a way of sneaking into our thoughts to make us doubt our service to the Lord and His love for us.

Daniel Prayed, God Responded

"The effective, fervent prayer of a righteous man avails much" (James 5:16). So said James, Jesus' brother and leader of the Jerusalem church. There is a wonderful cause and effect to prayer. When Jerusalem was about to experience the onslaught of Assyria's King Sennacherib, Judah's King Hezekiah prayed. God then sent Isaiah to Hezekiah to tell him, "Thus says the LORD God of Israel, 'Because you have prayed to Me against Sennacherib king of Assyria, this is the word which the LORD has spoken concerning him'" (Isaiah 37:21-22). The prophet then went on to share the promise of God's deliverance of the city.

The same relationship between prayer and response can be seen with the priest Zechariah. He and his wife Elizabeth were unable to have children, so they prayed fervently. The Lord heard their prayers and sent Gabriel with a message, saying, "Do not be afraid, Zechariah, for your prayer has been heard, and your wife Elizabeth will bear you a son, and you shall call his name John" (Luke 1:13 ESV). The prayers of this couple led to the birth of John the Baptist, the forerunner of the Messiah.

I depend on that cause-and-effect relationship to prayer. Daily, so many people pray for me and for the Behold Israel ministry. All of us on the team are truly humbled by such love and faithfulness. Great things are accomplished not because we are great people. Instead, we are just normal believers like you who can do great things because of the power of prayer.

This new and visually awe-inspiring messenger told Daniel that because the prophet had prayed, he had been sent by God:

> He said to me, "Do not fear, Daniel, for from the first day that you set your heart to understand, and to humble yourself before your God, your words were heard; and I have come because of your words" (Daniel 10:12).

Daniel prayed, and the messenger was sent, but it took him a long time to arrive.

The Reason for the Messenger's Delay

Remember that wonderful little word "but"? So often it refers to a positive change in circumstance. But not always. As it found its way into the angelic message, the "but" meant a delay:

> But the prince of the kingdom of Persia withstood me twenty-one days; and behold, Michael, one of the chief princes, came to help me, for I had been left alone there with the kings of Persia. Now I have come to make you

understand what will happen to your people in the latter days, for the vision refers to many days yet to come (verses 13-14).

Twenty-one days passed from the time God heard the need to the time the answer came. Why the delay? Many of us find ourselves asking God that same question. How many times have you prayed, then waited for God's response? And waited. And waited. Days turn into weeks, which turn into months, which become years. When that happens, it's tempting to conclude that your prayers have fallen on deaf heavenly ears. But when we stop to consider it, we know that's not who God is. If there is a delay, there must be a reason.

Sometimes God delays because we are not ready to receive the answer. Maybe there needs to be a maturing in us, spiritually or emotionally. He knows us better than we know ourselves. Thus, we can be assured that the time of His answer is always the best time for us, even when it doesn't feel that way.

Other times there are attitudes, relationships, or behaviors that we need to deal with before God is ready to say yes. When the Israelites were being oppressed by the Egyptians, they cried out for a redeemer. Moses, believing he was that redeemer and that the time had come for him to step forward, struck down an Egyptian who was oppressing one of his countrymen. He "supposed that his brethren would have understood that God would deliver them by his hand, but they did not understand" (Acts 7:25). They thought they were ready. Moses thought they were ready. But God knew they weren't yet ready.

Sometimes the delay is due to circumstances not quite being right. God may still be moving all the pieces into place. He is answering, but it is a work in progress. Other times, God is testing us. As we saw with Shadrach, Meshach, and Abednego, faith grows best in fiery places. And there are times when the answer is coming, but it hasn't arrived yet. Think of waiting for a package to come. You received an email that it shipped, but now you must patiently endure the travel gap between sending and delivering.

But there is one more reason for delay to occur, and it is one that we don't necessarily expect. This is the reason that Daniel found himself in God's waiting room. Sometimes our answer is interrupted due to spiritual warfare.

The Spiritual Battle to Suppress Prophecy

There are doctrinal areas where I feel on solid footing. Biblical prophecy is one of those. The gospel and the plan of salvation is another of my confident subjects, as is the inspiration and inerrancy of Scripture. In fact, in most topics, I feel very comfortable in my level of knowledge and understanding. The reason for my assurance is because I am a student of the Bible. And typically, the level of my doctrinal security is commensurate with the amount of God's Word devoted to the subject. A lot of Scripture, a lot of confidence. A little Scripture, much less conviction.

As I approach this passage on spiritual warfare, I will be telling you what I believe. However, because this passage is the only place we get this kind of detail on this specific aspect of the spiritual realm, any dogmatism I sometimes express will now be replaced by "what seems right."

Daniel's time of praying and fasting was the same duration as the messenger's delay. The holdup had to do with "the prince of the kingdom of Persia." Who or what is this prince? It appears that there are angels who are designated to specific countries. In this chapter, we learn that there is a prince of Persia (verse 13), a prince of Greece (verse 20), and "Michael your prince" (verse 21), who we can assume to be the prince of Israel. Isn't it interesting that Michael, the chief of all angels, has been assigned to Israel? This is one more proof that God has not rejected the Jews. They continue to be His people, and He puts them under the care of His best protectors.

This messenger angel, possibly Gabriel, had been battling against the angel of Persia. Once he completes his mission with Daniel, he will rejoin that battle. When that happens, both sides will be reinforced—Persia by Greece, and the messenger by Michael.

What did this battle look like? I wish we knew. It sounds fascinating, and a little bit scary. The fiction writer in me thinks of all the exciting scenarios I could create within its parameters. But this is nonfiction, and we need to keep our interpretation on the straight and narrow. What we can ascertain is the purpose for the warfare. The prince of Persia did not want Daniel to hear or know God's plan for His people. Isn't it interesting how the more things change, the more they stay the same? This very same battle is taking place even now as I write this, 2,500 years after Daniel's vision.

There are demonic spirits today that do not want anyone to know God's plan for Israel, the church, or the nations. In most churches, it is rare for a prophetic sermon to be preached. So many pastors who consistently teach on other Bible doctrines treat Bible prophecy like it's a chocolate sundae at a keto convention.

It's understandable, though, because only a handful of seminaries today have any courses on prophecy. And when it comes to Bible tools, aids to understanding prophecies and their fulfillment are few and far between. In the largest Bible software program available, you have to purchase the most expensive premium version before you will find a book on prophecy. Eight thousand books are included in that ultimate upgrade, only two of which are prophetic in nature.

You won't find much information in most study Bibles either, because the vast majority of biblical scholars who contribute to these tools do not interpret prophecy from a literal perspective. The excellent Jeremiah Study Bible, Ryrie Study Bible, and Tony Evans Study Bible are welcome exceptions to the allegorical and symbolic interpretive riffraff that is found in most.

Through Daniel's fervent prayers and the angel's determined fight, the messenger was finally united with his messengee. He told the prophet that his goal was to help him "understand what will happen to your people in the latter days, for the vision refers to many days yet to come" (verse 14). What Daniel will hear will not take place anytime soon. This has nothing to do with the Jews who have returned to Israel, nor will it deal with anything else during Daniel's lifetime. It is for "the latter days," a phrase repeated 15 times in the Bible. Typically, it refers to the end times. Isaiah said that a major geological shifting of the mountains in Jerusalem will occur "in the latter days" (Isaiah 2:2). Through Ezekiel, God prophesied to Gog that "it will be in the latter days that I will bring you against My land" (Ezekiel 38:16). Hosea spoke of the day of Israel's ultimate return to the Lord "in the latter days" (Hosea 3:5). These are all events that are yet to occur.

The Old Prophet Is Overwhelmed

We don't know the reaction the messenger expected from Daniel, but it was likely not the one he received.

> When he had spoken such words to me, I turned my face toward the ground and became speechless. And suddenly, one having the likeness of the sons of men touched my lips; then I opened my mouth and spoke, saying to him who stood before me, "My lord, because of the vision my sorrows have overwhelmed me, and I have retained no strength. For how can this servant of my lord talk with you, my lord? As for me, no strength remains in me now, nor is any breath left in me" (Daniel 10:15-17).

The messenger had tried to encourage Daniel with his words, telling the prophet not to be afraid and letting him know that God Himself had dispatched an answer to his prayer right away. But the old man was having none of it. Overwhelmed by the vision he had seen and by the messenger's words, Daniel turned his face back to the ground and shut his mouth. I have a friend whose Miniature Schnauzer tucks herself into a corner and faces the wall every time she goes to the vet. It's as if she is thinking, *If I can't see them, then they can't see me. And if they can't see me, then maybe this will all just go away.*

It doesn't work for the dog, and it didn't work for Daniel. The compassionate messenger understood that the old man was overwhelmed, and he stepped in to help:

> Then again, the one having the likeness of a man touched me and strengthened me. And he said, "O man greatly beloved, fear not! Peace be to you; be strong, yes, be strong!" So when he spoke to me I was strengthened, and said, "Let my lord speak, for you have strengthened me" (verses 18-19).

I am so thankful that God understands my weaknesses. He is not upset at my limitations. As the Creator, He put me together and knows better than I do what I can easily accomplish and what I'm going to struggle with. That is why He reaches into my life and strengthens me. Sometimes it is through prayer, and sometimes through His Word. Often it is through a friend or a pastor. Other resources the Lord uses are the tremendous number of letters, emails, and messages that I receive every day from faithful followers of Behold Israel. I can't tell you the times that just the right words are written by a person whom I've never met and who is living in a place I've never been. The result will be like hitting a light switch, and I'll turn from tired and discouraged to energized and joyful. That is the "one another" living that Jesus and the New Testament writers emphasized. God placed us in fellowship with each other so that we can encourage one another, support one another, strengthen one another, and, most of all, love one another.

Once Daniel had been strengthened and presumably was back on his feet, the messenger spoke:

> Do you know why I have come to you? And now I must return to fight with the prince of Persia; and when I have gone forth, indeed the prince of Greece will come. But I will tell you what is noted in the Scripture of Truth. (No one upholds me against these, except Michael your prince.) (verses 20-21).

I find it interesting that the messenger began with a question that he never answered. Instead, he went right into what was next on his agenda. But because we are all about context, we are not going to deal with that in this chapter. Even though these verses conclude chapter 10, they even more so open chapter 11. So we'll save them for then.

THE LONG JOURNEY TO THE ANTICHRIST

DANIEL 11

We all have our preferences in life. Some people like warm weather, and some like cold. There are those who prefer little to no meat in their diets, and others who don't feel it is a real meal unless some formerly breathing animal is involved. And there are those who love history, and those who would rather hike up Mount Everest barefoot than read an ancient account of long-dead kings and past battles.

If you are of the latter category, let me give you fair warning. This is the most history-ish of history chapters in the entire Bible. However, I would still encourage you to read it. The dual prophecy fulfillment it contains makes it well worth it. However, if I notice you skimming a little here and there, I won't be offended. Daniel 11 has likely been the source of more naps during seminary lectures than any other chapter in Scripture.

So why do we study it? Because everything that God has included in the Bible contains information He has deemed important for us to know. In this chapter, the Lord speaks through His messenger to tell us significant information about our past and the world's future. That alone makes it of great interest.

On the other side of the history coin, for those of you who are like me and love to delve into the past, this is a fascinating chapter that looks into a window of bygone years that is rarely opened. But remember, our past was still Daniel's future, which makes this portion of his book that much more amazing. Imagine me describing for you the next series of Israeli prime ministers up through the year 2250. That is akin to the supernatural feat the messenger of chapter 11 pulls off.

"Wait, Amir, you're contradicting yourself now! I've heard you say we are in the last generation before the rapture, but now you're talking about prime ministers for the next two hundred and more years." Relax, my dear friend. Yes, I believe the rapture is imminent. Yes, I believe we are in the last generation. I am giving a hypothetical illustration designed to highlight the miraculous nature of this chapter. In the messenger's words, we will find a timeline of how God has ruled over the affairs of Gentile countries for the purpose of carrying out His plans for the nation of Israel. Then, as a bonus, we'll also get a glimpse of how He plans to continue His work through today and into our future.

But first, we need to take a brief look at world history as it relates to Israel.

The Assyrian Empire

During the period of Israel's united kingdom under the rulership of Kings Saul, David, and Solomon, we don't read about any of the other world powers besides Egypt. They were around, but they were also irrelevant to God's work with Israel. But once the kingdom divided into the northern nation of Israel and the southern nation of Judah, we begin to learn about the significant empires that are developing in the area.

Located to the northeast of Israel and Judah were the Assyrians. They were a ruthless, violent people. It is no wonder that Jonah ran the other way when God told him to go preach repentance in the Assyrian capital of Nineveh. In the prophet's mind, the best thing that could happen to Israel was for the Ninevites to be on the receiving end of a heavy dose of God's judgment. When this vicious people responded to the prophet's message with repentance, the unexpected success of his mission sent Jonah into a depressive tailspin.

The Assyrians were originally friendly with the northern Israelites. However, they soon began to sour on them. King Tiglath-Pileser invaded the northern kingdom of Israel and carried a bunch of the people off to exile. Then in 722 BC, after a three-year siege, Tiglath-Pileser's son Shalmaneser took the capital city of Samaria and deported the rest of the northern kingdom's Israelites. This was all part of God's plan of judgment against the vile, idol-worshipping rebels. He had warned them through the prophets that He would do it, then He did it.

About a decade passed before King Sennacherib of Assyria, likely the grandson of Tiglath-Pileser, decided to have a go at the southern kingdom of Judah. It didn't end well. Hezekiah prayed, God acted, and the Assyrian king lost 175,000 of his soldiers in one night. That'll leave a sizable gap in any army. He hurried back home, where he was soon assassinated by two of his sons. Couldn't have happened to a nicer guy.

Then the glory of the Assyrian Empire began to fade. As it did, a new kingdom moved into ascendancy.

The Babylonian Empire

We've already dealt with the rise of the Babylonian Empire in an earlier chapter. In 612 BC, King Nabopolassar stomped Nineveh, effectively ending the empire. Then in 605 BC, crown prince Nebuchadnezzar killed off any pesky remainders of the Assyrians at the Battle of Carchemish. That same year, Nebuchadnezzar ascended to his deceased father's throne, taking the reins of what had become the new biggest, baddest bully on the block.

For Daniel and his peers, Babylon was their generation's empire. He was able to watch from the inside the ascendancy and decline of the kingdom Nebuchadnezzar built. After that great king had exited the scene, the power of the bloodline began to thin. Sooner than anyone could have expected, it was gone.

The Messenger Transitions to His Message

Moving forward, we need to begin with those final verses of Daniel 10 that we put off to this chapter. They combine with the first verse of chapter 11 to form one thought:

> Then he said, "Do you know why I have come to you? And now I must return to fight with the prince of Persia; and when I have gone forth, indeed the prince of Greece will come. But I will tell you what is noted in the Scripture of Truth. (No one upholds me against these, except Michael your prince. Also in the first year of Darius the Mede, I, even I, stood up to confirm and strengthen him.)" (Daniel 10:20–11:1).

As we mentioned before, the messenger presented a question, then declined to answer it.

"Know why I'm here?"

"No. Tell me."

"So, here's why I'm leaving…"

The messenger said he had to go because of a battle in which the spiritual princes of Persia and Greece were fighting against Michael and himself. Then he shifted from spiritual beings to a flesh-and-blood one, saying that after Darius overcame Belshazzar and quashed the

Babylonians in the first year of his reign, the messenger had strengthened "him." The question is, who is "him"?

There are two options. First, it could be that the messenger supported Darius. Grammatically, this is the best choice. Maybe he's saying that as part of God's punishment against the Babylonian Empire, it was this angel who helped to ensure that Belshazzar and his army were drunk and unprepared for the invasion by Darius. Or maybe to fulfill God's plan laid out in Nebuchadnezzar's statue dream and Daniel's ram-and-goat vision, the Lord sent this angel to protect Darius from harm as he was establishing his leadership.

The other option is that the "him" this angel strengthened was Michael the Archangel. This interpretation would see Michael and this angel teaming up to protect Israel from hostility. In a time of transition from the Babylonian to the Persian Empire, there would be numerous opportunities for Israel's enemies to plot revenge or act on personal grudges. Haman's genocidal hatred of the Jews only decades later, as told in the book of Esther, is an example of the potential harm one powerful man can cause when he has a personal vendetta against God's people.

Unfortunately, we don't know for sure who "him" is. Either possibility fits, and both options demonstrate the same truth. God sees His people, and He takes care of them. This protection is taking place in the physical realm as well as the spiritual.

The Persian Achaemenid Empire Is Born

The Medes were originally allies of Nabopolassar and Babylon back during their defeat of the Assyrians. But when that alliance ended, the Medes began looking south for friendship. Below them were the Persians, who lived in what is now modern-day Iran. A close partnership formed between the Medes and Persians, and their joint empire grew. But the Medes weren't as advanced culturally as the Persians, and eventually Medo-Persia became just Persia. The hard-to-spell name Achaemenid is simply a dynastic indicator of the Persian Empire based on an ancestor of Cyrus the Great, who was named Achaemenes. This is the combined empire that marched into Babylon that fateful evening when the hand wrote on the wall.

As the messenger began his explanation of Daniel's vision, he said, "And now I will tell you the truth: Behold, three more kings will arise in Persia, and the fourth shall be far richer than them all; by his strength, through his riches, he shall stir up all against the realm of Greece" (verse 2). These four kings are easily identifiable as Cambyses (529–522 BC), Pseudo-Smerdis (522–521 BC), and Darius I Hystaspes (521–486 BC), followed by the uber-wealthy Xerxes I (486–465 BC), also known as Ahasuerus.

Chances are that when you read that list you didn't find yourself saying, "Oh yeah, Pseudo-Smerdis! One of my favorite Persian kings!" However, it is possible that the name Xerxes may have sounded familiar. This monarch had a wife, Vashti, who publicly embarrassed him, so he went looking for a new queen. After a drawn-out search, he settled on a Jewish orphan named Esther.

The messenger had said to Daniel that this fourth king would stir up people against Greece. Xerxes was a warrior and a conqueror. Greece had become wealthy, and the Persian king wanted some of their stuff for himself. He invaded and was able to take control of Athens. However, he couldn't hold it long term and was forced to retreat. Later, he gave an invasion of Greece a second shot, but this time he was repelled.

The Greeks bore the scars of the Persian invasions, and when they began to grow in power, they decided it was time to settle old scores. They traveled east, attacked Persia, and crushed their enemy. We've already heard of this battle, both in dream and interpretation. The arrogant ram of Daniel 8 was trampled by the swift and powerful Greek goat—Alexander the Great. Here, the angel described the coming scenario by saying,

Then a mighty king shall arise, who shall rule with great dominion, and do according to his will. And when he has arisen, his kingdom shall be broken up and divided toward the four winds of heaven, but not among his posterity nor according to his dominion with which he ruled; for his kingdom shall be uprooted, even for others besides these (verses 3-4).

This is another one of those amazing nexus points where we see the perfect meeting of the prophetic future in Daniel 8, the prophetic future in Daniel 11, and the world's recorded history. Sometimes we get so used to the perfect accuracy of the Bible that we forget how remarkable it is. What other book ever written about the future has 100 percent accuracy? Or maybe 50 percent? Do I hear 25 percent? I'm starting to feel like Abraham bargaining with God for the salvation of Sodom. There is nothing that has ever been written that comes even close.

Alexander was a powerful conqueror, but he died young. If you'll remember, he had no succession plan, so his kingdom was divided four ways between four of his generals. Cassander ruled over Macedonia and Greece. Lysimachus was given Thrace. Ptolemy I, the bodyguard of Alexander, took Egypt. And Seleucus ruled over Syria.

Because this is all ultimately about Israel, you can say goodbye to Cassander and Lysimachus. They're out west and are thus irrelevant to the angel's message. The focus now is the kingdom of the north, the Seleucids of Syria, and the kingdom of the south, the Ptolemies of Egypt. If you're able to picture in your mind Syria and Egypt on a map, you'll know what lies directly between the two: the nation of Israel.

The Kings of the North vs. the Kings of the South

Now we come to a portion of Scripture that is truly extraordinary. We are about to read a detailed history book that was written before any of the events actually took place. In fact, it is so accurate that liberal theologians tear their hair out trying to prove that this portion of Daniel was written centuries after the rest. But it wasn't. How could this be? Our God, who exists outside of time, had already seen these events take place. So as He gave the message to the angel to pass on to Daniel, He was only relaying what He had witnessed before it had happened. It's quite beautiful and amazing.

Let's walk through the angel's message of future history:

> The king of the South shall become strong, as well as one of his princes; and he shall gain power over him and have dominion. His dominion shall be a great dominion (verse 5).

Here we see the formation of the Seleucid and Ptolemaic Empires. Ptolemy I Soter was one of Alexander's powerful generals. This "king of the South" was able to establish himself and his empire quickly. It wasn't so for Seleucus I Nicator. He had to fight hard for his territory. At one point, another of Alexander's generals, Antigonus, decided he should have Babylon instead of Seleucus. He attacked Seleucus's home base and came close to taking it. But before he could gain a victory, Ptolemy I rode in from the south and helped to drive Antigonus out. Soon after, Seleucus I was solidly established in his newly built capital city of Seleucia, where he began to grow in his "great dominion," just as the messenger spelled out in verse 5.

About six decades passed. Kings came; kings went. There was a battle here, a murder there. You gain a little territory; you lose a little territory. The one constant was the friction between Egypt and Syria due to their proximity to each other. After years of sniping back and forth, the two empires had a brief moment of common sense. They realized they had two options. They could either continue with their endless and fruitless battling, or they could formalize an alliance. They decided to try the latter.

> At the end of some years they shall join forces, for the
> daughter of the king of the South shall go to the king of
> the North to make an agreement; but she shall not retain
> the power of her authority, and neither he nor his authority
> shall stand; but she shall be given up, with those who
> brought her, and with him who begot her, and with him
> who strengthened her in those times (verse 6).

Welcome to this week's episode of *As the Eastern Mediterranean Turns*. Ptolemy II Philadelphus of Egypt and Antiochus II Theos of Syria hated each other, which made them perfectly matched to become in-laws. To keep themselves from destroying each other's empires, and their own in the process, they determined to "make an agreement." Cross-empire treaties were often sealed by marriage, so a big ceremony was planned. Ptolemy's daughter, Berenice, was blessed with the great joy of getting wed to Antiochus. The only problem was that Antiochus already had a queen, Laodice.

To Laodice it was explained that sometimes you just have to take one for the team. But the queen wasn't really a "take one for the team" kind of gal. Laodice knew people who could, wink wink, get stuff done. Chances are that if Berenice had read Daniel before her nuptials, she would have become a runaway bride. Soon, Berenice, the "daughter of the king," lay dead on the ground. Needless to say, that put a hamper in her retaining "her authority." Not long after, Antiochus was mysteriously poisoned. Now in control of the kingdom, mother-of-the-year Laodice placed her son, Seleucus II Callinicus, on the throne.

Was this the end of the whole sordid incident? Not even close!

> From a branch of her roots one shall arise in his place,
> who shall come with an army, enter the fortress of the
> king of the North, and deal with them and prevail. And

> he shall also carry their gods captive to Egypt, with their
> princes and their precious articles of silver and gold; and
> he shall continue more years than the king of the North
> (verses 7-8).

Remember, the "her" refers to Berenice, not Laodice. The "branch" of the dead short-timer queen was her brother Ptolemy III Euergetes. He was none too happy with how Laodice had done his sister wrong, and he set out to avenge her. The Egyptian king invaded Syria, killed Laodice, and made off with a pile of "silver and gold" and other spoils of war. Seleucus II attempted a campaign to the south to get all his shiny stuff back but failed. A decade-and-a-half later, while preparing for a campaign in another part of Asia Minor, the northern king fell from his horse and died, allowing Ptolemy III, the king of the South, to "continue more years than the king of the North." The Bible is always 100 percent accurate, even down to the historical details.

> Also the king of the North shall come to the kingdom
> of the king of the South, but shall return to his own
> land. However his sons shall stir up strife, and assemble
> a multitude of great forces; and one shall certainly come
> and overwhelm and pass through; then he shall return to
> his fortress and stir up strife (verses 9-10).

As we just saw, Seleucus II, the king of the North, launched a southern invasion, but was sent packing. After he died, his son Seleucus III Soter took over. But this 18-year-old was kind of sickly and didn't live up to the gruff, thick-armed military leader standard expected by the generals of the army. So they killed him after just a couple years and replaced him with his brother, Antiochus III, another son of Seleucus II. In this new king, the military found the manly general they were looking for. He had a gift for "stir[ring] up strife" with his great forces, then "overwhelming" and "pass[ing] through" any cities he came across.

Judea Comes into Play

Over the next years, there was a whole lot of back-and-forth between Egypt and Syria. The South had a new leader, Ptolemy IV, installed sometime after Antiochus III came to power. Antiochus III decided to take a shot at him, and it was now that another group joined the Seleucids against the Egyptians. Daniel was told that "violent men of your people shall exalt themselves in fulfillment of the vision, but they shall fall" (verse 14). Some pro-Seleucid Jews joined forces with the king of the North. The last part of the messenger's words indicates that it didn't go so well for them. Antiochus got turned back before he could do too much damage to the Egyptian Empire.

On his way back home, Antiochus III remembered the loyalty of the Jews. It was then that the king stood "in the Glorious Land with destruction in his power" (verse 16). Judea was now content to be part of the Seleucid Empire.

Antiochus III was strong, but a little bored. Egypt was a pain, but the payoff of another invasion wasn't worth the cost. He needed a new challenge. After all, conquerors need to conquer. It was then that another nation piqued the king's interest. But he couldn't go after them as long as Egypt could develop into a threat to the south. So he figured it was time for another treaty based on wedded bliss.

> He shall also set his face to enter with the strength of his
> whole kingdom, and upright ones with him; thus shall he do.
> And he shall give him the daughter of women to destroy it;
> but she shall not stand with him, or be for him (verse 17).

Antiochus gave his daughter, Cleopatra I, to marry Ptolemy V in 197 BC. Now, for those of you whose minds immediately went to

Elizabeth Taylor being pulled into Rome by hundreds of slaves on a massive Sphinx land barge, I'm sorry to disappoint. You're thinking of Cleopatra VII, who didn't show up for another 150 years or so. This Cleopatra was not even Egyptian. She was a Syrian treaty wife, and once again, the marriage didn't work out. The peace through matrimony failed, but by that time, Antiochus III had moved on to his new target—Greece.

> After this he shall turn his face to the coastlands, and shall take many. But a ruler shall bring the reproach against them to an end; and with the reproach removed, he shall turn back on him. Then he shall turn his face toward the fortress of his own land; but he shall stumble and fall, and not be found (verses 18-19).

It started so well. The Seleucids moved in and conquered the isles on the coast of Asia Minor. Antiochus III was Athens-bound, but then Rome intervened. While they weren't the big, bad Roman Empire yet, they were still formidable enough to sway the fight. Antiochus III was soundly defeated. After returning home, he was trying to mollify his wounded pride by capturing some tribute in Persia when he was killed. As the messenger said, "He stumbled, he fell, and he was no longer found."

Antiochus III's son, Seleucus IV Philopator, took his place. He is known for little, save for imposing "taxes on the glorious kingdom" (verse 20). Under a financial burden from Rome after his dad's defeat, he looked for a source of income to refill his coffers. The Jews were that source, and the heavy taxes he levied were oppressive. His reign was short-lived, though, and he was assassinated by his chancellor after only nine years.

Antiochus IV—Foreshadow of the Antichrist

Imagine hearing the trombones and percussion of Star Wars' "The Imperial March" sounding as we begin this next section. The trumpets would then begin their punctuated notes, and you would see Antiochus IV Epiphanes striding in, dressed in a black helmet and mask. Cloaked with a black cape, his breathing would sound loudly over the music—inhale, exhale, inhale, exhale.

The fact that Darth Vader existed in a "galaxy far, far away" makes it highly unlikely that he and our new antihero, Antiochus IV, ever had a chance to meet. However, they both would fit well Gabriel's description to Daniel of the rise of "a vile person" (verse 21). Actually, Darth might look at this new Seleucid king and say, "Hey, I may be vile, but come on..."

They don't get much more contemptible than Antiochus IV, who we've already met back in chapter 8. The ram-killing goat had lost his horn. In its place grew four more horns, and from one of those four came a small, obnoxious, egotistical horn that turned out to be the forerunner of the Antichrist. In the same way that this book, *Discovering Daniel*, has an accompanying workbook that gives you more detail than we have space for here, chapter 11 now gives you additional facts that the prophet didn't include in Daniel 8.

Antiochus IV was not in line for the throne, but he usurped it from his young nephew, seizing "the kingdom by intrigue" (verse 21). A few years after he took power, the Egyptians declared war on the Seleucids. But Antiochus was up to the challenge. He turned the attack around and plowed through Egypt, causing the Ptolemaic armies to "be utterly swept away before him and broken" (verse 22 ESV). He stopped short of Alexandria, though, possibly due to threats by or respect for the Roman army. Turning his army around, he marched back home. On his way was Judea.

Antiochus IV was not a fan of the Jews. The whole matter of heavy taxation on the temple by his brother Seleucus IV had not gone well.

There was hatred by the Jews for the oppressive assessments, and there was resentment by many in the Seleucid court for how difficult those in Judea felt they had to make everything.

The level of Jewish hatred toward Antiochus IV grew even more when he began meddling in their religious affairs. Onias III was the high priest at the temple, but the king removed him. This "prince of the covenant" (verse 22) was deposed in favor of his brother, Jason. The story goes that Antiochus IV auctioned off the position of high priest to the man who promised the most tribute. Jason outbid his brother, so he got promoted in 175 BC. That worked well for the new high priest until a man named Menelaus outbid him four years later. Not quite the system that Moses had presented to the Israelites all those centuries before.

Over the next years, there were ongoing battles between Antiochus IV and the Ptolemaic Empire down in Egypt. Some resulted in victories, allowing the Seleucid king to return "to his land with great riches" (verse 28). However, in 168 BC, the evil king went against the Egyptians one time too many.

> At the appointed time he shall return and go toward the south; but it shall not be like the former or the latter. For ships from Cyprus shall come against him; therefore he shall be grieved, and return in rage against the holy covenant, and do damage (verses 29-30).

Antiochus IV went south into Egypt. What he didn't know was that sailing in from Cyprus was a contingent from Rome. The king made it all the way to Alexandria, when he was met by a Roman consul named Gaius Popillius Laenas. The man demanded that Antiochus turn around. The Seleucid ruler, in an attempt to save face, asked for time to consider Rome's order. But Laenas used his staff to draw a circle in the dirt around Antiochus and said, "Before you leave this circle, you must give me a reply for the Roman Senate." Antiochus had no choice but to give in. The Seleucid king retreated.

Terror Unleashed Against the Jews

Unfortunately for the Jews, they were once again on Antiochus's homeward route. Humiliated, he took out his fury on Jerusalem, venting his "rage against the holy covenant."

> He shall return and show regard for those who forsake the holy covenant. And forces shall be mustered by him, and they shall defile the sanctuary fortress; then they shall take away the daily sacrifices, and place there the abomination of desolation. Those who do wickedly against the covenant he shall corrupt with flattery; but the people who know their God shall be strong, and carry out great exploits. And those of the people who understand shall instruct many; yet for many days they shall fall by sword and flame, by captivity and plundering. Now when they fall, they shall be aided with a little help; but many shall join with them by intrigue. And some of those of understanding shall fall, to refine them, purify them, and make them white, until the time of the end; because it is still for the appointed time (verses 30-35).

Gathering his troops, Antiochus IV joined with many of the Hellenized Jews who were in the city. These were Jews who had given up on the Torah and the ways of God. They had become secularized and more concerned with joining in the sins of the rest of the world than with remaining holy and separate.

If you were to go to Tel Aviv today, you would find a population of modern-day Hellenized Jews. Immoral, spiritually apathetic, and corrupt, they remind me of the lost masses Paul describes as filled with all unrighteousness, sexual immorality, wickedness, covetousness, maliciousness; full of envy, murder, strife, deceit, evil-mindedness; they are whisperers, backbiters, haters of God, violent, proud, boasters, inventors of evil things, disobedient to parents, undiscerning, untrustworthy, unloving, unforgiving, unmerciful; who, knowing the righteous judgment of God, that those who practice such things are deserving of death, not only do the same but also approve of those who practice them (Romans 1:29-32).

In the same way that you find in these liberal Jews an active hatred for the religious and cultural traditions of Israel, Antiochus IV found a ready-made alliance of those who wanted to tear down the old systems as much as he did. And just as Antiochus IV is the forerunner of the coming Antichrist, the progressive left in Israel will readily accept and support the coming one-world ruler.

The terror brought upon Jerusalem was appalling. Here's how the Jewish historian Josephus described it:

> For Antiochus the unexpected conquest of the city, the looting, and the wholesale slaughter were not enough. His psychopathic tendency was exacerbated by resentment at what the siege had cost him, and he tried to force the Jews to violate their traditional codes of practice by leaving their infant sons uncircumcised and sacrificing pigs on the altar. These orders were universally ignored, and Antiochus had the most prominent recusants butchered.[15]

It is from this terrible time that we get a pivotal piece of information. Jesus told His disciples on the Mount of Olives, "'Therefore when you see the "abomination of desolation," spoken of by Daniel the prophet, standing in the holy place' (whoever reads, let him

understand), 'then let those who are in Judea flee to the mountains'"
(Matthew 24:15-16).

This "abomination of desolation" occurred when Antiochus stopped
the Mosaic sacrifices and replaced them with the slaughter of a pig
on the altar. He then erected a statue of Zeus in the temple, dedicating the building to the Greek god. When Daniel heard of the "abomination of desolation," it was a prophecy about the future. But for
Jesus, it was both past and possibly twice in the future. It had been
200 years since it had been fulfilled by Antiochus IV on the Temple
Mount just below where Jesus was teaching His disciples from the
Mount of Olives. But His words were "when you see," once again
making clear the possibility of a dual fulfillment of this biblical prophecy. In AD 70, the Roman general Titus would burn the temple to
the ground. There are conflicting accounts as to whether the conflagration was unintended or it was part of a full-blown desecration
carried out by the general. What is unquestionable, based on Jesus'
description, is that a final desolation will occur in the future, which
will be perpetrated by the Antichrist.

Because of what Antiochus did by his violent and disgusting
acts in the temple, a man named Judas Maccabeus led an uprising
against the Seleucid Empire. He was "strong" and carried out "great
exploits." Thousands were killed in the process, but the temple was
recaptured and purified.

Now we come to a shift. Before verse 36, the messenger was speaking primarily about Antiochus IV. But this next section through to
the end of the chapter are mainly centered on the Antichrist. I purposely use the words *primarily* and *mainly* because throughout, you
can often see shadows, if not full outlines, of both.

The Coming Antichrist—Horror Beyond Imagination

On October 7, 2023, around 3,000 Hamas terrorists and Palestinian civilians invaded Israel from Gaza. The atrocities they committed

shocked the world. Jews were indiscriminately shot in their homes, on the streets, at a music concert. Towns and kibbutzim were assaulted. Hamas terrorists and Palestinian civilians broke into houses and tortured and slaughtered entire families. Parents were brutalized and murdered in front of their children, and children were brutalized and murdered in front of their parents. Two mounds were found in one location. Upon examination, each contained the bodies of ten children who had been rounded up and burned alive. Hundreds of people who were not killed were kidnapped and taken across the border into Gaza to be kept as hostages. There, the women in particular endured the most brutal horrors—worse than you can ever imagine.

In the past, when I would read about the evil that would be perpetrated upon the Jews once the Antichrist broke faith with them, I thought about the Holocaust. But while what was done to the Jewish people of Europe by Hitler and his Nazis was overwhelming in its numbers and brutality, what took place on October 7 took sheer barbarism to a whole new level. Now I have a new standard in my mind when I think of the hell that will be unleashed on the Jews. I understand Jesus' call in Matthew 24:15-18 for them to run without even returning home to get their things. I feel the depth of His "woe" spoken to women who are pregnant and those who are nursing (verse 19). Hamas introduced the world to just how deep depravity can go.

When the Antichrist comes, he will take it even deeper.

I just can't imagine…

Our world today is in a freefall. Not only do we have wars and rumors of wars, but we have chaos throughout the nations of the world. There is a vacuum of strong, righteous leadership that can lead us toward peace, stability, and unity. The mindset of most of the world is toward globalism. It's "Why can't we just get along?" on a worldwide scale.

Nations used to look to America for stability, but now the

exclamation mark of America's strength has been replaced by a question mark. The abandonment of Afghanistan and a slow response to Ukraine's cry for help has left Western allies nervous, wondering if an alliance with the US means that they may have to stand alone when the going gets tough or the politics become inconvenient. It is true that they came to Israel's aid in a big way after the October 7 attack. But Ezekiel 38 makes it clear that there will come a day when Israel will no longer be able to count on America. Is there anyone who has the character and charisma to give people hope again? I believe there is. I believe that he is alive, and our generation will see his rise. But even though it's my generation who will see him, I don't plan on being one of them. Neither should you.

> Then the king shall do according to his own will: he shall exalt and magnify himself above every god, shall speak blasphemies against the God of gods, and shall prosper till the wrath has been accomplished; for what has been determined shall be done. He shall regard neither the God of his fathers nor the desire of women, nor regard any god; for he shall exalt himself above them all. But in their place he shall honor a god of fortresses; and a god which his fathers did not know he shall honor with gold and silver, with precious stones and pleasant things. Thus he shall act against the strongest fortresses with a foreign god, which he shall acknowledge, and advance its glory; and he shall cause them to rule over many, and divide the land for gain (Daniel 11:36-39).

This lawless one will come to power by speaking words of comfort and peace. But there will come a time when his true colors show. As the messenger in Daniel foretells, he will exalt himself and speak against God. He will demand fealty and will ruthlessly put down any rebellion against his rule. But the defiance will be minimal because the world will be duped, at least for a while. As Paul wrote:

> The coming of the lawless one is according to the working of Satan, with all power, signs, and lying wonders, and with all unrighteous deception among those who perish, because they did not receive the love of the truth, that they might be saved. And for this reason God will send them strong delusion, that they should believe the lie, that they all may be condemned who did not believe the truth but had pleasure in unrighteousness (2 Thessalonians 2:9-12).

There are groups who will stand against him. One will be those who realize the error of their ways and give themselves to Christ. When they are found, they will be executed, and they will join the rest of the tribulation martyrs in the security of God's throne. A second group will be the Jews who will flee to the mountains to escape the wrath of this modern-day Antiochus IV. But there are others—nations—that will not fully buy into this leader, and that is part of what the rest of this chapter talks about.

The Tribulation's Final Battle and a Possible Scenario

Up to this point, the history in this prophetic passage has been easy to trace for the most part by comparing the words of Daniel with the historical events between the Ptolemies and the Seleucids. Verse 36 transitioned us to the future Antichrist, leading us to details that are not quite as easy to nail down. Now that we are arriving at verse 40, it is impossible to find these events in any historical record because they have not yet occurred.

When this new king of the North establishes his throne, there are those who will not be ready to give up their own power. Battles will be fought. But because he carries the power of the prince of this world, the Antichrist will overcome.

> At the time of the end the king of the South shall attack him; and the king of the North shall come against him like a whirlwind, with chariots, horsemen, and with many ships; and he shall enter the countries, overwhelm them, and pass through. He shall also enter the Glorious Land, and many countries shall be overthrown; but these shall escape from his hand: Edom, Moab, and the prominent people of Ammon. He shall stretch out his hand against the countries, and the land of Egypt shall not escape. He shall have power over the treasures of gold and silver, and over all the precious things of Egypt; also the Libyans and Ethiopians shall follow at his heels. But news from the east and the north shall trouble him; therefore he shall go out with great fury to destroy and annihilate many. And he shall plant the tents of his palace between the seas and the glorious holy mountain; yet he shall come to his end, and no one will help him (Daniel 11:40-45)

What is going on here? I believe that what we are seeing in this passage is part of an incredibly sinister plot between Satan, the Antichrist, and the false prophet to try to stop the second coming of Christ. Now, let me say this as I begin to spell this out: We are fully in the area of speculation. I've always promised you that I'll tell you the difference between what is crystal clear in Scripture and what I'm surmising from my years of studying Scripture. There is plenty of wiggle room doctrinally in the passage above and in my particular scenario because the Bible doesn't say a whole lot either way. So take this not as what is, but as what may be. Okay, qualification done. Let's go.

The Antichrist will rule from Jerusalem. The Jews will have fled by this time, and he will have established Antichrist-worship in the temple. Not every nation will be on board with this, but what will he care? Because of his satanic backing, no one on earth will be powerful enough to mess with him. But those words "on earth" are a huge caveat. The Antichrist and false prophet serve Satan, and Satan knows the words of Scripture likely better than any theologian in any seminary on earth. He knows the tribulation will come to an end. He also recognizes that when it does, Jesus will come back, his two minions will be tossed into the lake of fire, and he's getting a 1,000-year hiatus from doing nasty things while he's locked away in the abyss. The only possible chance of preventing that collapse of his evil empire is to stop Jesus from taking over in Jerusalem. Satan knows he can't stop the second coming. But what if he is able to take out Jesus as soon as He gets here?

That's a big task. Satan managed to kill Jesus once, but that plan kind of backfired. Maybe if he did it a second time, it would stick. But to do that he would need an army—a huge army. The problem will be that the nations will have started to tire of his guy in Jerusalem. But what if he could turn their Antichrist-fatigue to his advantage? Imagine Satan comes up with a plan and reads the Antichrist and false prophet in on it. The Antichrist is a little miffed at first. Are there really people out there who don't like him? And, if there are, can't he just have the false prophet go and kill them? Eventually, though, he sees the big picture and comes on board.

The plan is implemented:

> The sixth angel poured out his bowl on the great river Euphrates, and its water was dried up, so that the way of the kings from the east might be prepared. And I saw three unclean spirits like frogs coming out of the mouth of the dragon, out of the mouth of the beast, and out of the mouth of the false prophet. For they are spirits of

demons, performing signs, which go out to the kings of the earth and of the whole world, to gather them to the battle of that great day of God Almighty...And they gathered them together to the place called in Hebrew, Armageddon (Revelation 16:12-14, 16).

The armies are gathering in Armageddon. But who are they gathering to fight? There is only one king in Jerusalem in that time, and that is the Antichrist. So the armies march on Jerusalem, just as the triumvirate of evil intended. Why would the Antichrist have joined in sending out the unclean froggy spirits to stir the people up to come and attack him? Again, he sees the big picture. He doesn't care how many Jerusalemites are killed. He just needs a ready army nearby. Zechariah prophesied about the violence and destruction that will occur when the army attacks the holy city:

> Behold, the day of the Lord is coming,
> and your spoil will be divided in your midst.
> For I will gather all the nations to battle against Jerusalem;
> the city shall be taken,
> the houses rifled,
> and the women ravished.
> Half of the city shall go into captivity,
> but the remnant of the people shall not be cut off
> from the city (Zechariah 14:1-2).

The combined armies of the nations will be enjoying their easy victory when an event will occur that will take them utterly off guard. But it is what Satan's three-part axis of evil had planned for. Satan understands the Scriptures, so he knows that at the Feast of Tabernacles, seven years after the advent of the tribulation, Jesus the Messiah will return. This time, He will come as Revelation's Lion of Judah rather than Isaiah's suffering servant. The nations, having been duped into coming to Jerusalem, will now be forced to align their militaries with the armies of Satan and the Antichrist to battle Jesus and the host that has returned with Him.

It was a bad plan from the beginning. Satan came up with it out of desperation, but he was doomed to fail. No one can go up against the Almighty Creator and win.

> I saw the beast, the kings of the earth, and their armies, gathered together to make war against Him who sat on the horse and against His army. Then the beast was captured, and with him the false prophet who worked signs in his presence, by which he deceived those who received the mark of the beast and those who worshiped his image. These two were cast alive into the lake of fire burning with brimstone. And the rest were killed with the sword which proceeded from the mouth of Him who sat on the horse. And all the birds were filled with their flesh.

> Then I saw an angel coming down from heaven, having the key to the bottomless pit and a great chain in his hand. He laid hold of the dragon, that serpent of old, who is the Devil and Satan, and bound him for a thousand years; and he cast him into the bottomless pit (Revelation 19:19–20:3).

As it was prophesied, so it was done. Is my scenario the right one? Maybe. But maybe not. What we do know for certain is that the Antichrist will rise. People will flock to him, including the Jews. Halfway into his seven-year stint, he will show his true colors. The Jews will run and hide, but most of the world will celebrate him. However, over time, the nations will sour against him. At the end of the tribulation, armies will gather to march on Jerusalem. They will attack, Jesus will return, the nations will be defeated, the Antichrist and false prophet will be cast into the lake of fire, and the devil will go into the abyss for 1,000 years. That is what you can take to the bank because that is what the Bible clearly prophesies.

Seems like we could wrap it all up right here in a nice, clean little package. But the messenger is not quite done talking. That means Daniel is not quite done writing. And if Daniel isn't done writing, then we are not done reading. We've still got a couple more people to meet and a few more numbers that need to be dealt with.

CHAPTER 12

A FINAL MESSAGE OF HOPE

DANIEL 12

W hen I guided tours through Israel, I always liked to leave the visitors on a high note. Often, journeys through Israel begin with Jerusalem, then head south toward the Dead Sea, north to Galilee, and, finally, west to Caesarea. My preference was to reverse that order so that our final days were in Jerusalem. As the pilgrims wrapped up their time in the Holy Land, I would take them to the Garden Tomb, which I believe is the genuine site of the resurrection of Christ. It is inevitably a spiritually moving time. We would sing hymns and take communion. Then I would allow the folk to spend some time quietly enjoying the presence of the Lord in that powerful place. For many, it is that experience that stays strongest with them as they return to Ben Gurion Airport for their flight home.

We are now entering the final leg of our tour of Daniel. We have heard great stories of faith, seen the protective power of God, witnessed spectacular visions, and been invited to share in the wisdom of heavenly interpretations for the wildest of dreams. We've celebrated

God's faithfulness, marveled at His understanding, been awed by His power, and felt tremendous gratitude for the saving nature of His grace. But we are not done yet. God still has a little bit left before He's ready to call this prophetic book a wrap. And, if He's saved it for the end, then it is undoubtedly a message He wants us to remember.

As Daniel 12 begins, it does so with a warning:

> At that time Michael shall stand up,
> the great prince who stands watch over the sons
>   of your people;
> and there shall be a time of trouble,
> such as never was since there was a nation (verse 1).

Michael, the protector of Israel, will get to his feet. He will not stand to stretch his legs or to better see the view. He will rise because the enemy is attacking, and he is in for a battle of the ages. He knows his enemy. We know of at least one time in the past when Michael contended "with the devil, when he disputed about the body of Moses" (Jude 9). That is one of those little tidbits of insight into the spiritual world upon which I wish the Holy Spirit had elaborated. John also speaks of a time when Michael will fight "with the dragon" (Revelation 12:7), leading to Satan being cast down to earth.

The setting in which the archangel finds himself this time is one when God's chosen people will face incredible punishment and sorrow. The great tribulation is coming, and its purpose is to shake up the Jews to such an extent that they will be ready to repent and turn back to God:

> Alas! For that day is great,
> so that none is like it;
> and it is the time of Jacob's trouble,
> but he shall be saved out of it (Jeremiah 30:7).

Michael will need discernment and an open path of communication with the Lord so that he can know what happens to be the Father's discipline of His children and what is simply a vicious attack from an enemy who wants nothing more than to annihilate the Jews.

The Tribulation—Israel's Great Distress

As we addressed in the previous chapter, the people of Israel have experienced many times in their history when they became the victims of those who hated them just because they were Jews. But all those other times, including that of October 7, 2023, will pale in comparison to what awaits them during the tribulation. The persecution of Israel will be on a level "such as never was since there was a nation." The history of the Jews includes destructions by Assyria and Babylon, Antiochus IV and the Roman emperors, the Holocaust and the Eastern European pogroms, and, once again, the heart-tearing atrocities perpetrated by Hamas. While the entire population of the world will suffer under the righteous judgments of the seals, trumpets, and bowls, Jews around the globe will additionally have all the forces of evil out to get them. That is what this chapter is about.

The center of global attention will not be Moscow, Tehran, Beijing, Istanbul, or Washington, DC. The world's focus will be on Jerusalem. All the major networks, all the social media news sources, all the bloggers and YouTubers and Telegrammers will gather in that city. They'll go there looking for answers. What happened to the millions of "religious people" who suddenly disappeared? Were they kidnapped by aliens, or taken underground in some global government action? For some reason, many will believe that the answers lie in Israel's capital city.

Whatever it is that draws them to Jerusalem, they cannot be in a better place to report on the action. That is, if they survive:

[The beast] was given a mouth speaking great things and blasphemies, and he was given authority to continue for forty-two months. Then he opened his mouth in blasphemy against God, to blaspheme His name, His tabernacle, and those who dwell in heaven. It was granted to him to make war with the saints and to overcome them. And authority was given him over every tribe, tongue, and nation. All who dwell on the earth will worship him, whose names have not been written in the Book of Life of the Lamb slain from the foundation of the world (Revelation 13:5-8).

In the middle of the tribulation, an already-turbulent world will have its violence meter cranked up to high. Those who oppose the Antichrist will face a buzzsaw of punishment. The postexilic prophet Zechariah described the horrors that will be directed specifically at the Jews, writing,

"It shall come to pass in all the land,"
says the LORD,
"that two-thirds in it shall be cut off and die,
but one-third shall be left in it:
I will bring the one-third through the fire,
will refine them as silver is refined,
and test them as gold is tested.
They will call on My name,
and I will answer them.
I will say, 'This is My people';
and each one will say, 'The LORD is my God'"
(Zechariah 13:8-9).

Ready for some tragic equations? If we are considering only the 7.2 million Jews who are currently living in Israel,[16] that means

4.8 million will be killed during the time of Jacob's trouble. When we expand it to all 15.7 million living worldwide,[17] we're looking at 10.5 million Jews who won't survive the seven years. The blood will flow in the streets. There are times when I make the drive from my home to Jerusalem, and I try to picture what it will be like in those days. Then to think that they are not that far away! There are people who I see on the street during my drive who will be subject to the terrors of this biblical prophecy. The thoughts can get so overwhelming that I am forced to turn on the radio to try to distract myself.

The one hope we can cling to for that time is that there will be 5.2 million Jews who will survive the time. It is they who will call on God's name, receive Him as Lord and Savior, and hear the voice of the Almighty say, "This is My people." These are the ones of whom the messenger said, "At that time your people shall be delivered, every one who is found written in the book" (verse 1).

A 1,000-Year Leap

There is a time gap between verses 1 and 2 of Daniel 12. Leaving the tribulation, the messenger jumped forward 1,000 years to the conclusion of the millennium. He told the prophet, "Many of those who sleep in the dust of the earth shall awake, some to everlasting life, some to shame and everlasting contempt" (verse 2). That people are returning to life tells us that we are dealing with a resurrection. The fact that it is a mixed company of saved and unsaved souls identifies the specific resurrection. There is only one resurrection when the unsaved will be given their incorruptible bodies, and that is just before the final Great White Throne judgment.

For years, I've been accused by tour groups of moving too fast. So before I hear any of you pleading, "Slow down, Amir!," let me hit the brakes here. Daniel's messenger is talking about a general resurrection—a resurrection of all who are dead, whether saved or unsaved.

There is only one of those. All prior resurrections are for believers only. Paul laid out the timeline:

> Now Christ is risen from the dead, and has become the firstfruits of those who have fallen asleep. For since by man came death, by Man also came the resurrection of the dead. For as in Adam all die, even so in Christ all shall be made alive. But each one in his own order: Christ the firstfruits, afterward those who are Christ's at His coming. Then comes the end, when He delivers the kingdom to God the Father, when He puts an end to all rule and all authority and power (1 Corinthians 15:20-24).

When Jesus rose from the grave at the Garden Tomb, He inaugurated the first resurrection in which believers are given new bodies like His—the upgraded models that are incorruptible and untainted by Adam's sin. The first time these bodies, prototyped by Jesus, will begin their wider distribution is at the rapture, when "the dead in Christ will rise first. Then we who are alive and remain shall be caught up together with them in the clouds to meet the Lord in the air" (1 Thessalonians 4:16-17). After that, there will be a series of resurrections involving the two witnesses during the tribulation, and the Old Testament saints (including Daniel) and tribulation saints at the second coming of Jesus. Those are all elements of the first resurrection.

The resurrection that the messenger is referring to is the one that Jesus spoke of when He said, "The hour is coming in which all who are in the graves will hear His voice and come forth—those who have done good, to the resurrection of life, and those who have done evil, to the resurrection of condemnation" (John 5:28-29). Included in this group are the believers from the time of the millennium and the unbelievers from all time. This is the event of which John wrote:

I saw the dead, small and great, standing before God, and books were opened. And another book was opened, which is the Book of Life. And the dead were judged according to their works, by the things which were written in the books. The sea gave up the dead who were in it, and Death and Hades delivered up the dead who were in them. And they were judged, each one according to his works. Then Death and Hades were cast into the lake of fire. This is the second death. And anyone not found written in the Book of Life was cast into the lake of fire (Revelation 20:12-15).

There are some whose names will be found in the Book of Life. But because this is the time when those who rejected God throughout history will be judged, the vast majority will not receive the mercy that will be accorded to those whose names are listed. This is a truth that so many people simply do not understand. Resurrection is not just for believers. All are destined to rise again into a body that will endure for all time. The only question is whether they will forever experience the joy of God's presence in heaven, or the torments of eternal damnation in hell? I shudder when I think of that.

The Most Important Decision of Your Life

Has there ever been a sleep from which you have not awoken? That you are reading this sentence tells me that the answer to that question is no. The very nature of sleep includes an end point. When your eyes first open and awareness creeps back through your brain, your first thoughts will likely differ depending on what's awaiting you for the day. Maybe you're on vacation and you know that the day ahead will bring wonderful times of making memories with your family. As you lay there you may feel joy, excitement, or anticipation.

But maybe you are filled with dread as you face a difficult day ahead at a job you don't like, working for a tyrannical boss. Or possibly you have just lost a spouse or a child, and those first moments of awareness bring a flood of sorrow, hopelessness, and the dread of being alone. There may be those mornings you lay in bed wishing you could go back to sleep, but you know you have to get up. So often, these difficult mornings are the result of situations beyond our control. Life has caught up to us, and we just have to move forward.

The Bible often compares death to sleep, as does the messenger in this passage. And, before I get letters, let me say that in the following paragraph I am in no way advocating a doctrine of soul sleep in which we are essentially "unconscious" from the time of death to the time of our resurrection. Jesus' story of the rich man and Lazarus, as told in Luke 16:19-31, is evidence enough that we have full awareness after our death.

What Scripture teaches us is that a time is coming when we will experience our final, great wakeup. It is then we will open our eyes to experience our eternity. Where this return to consciousness differs is that what we wake up to is entirely our choice. Actually, let me phrase that better: What we wake up to then at the resurrection is entirely based on our choice now. If we choose to receive the free gift of salvation that Jesus offers to us by grace through faith, then our resurrection will be like waking up to the best morning of the greatest day ever. But if we choose to ignore Jesus or reject Him, our resurrection will mean waking up to guilt, regret, and a knowledge that we are about to receive the just punishment for our rebellion against our Creator.

The only time allotted for making that eternal decision is in this life. The writer of Hebrews tells us that "it is appointed for men to die once, but after this the judgment" (9:27). That means that at the moment our temporal life on this earth ends, our spiritual life in eternity has been determined.

Because deciding whether to follow or reject Jesus is the most important decision a person will ever make, the Lord has always kept His witnesses in the world. The truth of His gospel has continuously been extant, and the reality of His existence has always been "clearly seen, being understood by the things that are made, even His eternal power and Godhead, so that [people] are without excuse" (Romans 1:20).

God will even extend His witness through the tribulation. Into the insanity of the Antichrist's world, He will send "one hundred and forty-four thousand of all the tribes of the children of Israel" (Revelation 7:4) to spread the gospel. These are the ones that Daniel's messenger said will "shine like the brightness of the firmament, and those who turn many to righteousness like the stars forever and ever" (Daniel 12:3).

Box It Up Until Later

The messenger's interpretation of Daniel's vision was coming to a close. As he wrapped up, the angel said something quite surprising. "But you, Daniel, shut up the words, and seal the book until the time of the end; many shall run to and fro, and knowledge shall increase" (verse 4). What is that about? Did God send the messenger with an interpretation of the vision that was solely for the prophet's personal consumption? And did Daniel sin against God by making it available to the masses?

The answers to the last two questions are no and no. God's intention from the beginning was for the truth of this vision to get to the world. The admonition to Daniel was for him to protect and preserve the contents of the angel's message until a time came when it could be clearly understood. This was not a command to hide the truth; it was a recognition that the truth will not be fully understood until God reveals more of the puzzle.

Suppose you order a jigsaw puzzle online. When it arrives, it is in a plain brown box. *Strange*, you think. But still, you're excited as you pull off the plastic wrap and work to lift up the box's lid. Puzzle pieces spill out, and immediately you begin to sort them. As you do, however, you quickly discover that all you've been sent are the edges. Immediately, you call the company to complain. The representative apologizes. They've had some manufacturing problems. They'll have the rest of the pieces sent to you in three weeks' time. As you begin your wait, what will you do with the edge pieces you've already been sent? Will you leave them spread out on the kitchen table? No, you'll dump them back into the box and put on the lid so that they will remain protected while you wait to receive the rest of the puzzle.

This is the angel's admonition to Daniel. Seal up this vision in the puzzle box. In the future, more pieces will come. At that time, you can once again pour out the edges and see how they fit into the big picture. When will that time be? Well, hopefully by now you'll have caught on to the unbreakable link between Daniel and Revelation. While the messenger of Daniel said, "Seal the book," John's angel said, "Do not seal the words of the prophecy of this book, for the time is at hand" (Revelation 22:10). With the added insight of John's revelation, we can finally understand Daniel. And with Daniel's vision, we can lay a foundation for the apocalyptic experience of John.

There is one last aspect to address from the message given to Daniel. The angel stated that "many shall run to and fro, and knowledge shall increase" (verse 4). The words translated "run to and fro" are the Hebrew יְשֹׁטְטוּ רַבִּים (*yeshotetu rabbim*) and depict wandering around without purpose. This picture of people scurrying aimlessly is seen elsewhere in the Bible. In the book of Amos, we find a prediction of this same thing happening:

> "Behold, the days are coming," says the Lord GOD,
> "that I will send a famine on the land,
>   not a famine of bread,
>   nor a thirst for water,
> but of hearing the words of the LORD.

They shall wander from sea to sea,
and from north to east;
they shall run to and fro, seeking the word of the LORD,
but shall not find it" (Amos 8:11-12).

The prophet Jeremiah speaks similar words, saying, "Run to and fro through the streets of Jerusalem; see now and know" (Jeremiah 5:1). What are they wandering around looking for? The Word of the Lord. There have been many times in history when there was a famine of the Word of God. People may have wanted it, but could not find it. Even today there are many people groups who do not have the Bible in their language.

But for most of the world, the Bible is readily available. We have the full canon of Scripture that we can access in print or on our computers or from our smartphones. We can even listen to it played through our car radios on our way to work. The problem is that so few people are studying it. Our world today has more knowledge available to it than at any other time in history. Yet people are more lost and confused than ever. The greatest challenge to our culture today is living in a world filled with technology and information, yet in the midst of all that, focusing on the things that matter.

This is as true in the church as it is in the secular world. How much time do Christians spend looking at their screens? Don't get me wrong; there is much great information that is available through digital media. But are we using that screen time well, or frivolously? Are we succumbing to sensationalism and clickbait? Are we following after conspiracy theories and sloppy biblical interpretation? Are we using our time to attack other Christians because they may disagree with us on an issue that has nothing to do with salvation?

Instead of running to and fro, Paul said we must "walk circumspectly, not as fools but as wise, redeeming the time, because the days are evil" (Ephesians 5:15-16). This means being intentional about how we spend our time and exercising care over the kind of information we take in during our limited waking hours.

Once again, we are blessed to live in a time when we are surrounded by an abundance of biblical resources. There is no excuse for any believer to be biblically illiterate. Let me encourage you right now by acknowledging that the very fact you are reading this book says a lot about your passion for the Word of God and your desire to know His plans for this world. Well done, truth seeker—keep up the good work!

How Long?

The angel had said all he had been sent to say, so he began his departure, leaving Daniel to ponder over all that he had heard. But before the messenger could fly off to help Gabriel in his fight against the princes of Persia and Greece, a voice stopped him. Daniel looked toward the river "and there stood two others, one on this riverbank and the other on that riverbank. And one said to the man clothed in linen, who was above the waters of the river, 'How long shall the fulfillment of these wonders be?'" (Daniel 12:5-6).

How long, Lord? This is the answer we always want to know. How long until I am well again? How long until my family is reconciled? How long until I'm out of this financial mess? We know God is faithful and that He loves us. But we're ready for that fatherly compassion to express itself in a more tangible way. This cry echoes the prophets and the psalmists who longed for the day when God's hand of discipline would be replaced by His hand of mercy.

The old saying goes, "The devil is in the details." If the enemy is the opposite of all things God, then I suppose we can assume that "God is in the lack of details." That certainly plays itself out in the nature of faith being the "substance of things hoped for, the evidence of things not seen" (Hebrews 11:1). We don't see God's calendar, we don't know His agenda, we can't observe Him physically as He works—which is why we must trust that He is there.

That is why it is so wonderful that Daniel's messenger stopped above the waters of the river to give the old prophet an answer:

> I heard the man clothed in linen, who was above the waters of the river, when he held up his right hand and his left hand to heaven, and swore by Him who lives forever, that it shall be for a time, times, and half a time; and when the power of the holy people has been completely shattered, all these things shall be finished (Daniel 12:7).

The angel swore an oath, confirming the truthfulness of what he was about to say. Then he gave us a window of time that by now is familiar to us all: "a time, times, and half a time," or three-and-a-half years. Daniel and Revelation, once again showing us that they are BFFs. This is speaking of the same time pointed to by John's bizarre sign of the dragon and the eagle-winged woman. The dragon (Satan) persecuted the woman (Israel), but she escaped to hide in the wilderness, where she was taken care of "for a time and times and half a time" (Revelation 12:14). But while she was hidden away, "the rest of her offspring" (verse 17)—the Jews who were not safe with her—were severely persecuted. This future persecution will take place until "the power of the holy people has been completely shattered" (Daniel 12:7). At that time, the end of the tribulation will come.

You've got to feel for Daniel with what happened next. Maybe you're reading this book, saying, "Okay, Amir, I get it, but I don't quite get it. It's certainly clearer than it was before, but we're still talking old aquarium water as opposed to pure Rocky Mountain snowmelt runoff." That's totally understandable, and I promise to attempt to clarify, as much as possible, the answer that the angel gave to Daniel.

> Although I heard, I did not understand. Then I said, "My lord, what shall be the end of these things?"

And he said, "Go your way, Daniel, for the words are closed up and sealed till the time of the end. Many shall be purified, made white, and refined, but the wicked shall do wickedly; and none of the wicked shall understand, but the wise shall understand" (verses 8-10).

When the old prophet asked for a little more clarification, the angel responded, "Off you go, Daniel. I've said all I'm going to say." And you can't blame him. Michael the Archangel was waiting on his help. But then the angel pulled the oldest trick in the preacher handbook. He said, "Oh, I see my time is almost done" before going on for another 20 minutes. I, for one, would never do that. I try to limit my going-over cheat time to 10 minutes max.

I love the angel's next words. They are so obvious, but so wise. He tells Daniel that the end times will produce two groups of people. There will be those who realize the truth, repent, are forgiven, and become part of God's family. Then there will be the wicked, who will keep doing the same stupid stuff they've always done.

There are two ways to interpret the second part of verse 10. One sees in the angel's words the fact that the wicked ones won't understand why all the bad tribulation stuff is happening to them. "It's not fair. I don't deserve this. God is just mean." They'll be angry and bitter, but they'll never quite get to the point where they realize that it's all their fault. As you may have heard people say, "Stupid is as stupid does."

But the wise ones will understand that there are consequences to one's actions. When a person rejects God, they should expect repercussions. It is that Holy Spirit-level understanding that leads to repentance and salvation. King Solomon made the angel's point centuries before when he wrote, "The fear of the LORD is the beginning of knowledge, but fools despise wisdom and instruction" (Proverbs 1:7). Like Nebuchadnezzar, when he finally looked up to God from his animalistic state, it is when we are looking upward that we can see what is really going on around us.

That interpretation certainly works, but there is another that just might fit the context better. Daniel's angel divides the Jews into two groups. There are those who will be "purified, made white, and refined," and there are the wicked. For the first group to come to that future point of salvation, they must be the ones who escape Jerusalem when the Antichrist reveals his intentions. Wisely, they will see what's coming, understand that they have only a short time to flee, and escape to the wilderness while the getting is good. But the wicked will have no understanding. They will have no discernment. They will stay in Jerusalem, holding on to the hope that the Antichrist will remain true to his original word. They'll stay until their deaths.

The angel then referred to that horrible time of genocidal persecution, saying,

> From the time that the daily sacrifice is taken away, and the abomination of desolation is set up, there shall be one thousand two hundred and ninety days. Blessed is he who waits, and comes to the one thousand three hundred and thirty-five days" (Daniel 12:11-12).

This is the third time that phrase "abomination of desolation" is used in Daniel's book. Once again, it refers to the time when the Antichrist removes the sacrifice of God from the temple and places himself in the position of the recipient of worship. From the time of the removal of the sacrifice to the time of the end there will be 1,290 days.

We've seen three-and-a-half years. We've seen 42 months, 1,260 days, and time, times, and half a time. All of those are different ways of saying the same number. But now, right before the end of the book, the angel suddenly drops 1,290 and 1,335. Really, Mr. Messenger? What is up with that?

Once again, we are forced into the realm of educated speculation. The best explanation I've seen was written by Ron Rhodes, president of Reasoning from the Scriptures Ministries:

> A 75-day interval apparently separates the end of the tribulation period from the beginning of the millennial kingdom. During this brief interim, a number of significant events transpire. For example, the image of the antichrist that had caused the abomination of desolation at the midpoint of the tribulation will be removed from the temple after 30 days. "From the time that the regular burnt offering is taken away and the abomination that makes desolate is set up, there shall be 1,290 days" (Daniel 12:11). The last half of the tribulation lasts only 1260 days (or three and a half years), so the abomination that makes desolate is removed from the Jewish temple 30 days after the tribulation ends. An additional 45 days must also be added into the prophetic timetable: "Blessed is he who waits and arrives at the 1,335 days" (verse 12). The 1335 days minus the 1290 days means another 45 days are added into the mix. Apparently, this is when the judgment of the nations takes place (Matthew 25:31-46). The Jewish survivors of the tribulation period will also be judged.[18]

Whether the inclusion of these extra days made sense to Daniel, we don't know. Still, the old prophet faithfully included these details into the record, as instructed, so that they could be better understood at a later day. Then as he departed, the angel left Daniel with a wonderful promise. Knowing that the wise man's time on earth was coming to a close, the messenger said, "You, go your way till the end; for you shall rest, and will arise to your inheritance at the end of the days" (verse 13).

Daniel was separated from his family at a young age, raised in a foreign land, and forced to serve idol-worshipping king after idol-worshipping king his entire life, all while being denied any opportunity for experiencing the joy of marriage and fatherhood. He had accomplished much, but it was always for someone else. Knowing this, the angel had promised him that a time of rest was coming his way. Death would take him, but it would not keep him. Resurrection would come, and when he arose, it would be to the spectacular inheritance he had earned through being a servant of the true King as well as His Son.

This reminds me of my father-in-law, Hanan Lokes. For years, he was a leader of the church in Israel. He touched so many lives and sacrificed so much. When he passed away in 2022, he left a gaping hole in our family and in the Israeli church. Still, we rejoiced for him, knowing that after his dedicated sojourn on this earth, his inheritance was waiting for him in heaven.

Each of us should have that same level of commitment and sacrifice. What are you doing for the Lord? How are you serving Him? Daniel was a man no different than us. He just had a determination not to waste his life chasing the things of this world. When God presented him an opportunity to serve, he jumped at it. As a result, he accomplished great things. The Lord is ready to use each of us the same way.

A Final Message of Hope

What a tour this has been! We've enjoyed amazing stories of God's faithfulness and experienced wild visions that point to the time of Daniel and to our generation as well. Most exciting of all, we've seen the deep ties that exist between Daniel and Revelation. Both have great portions of encouragement and application. Both explain clearly various aspects of God's scenario for the end times. However, as thorough as they may be in certain areas, neither book is comprehensive in its coverage of biblical prophecy. But bringing the two together fills in most of the gaps that one or the other may leave on its own.

God wants us to understand His plans. That is obvious by the large percentage of Scripture that He commits to informing us about what He is going to do. I like Paul's exhortation, "I do not want you to be ignorant, brethren, concerning those who have fallen asleep, lest you sorrow as others who have no hope" (1 Thessalonians 4:13). What a blessing it is to realize that we have everything we need to know about the end times right in our Bibles! According to Paul's words, that truth is a source of hope and of comfort.

It is those words that reveal the true purpose for the prophecies God gave in Daniel and the book of Revelation. The Lord wants you to be able to look around at the insanity of this world and say, "I won't be afraid, because I know that God has a plan." When horrors take place like what happened in Israel on October 7, 2023, you can rest assured that evil does not win. God has shown you that as a believer, you will be taken up to Him at the rapture. How do you know He won't forget you? Because He has made it clear how, through the tribulation, He will not forget His people Israel, and how, at the end of the seven years of discipline, He will bring them to Himself. He is a promise-keeping God—He has demonstrated this throughout history, and He has assured it into the future.

So hold on to your hope, my friend. Trust in the Lord. Don't lean on your own understanding of what is taking place in this world. In all your ways, live for Him as your Lord and Savior, knowing that when the time comes, He will open that path straight into His presence.

NOTES

1. John F. Walvoord, *Daniel* (Chicago, IL: Moody, 2012), 58-59.

2. John C. Lennox, *Against the Flow* (Oxford, UK: Monarch Books, 2015), 88.

3. Richard Dawkins, *The God Delusion* (New York: Houghton Mifflin Company, 2006), 187.

4. Henry Petroski, "Moving Obelisks," *American Scientist*, https://www.americanscientist.org/article/moving-obelisks#:~:text=According%20to%20one%20survey%20of,height%20specification%20of%201%3A10.

5. Henry Petroski, "Moving Obelisks," *American Scientist*, https://www.chards.co.uk/guides/density-of-gold-and-other-metals/377#:~:text=A%20cubic%20centimetre%20of%20gold,weigh%20 1188.6%20pounds%20(avoirdupois).

6. John Schmidt, "Gold Price Today," *Forbes*, updated November 15, 2023, https://www.forbes.com/advisor/investing/gold-price/.

7. Hye-soo Kim, "Kim Family Regime Portraits," *HRNKInsider*, April 13, 1018, https://www.hrnk insider.org/2018/04/kim-family-regime-portraits.html.

8. Clarence Larkin, *The Book of Daniel (Illustrated)* (CreateSpace, 2017), 63. Kindle edition.

9. "Clay cylinder," *The British Museum*, https://www.britishmuseum.org/collection/object/W_K-1689.

10. Keaton Halley, "Belshazzar: The second most powerful man in Babylon," *Creation.com*, July 2015, https://creation.com/archaeology-belshazzar#:~:text=First%2C%20in%201854%2C%20 four%20clay,inscriptions%20were%20excavated%20from%20Ur.&text=These%20 Nabonidus%20Cylinders%20contained%20Nabonidus,and%20heir%20to%20his%20throne.

11. Dr. Seuss, *How the Grinch Stole Christmas* (New York: Random House, 1985), Kindle loc. 12 of 33.

12. Mark Moore, "'Promises' slogan was used long before Trump and de Blasio," *New York Post*, updated August 21, 2018, https://nypost.com/2018/08/21/promises-slogan-was-used-long-before-trump-and-de-blasio/.

13. Dwight J. Pentecost, "Daniel," *The Bible Knowledge Commentary: Old Testament*, eds. John F. Walvoord and Roy B. Zuck (Wheaton, IL: Victor Books, 1985), 1:1363.

14. Sir Robert Anderson, *The Coming Prince: The Marvelous Prophecy of Daniel's Seventy Weeks Concerning the Antichrist* (Trumpet Press, 2016), Kindle edition.

15. Josephus, *The Jewish War* (Oxford, UK: Oxford University Press, 2017), 6. Kindle edition.

16. Times of Israel staff, "Global Jewish population hits 15.7 million ahead of new year, 46% of them in Israel," *The Times of Israel*, September 15, 2023, https://www.timesofisrael.com/global-jewish-population-hits-15-7-million-ahead-of-new-year-46-of-them-in-israel/.

17. Ibid.

18. Ron Rhodes, *The End Times in Chronological Order: A Complete Overview to Understanding Bible Prophecy* (Eugene, OR: Harvest House, 2012), 178. Kindle edition.

This workbook companion to *Discovering Daniel* offers a wealth of additional content to further enrich your study of Daniel and will help you apply this book of the Bible to your daily life, emboldening you to live with hope and confidence.

Amir Tsarfati, with Dr. Rick Yohn, examines what Revelation makes known about the end times and beyond. Guided by accessible teaching that lets Scripture speak for itself, you'll see what lies ahead for every person in the end times—either in heaven or on earth. Are *you* ready?

This companion workbook to *Revealing Revelation*— the product of many years of careful research— offers you a clear and exciting overview of God's perfect plan for the future. Inside you'll find principles from the Bible that equip you to better interpret the end-times signs, as well as insights about how Bible prophecy is relevant to your life today.

In *Israel and the Church*, bestselling author and native Israeli Amir Tsarfati helps readers recognize the distinct contemporary and future roles of both the Jewish people and the church, and how together they reveal the character of God and His perfect plan of salvation.

To fully grasp what God has in store for the future, it's vital to understand His promises to Israel. The *Israel and the Church Study Guide* will help you do exactly that, equipping you to explore the Bible's many revelations about what is yet to come.

As a native Israeli of Jewish roots, Amir Tsarfati provides a distinct perspective that weaves biblical history, current events, and Bible prophecy together to shine light on the mysteries about the end times. In *The Day Approaching*, he points to the scriptural evidence that the return of the Lord is imminent.

Jesus Himself revealed the signs that will alert us to the nearness of His return. In *The Day Approaching Study Guide*, you'll have the opportunity to take an up-close look at what those signs are, as well as God's overarching plans for the future, and how those plans affect you today.

Bestselling author and native Israeli Amir Tsarfati provides clarity on what will happen during the tribulation and explains its place in God's timeline.

With this study guide companion to *Has the Tribulation Begun?*, bestselling author and prophecy expert Amir Tsarfati guides you through a biblical overview of the last days, with thought-provoking study and application questions.

AMIR TSARFATI WITH BARRY STAGNER

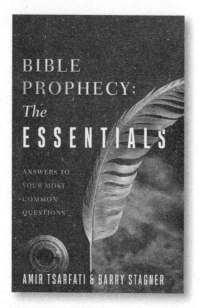

In *Bible Prophecy: The Essentials*, Amir and Barry team up to answer 70 of their most commonly asked questions, which focus on seven foundational themes of Bible prophecy: Israel, the church, the rapture, the tribulation, the millennium, the Great White Throne judgment, and heaven.

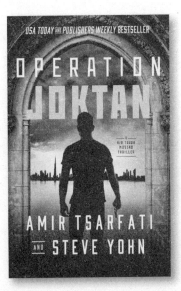

Book 1

"It was the perfect day—until the gunfire."

Nir Tavor is an Israeli secret service operative turned talented Mossad agent.

Nicole le Roux is a model with a hidden skill.

A terrorist attack brings them together, and then work forces them apart—until they're unexpectedly called back into each other's lives.

But there's no time for romance. As violent radicals threaten chaos across the Middle East, the two must work together to stop these extremists, pooling Nicole's knack for technology and Nir's adeptness with on-the-ground missions. Each heart-racing step of their operation gets them closer to the truth—and closer to danger.

In this thrilling first book in a new series, authors Amir Tsarfati and Steve Yohn draw on true events as well as tactical insights Amir learned from his time in the Israeli Defense Forces. For believers in God's life-changing promises, *Operation Joktan* is a suspense-filled page-turner that illuminates the blessing Israel is to the world.

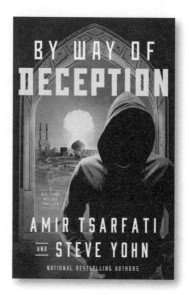

Book 2

The Mossad has uncovered Iran's plans to smuggle untraceable weapons of mass destruction into Israel. The clock is ticking, and agents Nir Tavor and Nicole le Roux can't act quickly enough.

Nir and Nicole find themselves caught in a whirlwind plot of assassinations, espionage, and undercover recon, fighting against the clock to stop this threat against the Middle East. As they draw closer to danger—and closer to each other—they find themselves ensnared in a lethal web of secrets. Will they have to sacrifice their own lives to protect the lives of millions?

Inspired by real events, authors Amir Tsarfati and Steve Yohn reteam for this suspenseful follow-up to the bestselling *Operation Joktan*. Filled with danger, romance, and international intrigue, this Nir Tavor thriller reveals breathtaking true insights into the lives and duties of Mossad agents—and delivers a story that will have you on the edge of your seat.

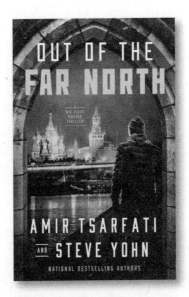

Book 3

Tensions are at a breaking point. The Western markets that once relied on Russian gas have turned to Israel for their energy needs. Furious, Russia moves to protect its interests by using its newfound ally, Iran, and Iran's proxy militias.

As Israel's elite fighting forces and the Mossad go undercover, they detect the Kremlin is planning a major attack against Israel. Hunting for clues, Mossad agents Nir Tavor and Nicole le Roux plunge themselves into the treacherous underworld of Russian oligarch money, power, and decadence.

With each danger they face, le Roux's newfound Christian faith grows stronger. And battle-weary Tavor—haunted by dreams from his past—must confront memories and pain he'd sought to bury.

In this electrifying thriller, hostilities explode as Tavor and le Roux fight to prevent a devastating conflict. Will they be able to outwit their enemies, or will their actions have catastrophic consequences?